THROUGH
THE
NARROW
GATE

THROUGH THE NARROW GATE

by
KAREN ARMSTRONG

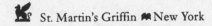 St. Martin's Griffin ♞ New York

www.stmartins.com

Library of Congress Cataloging-in-Publication Data

Armstrong, Karen.
    Through the narrow gate / Karen Armstrong.
        p. cm.
    ISBN 0-312-34095-8
    EAN 978-0312-34095-7
    1. Armstrong, Karen. 2. Ex-nuns—Biography. I. Title.

BX4668.3.A75A3 1995
271'.9—dc20
[B] 94-35980   CIP

10 9 8 7 6 5 4 3 2

Acknowledgments

I should like to thank all my friends who have listened to me during the last few years and helped me to adjust to the world, and who encouraged me to write this book.

In memory of my father

Enter by the narrow gate, since the gate that leads to perdition is wide, and the road spacious, and many take it; but it is a narrow gate and a hard road that lead to life, and only a few find it.

—*Matthew 7:12*

CONTENTS

INTRODUCTION

Through the Narrow Gate was my first book. It told the story of my seven years as a nun in a Roman Catholic teaching order, but was not intended to be an exposé. The decision to leave my order had been very difficult, and for about six years I existed in a state of grief and depression probably not dissimilar to the experience of a bad divorce or a major bereavement. But when I sat down to write this memoir in 1979, some twelve years after leaving the religious life, I felt that I was beginning to recover. But I was also aware that I needed to review those convent years, and recover the memory of that time before the details were lost to me forever. People often asked me to tell them about my years as a nun, but the issues raised were too deep and complex to recount at a dinner party. I tried to fob people off with an amusing anecdote, and found that I was trivializing this very formative period. This was not right, and so I decided to revisit the convent experience and find out what—if anything—it had meant to me.

It was a difficult book to write. I had no ambitions to become a professional author, but had wanted to be an academic. Apart from the usual undergraduate essays, I had produced only a dry-as-dust thesis, so my first attempt was somewhat abstract and professorial. I had been trained to keep some distance between myself and my material, but I soon realized that this would not work in a memoir, so I started again. This time my story was very angry indeed. When I showed it to my agent, she asked why, if the experience had been so terrible, I had stayed in the order for seven whole years. After all, when I finally decided to leave none of my superiors had put any pressure on me. What had kept me inside so long?

It was a very good question, so I put a line through the second draft and started again. It had been important to express my anger and disappointment; writing it all down had been cathartic, and I felt lighter. A hard knot of rage had been released. In my third draft, I tried to dig a little deeper, and found that I recalled many good things that had been buried under the rubble of resentment and bewilderment: I remembered the excitement of my first days as a Postulant, when felt that I had embarked on a wonderful spiritual adventure; I remembered the beauty of the liturgy, and the kindness of some of my superiors. So writing *Through the Narrow Gate* was an act of redemption. I had rescued the experience, purified it and allowed it to speak to me in the present. When I wrote the epilogue, I realized that even though the convent years had been difficult, I would not have missed them for the world.

I had assumed that *Through the Narrow Gate* would be my one and only book. I also thought that I had finished with religion. After I left the convent, my faith seemed to slip away and by the 1980s, when this book was published, I wanted nothing to do with the church, and did not, as I thought, believe in God or the supernatural. I was finished with all that. And yet as I recovered my memories of convent life, I felt again that yearning for transcendence that had impelled me into the religious life in the first place. That old longing had been reinvigorated, but I did not know what I could do with it. At the end of the book, I said that I thought that, paradoxical as it might sound, I was a better nun in the world than I had ever been in the cloister and that in some ways I felt that I should be a nun all my life. I had never married, but lived alone and seemed to have an inbuilt hunger for spirituality. Yet what did this mean? How could I seek a nonexistent God? Could there be holiness for a secularized nun?

I have spent the last twenty-five years trying to answer these questions. Writing *Through the Narrow Gate* started something that I did not expect. Almost by accident, I did become a writer, began to explore the history of the great world religions, and to investigate the notions of God and the sacred. I have told the story of this post-convent quest in *The Spiral Staircase*. But the search began here, in this first memoir. I am glad that I wrote this book, that I struggled to assess my past accurately and make peace with it. The experience has taught me that it is very important to look honestly at your personal life, to unravel the web of pain and anger, and see it as it really was. Until you have achieved some sense of continuity with your former selves, you cannot move forward into the future.

I am also very grateful to the nuns who trained, advised, scolded, and befriended me. I now know that I entered the religious life at a very difficult time, and was one of the last people to go through the old system before it was reformed by the Second Vatican Council. It was a time of transition: one way of life was dying and nothing had yet appeared to take its place. We were all—young nuns and old—living in a vacuum, a cloud of unknowing. Not surprisingly, we all had our struggles, our pain, and our bewilderment. We all made mistakes. But my superiors did their best for me, and some of the people who have appeared in these pages—especially the superior I call Mother Bianca—have been a major source of inspiration to me throughout my life.

I entered the Postulantship far too young for the vast task I had set myself. I was not suited to the life, and many of the difficulties that I describe were caused by my own immaturity. Nevertheless I regard my convent life as a gift. It was not a mistake. I entered my order because I wanted to find holiness, and now that I am entering my sixties I believe that the life I have now—constantly writing, thinking, and speaking about the sacred—may have been what I was looking for all those years ago, when I packed my suitcase, and made my first attempt to enter through the narrow gate.

1 · BEGINNINGS
1962

It was 14 September 1962, the most important day of my life. On the station platform my parents and my sister, Lindsey, were clustered together in a sad little knot, taking their last look at me. I was seventeen years old and was leaving them forever to become a nun.

Kings Cross station was a confused flurry of shouting porters, whistles, people dodging and tearing through barriers. A disembodied voice announced arrivals and departures. An old lady walked down the platform, smartly dressed, leaning on her stick and looking fixedly at the ground, lost in her private world. A group of soldiers drinking beer from bottles laughed gustily at the far end of the platform. A young girl and a boy were standing with their arms draped clumsily round each other, whispering intensely. Saying good-bye.

I looked at this from the windows of the train, but it was like watching a film or seeing it all through a thick glass screen. The whole day had been like this. I had gotten up that morning early, packed my suitcase and stripped my bed, folding the sheets and blankets neatly, conscious somewhere that this was the last time. I took a last look round the house, knowing that I ought to be feeling something, but actually feeling very little. Just a numbness, a blocking of all responses. But underneath all that I was aware of a fluttering excitement. At last the day had come. For the past year I had been looking forward to it with an intensity I had never experienced before, terrified that something would happen to stop it. I was beginning a huge spiritual adventure.

The night before I had read Monica Baldwin's book *I Leap Over the Wall,* written after twenty-eight years in a convent. It was a book that was legendary to me. The nuns at school had always spoken of it in tones of dire disapproval mixed with a kind of pity. "Poor woman," they had always said, "it's so obvious that she hadn't got a vocation." Somewhat guiltily I had bought a copy and devoured it in the privacy of my bedroom. It was my last chance to read it and I felt compelled by furtive curiosity. I say I read it, but I skipped large chunks. I wasn't interested in the author's adventures after leaving her convent. I wanted to know what had happened to her inside. Her account of the austerities of the life didn't put me off for a moment. I knew that it was going to be hard; I wanted it to be hard. It wouldn't be worth doing otherwise. What were a few hardships if they led to a close relationship with God? I felt sorry for Monica Baldwin. How could she have given up?

I glanced impatiently at my watch and then instantly felt contrite. This was a wonderful day for me, but my family had not chosen this. For them it was not a glorious beginning but an end. I looked down at them, knowing sadly that even now they were hoping against hope that I would change my mind at the last minute. None of that showed, however. My parents, tall and elegant, smiled bravely up at me. My sister was looking at me with awe mingled with horror, hardly able to believe that this was really happening. She was three years younger than I but already she was far taller and looked much older. Even at fourteen she possessed a physical poise and confidence that marked her as the sort of child my parents should have had. Like them she loved life; nothing was going to make her enter a convent. But I wasn't like that. To me the world had proved an unsatisfactory place. It wasn't enough. Only God with His infinite perfection could complete me. "Thou hast made us for Thyself, O God, and our hearts are restless till they rest in Thee." St. Augustine's words in his *Confessions* expressed what I felt exactly. I had read them for the first time a few months ago, during the school retreat. If the Gospels were true, it seemed to me, then logically there was nothing else to do but become a nun and give my whole life to God. Only He could satisfy me.

My parents could not really understand my decision. They were Catholics and knew that if I had a religious vocation it was their duty to let me go. But for them religion meant Sunday morning Mass and a decent morality. They were bewildered at my decision to abandon all the good things of life and embrace an asceticism that they could only see as impoverishing. However, they had made up their minds to let me enter the convent and were determined to see it through with as good a grace as they could.

They had driven me down from our home in Birmingham that morning to see me off at Kings Cross. It was our last time together as a family, and our knowledge of this filled the car. Outside on the highway the traffic swooshed past with heartless speed. I looked out the window, mechanically counting the bridges. Lindsey, huddled at the other end of the back seat, as far away from me as possible, stared with deliberate nonchalance out the window. She had been horrified when my mother told her. "How ghastly! I can't think of anything worse," and she had refused to talk to me about it at all. It's almost as though she thinks a religious vocation is infectious, I thought wryly, looking at her averted head.

"All right in the back, there?" my father asked with forced heartiness. A useless question but an attempt to communicate.

"Yes, thanks," we chorused obediently. There was silence except for the engine's purring.

"Daddy," said Lindsey peevishly, "do you think we could have the window shut? My hair's blowing all over the place—and so is Karen's."

"You girls!" my father sounded at the end of his tether. "What the hell does it matter what your hair looks like? Nobody's looking at you at the moment, are they? Why has every bloody hair got to be in place the whole bloody time! Nobody notices. You're fanatical about your hair—both of you! Yet you never think of cleaning your shoes. People notice dirty shoes far more than untidy hair, let me tell you!"

We let the outburst go. It was one of his favorite hobby-horses. But he wasn't really angry about our hair or our shoes. He was angry with God for taking his daughter.

"Would anyone like a piece of candy?" my mother asked soothingly. It was strange hearing her be the peacemaker. Usually it was she who got irritated and my father who calmed her down.

It was odd, I thought, how she felt the need to fill us up with glucose while we were on a journey. Anyone would think we were climbing Mount Everest. But it had always been the same, one of those odd quirks of family life that would be closed to me forever

3

after today. It was the sort of thing you probably quite forgot. In a few years perhaps all my life at home would seem unreal.

"We'll just be in time to have lunch somewhere nice," my mother said cheerfully.

We made pleased noises. I felt too excited to eat anything at the moment, but this was another ritual that would have to be gone through. The Last Meal.

"I wonder what the food's like in there?" mused my father gloomily. The *in there* was delivered in a dropped intonation as though it meant a prison.

"Terrible, I should think," said Lindsey grumpily. She was still feeling sore about her hair and my father's attack. "It'll be just like school food. You remember, Karen, the nuns always said they ate the same food as us. Imagine school food every day of your life!"

Gloom filled the car. It was not the moment, I knew, to hold forth on the unimportance of physical comforts. At the moment the issue of food seemed trivial. It would be like the fairy godmother urging Cinderella to sit down to a sensible supper before she set off for the ball, a distraction from the real issue.

"But I'm sure you must have nice food sometimes, Karen," my mother was saying. "I wonder if you'll have turkey and plum pudding on Christmas Day."

"Mmm," I murmured vaguely. How did I know? These random speculations were serving to impress on all of us the barrier that was so soon to divide us from one another.

"I wonder what you'll be doing this time tomorrow," my mother went on, desperate to keep up the conversation at all costs. Silence was much too difficult to handle.

"Unpacking, I expect," I suggested cooperatively. "General settling in. And then perhaps we get down to normal duties. Mother Katherine said that postulants spend most of the time doing housework."

"Good God!" said my father, "do they realize how bad you are at housework? You're always dropping things and you never seem to see the dirt. I don't expect they'll keep you long," he added facetiously, but he sounded suddenly hopeful. Somehow I knew that he would actually be angry if the Order sent me home like an unwelcome parcel. But, "You probably won't stand that for long," he added quite cheerfully.

4

"Oh, it won't be too bad," I added firmly.

There was silence once more. Then my father cleared his throat. I knew he was trying to say something important.

"Look!" he said awkwardly, swerving dangerously round a truck. "You mustn't be ashamed if you decide that the life isn't for you. Don't feel, will you, that anyone will think any the less of you if you don't stick it out. It'll be hard to admit that you've made a mistake. But if you find that you have, we'll still be proud of you— even more proud of you, if you see what I mean."

Lindsey shuddered as though some indecency had been spoken. The air hummed with embarrassment. As a family we just did not say that kind of thing to one another. Reserve characterized our conversations entirely. We chatted endlessly about trivia but left the big things unsaid. My father, I knew, had said something important, but none of us knew how to cope with it. How sad it all is, I thought. Each of us is locked away from the others. And now we'll never learn to talk deeply. So many things will never be said. Because now it's too late.

"Candy?" asked my mother again, and this time we all accepted, filling the void with the business of unwrapping and sucking.

And now here we were at Kings Cross, still smiling cheerfully, more anxious than ever not to mar these very last moments with tearfulness and grief. Five more minutes. We ought to say something memorable, something to mark the occasion as a momentous one. *I* should speak this time; my father had done his bit. He was glancing round the station, trying to focus his attention on something that would distract him from what was really happening. What *could* I say to them? "Thank you for all you have done for me"? "I'll be thinking of you and praying for you always"? It sounded so glib and meaningless, though I meant it all.

"Well," my mother said brightly, "the train's going to leave on time. That's perfect. We'll just have time to get to the theatre."

They were all going to a matinee performance of *The Sound of Music.* We had the record at home. Those pretty nuns, that irrepressible postulant, the wise superior. A good choice in many ways. The religious life cut down to fit the limitations of the stage—cozy, comprehensible, and painless. I knew that the real thing wasn't

5

going to be like that. The nuns I was joining in a couple of hours must smile at it. Of course it would be different.

"Got your suitcase?" asked my father helplessly, though he had put it on the rack with his own hands.

"Yes!" I said heartily. "There it is."

"What time do you get there?" asked Lindsey, making a huge effort. She still looked at me, lost in a dream of horror.

"Four-fifteen," I replied, though we had been through all this hundreds of times already. "I'll be there in time for tea."

We looked at one another.

Silence.

"I do hope you enjoy it," I said. *The Sound of Music,* I mean. You'll have to tell me all about it when you write."

God, couldn't I think of anything better than that?

We gazed at one another for five long seconds. The smiles never once faltered. If only we could get this all over with, I thought sadly. It'll be so much easier for them once I've really gone. I couldn't bear what I was doing to them. In a way their cheerful bravery was a reproach. If only they'd behaved a little less impeccably so that I could feel a bit cross with them. But that wasn't fair, I knew. The next few minutes stretched ahead like a lifetime, filled with sadness and ambivalence. After that, once the train had disappeared in a smooth curve, there would be nothing between me and the convent. These last miserable moments were the first step along the road of sacrifices that would take me to God and a happiness and significance that were too great to imagine. In the meantime my family and I stared at one another, still smiling.

Then a whistle. Slamming doors. A hiss of steam.

"Good-bye!" I screamed, and at that terrible moment a feeling of panic and grief hit me like a physical force. I really was going. I'd done it now. I leaned perilously out the window, kissing my mother, my father quickly, snatching the last moment before I was torn from their embrace by the train carrying me slowly but irrevocably away from them.

"Good-bye, darling," said my baffled father. "I know you'll be very happy."

I continued to wave, fighting back the tears that stung my eyes as we pulled out. For the first time in my life my family suddenly looked very small and distant. Finally they disappeared.

How had it all begun?

I was born in Worcestershire, some fifteen miles outside Birmingham in a little place called Wildmoor. Now it has been swallowed up in housing projects. Then it consisted only of a row of small artisans' cottages half a mile from a little shop that sold everything from fuel oil and candles to groceries and sweets. On the third point of the triangle, two suburban semidetached houses stuck out incongruously. We lived in one of these. It was tiny, but it had a large garden that backed onto a ploughed field. This was also the local cess pit, for on Mondays huge pipes conveying the local sewage flowed through our garden, filling the house with a subdued but acrid stench. It was quite primitive. There was no running water downstairs and kitchen water had to be jacked out of a little pump in the garden. Every day my father would drive off to Birmingham to work and leave my mother alone in the house.

My mother so wanted to create a happy home for me, shielded from the disturbance that had been too much a part of her own childhood. She was the second daughter of a pharmacist and had grown up in Essex. Her elder sister, Mary, was my grandmother's favorite—not my grandfather's. I rarely remember him as preferring anybody or anything much to anyone else. He was a quiet, scholarly man. He should have gone to college, but there was no money, and he contented himself with reading—especially history. As the years went on his reading became a retreat. He had plenty to retreat from, poor man. My grandmother, a small, vital woman, was notoriously unfaithful to him and from my mother's earliest years had a string of lovers, one being the father of her best friend at school. When Eileen, my mother, was twelve, Granny got tuberculosis—all her family died of it—and went to live in a sanatorium in Switzerland for two years. My mother went with her, thus wrecking her education. She learned skiing and Swiss-German but little else. There's a cartoon at home done by one of the other patients there at that time. It shows my grandmother clasped passionately in the arms of a faceless man and my mother standing looking at them, a plain little girl with a skirt far too short for her, knickers showing. The caption reads: "I think I had better go to bed now, Mummy."

On their return to England the procession of men resumed but, an added horror, my grandmother started to drink. By the time the war broke out she was an alcoholic, secretly drinking neat gin in the

7

bathroom. From the time she was fifteen my mother felt she was in charge of the whole mess. But she escaped. My great-uncle, with whom she stayed sometimes, used to frequent the local pub, and, after closing time, he would gather up all his drinking companions and take them back to his house. There the drinking continued and my mother played the piano for them when she was on leave. On one of these evenings she met my father, who fell in love with her while she was playing the piano and singing a song called "Little Brown Bird." Almost a Victorian set-piece.

My father, however, was no callow romantic. At this time he was in his forties, twenty years older than my mother, and a bit of a rake. At the age of four he had come over to England from Ireland, where his father had run a village post office and was a respected member of the little community. He never made it in England, however. My father grew up in a Birmingham slum, left school at fourteen, and, after various fits and starts, eventually began a quite successful business as a scrap metal merchant.

When my mother met him there had been many women in his life, but she nailed him. He was a handsome man. Very tall—well over six feet—he stood broad-shouldered and solid, with a firm face and a lot of black, wavy hair. He loved clothes and decked himself out with flamboyance.

The match came in for heavy opposition. My grandmother refused to have anything to do with it, and her family told my mother firmly that she was neglecting her responsibilities and was mad to marry a man so much older than herself who would never, it was clear, be much of a success. She stood firm, though. My father paid for the wedding, which was poorly attended on my mother's side. And a very successful marriage began.

My father loved life and the things of this world. He adored good food and drink. He used to draw and paint and developed an interest in antiques, which he sought out with the zeal of a lover, filling the house with beautiful things. He loved travel and would frequently whisk my mother off to the French Riviera. He made quite a lot of money from scrap metal but never saved a penny of it. What he had he spent recklessly and generously. When their friends asked him how on earth he could afford to take us all to the south of France every summer, he smiled charmingly and replied, "I can't." He rescued my mother from the grimness of her youth and taught her to enjoy herself. Neither of them ever looked at anyone else.

Under his influence my mother opened out like a flower. From a pudgy adolescent, she became a slim, glamourous woman. She had dark hair, bright alert eyes, and a full mouth. With my father she ate and drank like a princess, entertained his enormous circle of friends, and went with them on perilous midnight tobogganing expeditions where, clinging to my father, she hurtled dangerously through the darkness. My earliest memories are of lying upstairs on my cot, listening to the hum of voices downstairs, the laughter of the assembled company, and the clinking of glasses.

At the outset of her married life, my mother was an indifferent housekeeper. Unlike her neighbors, she sat quite happily amid the breakfast debris, reading the paper until well into the morning. She scandalized Mrs. Jefferson next door by not getting her washing out to dry until Saturday. What cleaning there was was done by Mrs. Meacham, a fat, gingery woman with a loud cheery voice who came in daily from the cottages. "Meachey" was not much of a one for cleaning either. When she had had enough she called to my mother, who was reading in the back room: "I'm just going to take Karen to see the pigs!" and my mother would agree happily, settling back to enjoy a peaceful half-hour, knowing that I would be well looked after. Meachey would put me on the handlebars of her bicycle and wheel me to her cottage. I loved her, purely and simply. We went through the front door straight into the downstairs room where I was given a glass of orange juice. Then, as a part of the ritual, I visited the outside privy, which I considered a great treat. Finally we went down the narrow strip of garden to a corrugated fence and Meachey lifted me up. There, inside the little enclosure, were the pigs: one pink and one black and white, snorting and messy. I used to look at them solemnly, thinking what a nice, sensible life they led, wallowing in the mud and straw. Sometimes I helped to feed them and relished the decaying smell of the sloppy food. It was even more special when there were squealing little piglets, too, shrieking and sleek, fighting to be first at the trough, hankering for life. Next time I went they had disappeared, and some instinct of self-preservation told me not to ask where they had gone. The sty seemed very empty.

Apart from my parents, Meachey, and the pigs, I had no other companions. There were no children of my age in Wildmoor and

I lived in a little cocoon of family. I was never lonely. As soon as I could walk and talk I lived an intensely imaginative life. On Sunday afternoons my father would take me for a walk. This was a special event. We went right down to the little brook and played "pooh sticks," and on my way home I visited all my "friends." Certain bushes and trees along the country lanes housed fairies, and we used to knock at a bush, enter, and have tea and a chat. I always felt very proud to show my handsome father to these friends of mine, and he patiently sat there, crouched on a tree stump, pretending to drink tea, entering gamely into the spirit of the thing. He had not been keen to have children initially; he felt he was too old to adapt to their demands, but once we arrived he loved being a father. He never wanted sons.

When I was three and a half my mother presented me with a sister, Lindsey Madeleine. She was too young to play with for a long time. She was a noisy, vivacious baby and extremely restless. As soon as she could sit up, she ruined the pram by forcing her head through the canvas hood. We must have looked an odd trio on our afternoon walks, my mother pushing a battered and muddy pram with Lindsey's head thrust through the hole in the hood, like the figurehead on the prow of a ship, waiting patiently while I stood chattering into a thornbush.

When he got home in the evening, my father always read to me before I went to bed. My mother also read to me during the day, and together we listened to the story on "Listen with Mother," and later I joined her for the story on "Woman's Hour." No matter that I could not understand it; I loved the words. My father bought me a lot of books and I quickly knew them by heart, we read them so frequently. If my mother tried to skip a page, I knew instantly and made her go back and read the thing through in full. Reading was not just a matter of finding out what happened in a story; it was a ritual. It was the words that mattered. The characters of the books became realities to me when I played alone. I had endless conversations with Little Grey Rabbit and her *ménage.* There was one book that was a special favorite. It concerned a hedgehog called Harry and featured human beings as creatures called "mortals." I can't remember much about the story, but the word *mortal,* once I knew what it meant, colored the rather somber story with melancholy. Whenever my mother or Meachey offered to read to me, I produced

Harry the Hedgehog till they both got heartily sick of it. But it was no use offering me anything else. My mother thought the book was morbid and quietly disposed of it. I noticed its absence and guessed what had happened. It was no use complaining. Adults were omnipotent and I mourned the lost book, trying to recapture the beautiful sadness as best I could. I bided my time.

One day when my grandmother was staying with us, she took me on the village bus into a nearby market town for tea. We did some shopping and she offered to buy me a book, which was the best present I could have. In the children's department I scoured the shelves with eagle eye. I knew exactly what I was looking for. Granny offered me one or two books, but I shook my head. At last I saw it. I couldn't read but I recognized Harry himself on the cover.

"That one!" I cried.

Granny looked at it.

"*Harry the Hedgehog*?" she read. I nodded firmly.

"Are you sure that's the one you want, dear?" She was puzzled by my insistence but finally agreed.

My mother and Meachey were having a cup of tea when we returned. I tried not to look too triumphant. I wanted to be generous in my victory.

"Granny's bought me a new book!" I said, cuddling up to my mother with a winning smile.

"Aren't you a lucky girl! Say thank you to Granny!"

"I already have," I answered truthfully and produced my parcel. "Look, Meachey!" I said innocently.

She looked. "Oh, no!" she wailed. "Oh, my God! Not *Harry the Hedgehog*! Oh, Mrs. Armstrong! I can't stand it!"

"It *was* a pity we lost the old one," I said sweetly. "Isn't it kind of Granny? Let's have it tonight."

But mortality had already entered our safe little home. I had been told that my mother would be bringing home a new baby. She prepared me for the event very carefully and bought me a doll, a crib, and a pram, so that I could be occupied with my baby and not feel jealous. The baby, alas, was a breech birth, and the little blonde girl, christened Caroline, died of a lung infection. I remember nothing of my own expectations about the baby, nor my disappointment when my mother came home alone. But I do remember the sadness and the sense of loss that pervaded the house, bravely hidden but strongly felt. I once came upon Meachey and an aunt in close conversation in the kitchen.

"It's a shame," Meachey was saying, "a crying shame!"

There was nothing unusual in this. Meachey's conversation tended to be rather lugubrious at the best of times. What was different was the way they both stopped talking as soon as they saw me, bustled me out of the room, and talked with affected cheerfulness of something else. Something was being kept from me, something sad, and I felt frightened and excluded. I took to carrying around the house the doll my mother had bought me. Her name was Trudi and she went everywhere with me. I felt obscurely that it was vital to keep Trudi safe, and that if I kept a stern eye on her it would ward off this terrible thing that had entered the house. I found great comfort in the fact that Trudi was rubber.

"She won't ever break, will she?" I pestered my father. "She'll be with me always, even when I'm old?"

"No, she won't break," he answered.

"Will she break if I drop her?"

"No. Try it and see."

I closed my eyes tightly and flung Trudi on the ground and then dared not look. "It's all right," my father promised. It was. Trudi lay there on the ground, undignified and outraged but still miraculously whole.

"It's all right," I promised her that night. "I'll always look after you. Nothing will ever happen to you."

My mother was in bed for a long time after she came home from the hospital, and I felt that I must be near her to keep this thing, whatever it was, at bay, to assure myself that everything was really just the same as ever. (Of course, once death entered my life, nothing would ever be quite the same again.) Book in hand, I waddled sternly into her bedroom, climbed up onto the bed, and nestled down near her. The closer I got, the safer she'd be. "Sing it! Sing it!" I demanded, thrusting the book firmly into her hand. Sensing my need of her, my mother read on bravely, hour after hour. Sitting close together, we made a cocoon of security. It was an incantation holding away the sadness of life.

To all intents and purposes life continued smoothly in the same peaceful, uneventful way. Yet fear, dating perhaps from Caroline's death, was always there and emerged in my dreams. Dragons pursued me endlessly over terrifying, undulating hills night after night. I remember dreaming once that my father was dead, and a desolation filled me as I knelt beside his strangely changed body, weeping, "Come back, Daddy! Come back!"

It must have been about this time that I hit upon a magical way of leaving this frightening world behind and entering into my own world of beauty and order. Sometimes on weekends or on summer evenings when my father got home we went for a picnic in the nearby Farley woods. Once we hit upon a perfect place, but we never went there again. It was a beech wood and it was bluebell time. The little glade was completely enclosed by walls of pale green leaves broken only by sharp shafts of sunlight. The ground was a blurred mass of blue. It was the most perfect place I had ever seen. It was not just the beauty, it was the peace. The fears and that horrible shadowy reality that now lurked at the corners of my life were shut out and I was safe with my parents. They were talking together and I was left to listen or to think as I chose, knowing that they were there. I gave the experience of that hour a private name. I called it "putsh." Peace, safety, beauty, and privacy.

"Putsh" became an important concept for me. Whenever I thought we were near the woods, I called out "Putsh!" from the back of the car, to my parents' bewilderment. Whenever life became troublesome, I repeated the word over and over again as a talisman, trying to bring that beauty and order back into my life. Nobody could understand what I wanted, but I didn't want them to. It was like a magic secret. If I told anyone, the magic would go away.

Though I longed to go back to the little glade, there was one special means I discovered for arriving at "putsh" inside my own head. We had an old wind-up Gramophone, and I learned to work this myself. I found the exact spot on the carpet, and then, crouched in a fetal position, I rocked backward and forward to the music. Swaying to and fro like that, I found I could empty my mind of everything but a heightened sense of things. Death and sadness no longer existed and I moved in an atmosphere of limitless perfection. This lasted for years and left in me a hunger for infinite horizons that later I learned to transfer to religion. After all, God is the ultimate perfection, and as the world grew more and more distressing when I grew older, I found myself searching for Him to find that peace permanently.

The seclusion of my childhood ended abruptly on the day I first went to school. I'd looked forward to it for weeks. My mother had told me enthusiastically what fun I would have. I felt important trying on my school uniform—bottle-green gym slip, bulky tie, fawn sweater, all several sizes too big for me to allow for growth. But now, as I sat next to my father in the front seat of the car, the thick Harris tweed coat felt like a suit of armor. It was a wet, dark morning, and the long journey into Birmingham seemed a trek from one world into another. I peered with difficulty from under the huge brim of my green velour hat and saw the trees straining despairingly in the wind, which blew shrilly and threateningly.

The windshield wipers shrieked as they made their jerky journey backward and forward, sloshing the rain into deep pools and rivulets.

"How does the uniform feel?" Daddy asked. I could hear the strained heartiness in his voice and tried to reassure him.

"Very nice, thank you, Daddy." My voice seemed squeaky and came out in a rush as though it didn't belong to me. I swallowed and felt a great lump in my throat, and when I tried to breathe my chest was constricted with fear.

My father looked at me. Pigtails stuck out awkwardly beneath the hat. My face, never very rosy, was now almost the same greenish hue as my uniform, and the sprinkling of freckles across my nose stood out in stark relief. They seemed an incongruous memento of a carefree summer.

"You do look smart!" he said. "The nuns *will* think you look nice! Just like a proper schoolgirl."

I did my best to smile. The nuns. What a strange word that was! I had heard a lot about them recently. I must call them "Sister" or "Mother," and they loved Jesus and would teach me to read. They were very kind people and I would love them dearly.

Clutching my father's hand I made my way down the school drive. Everywhere there were little girls. But they didn't seem little to me. Most of them towered above me. Still trying fiercely to smile, I let go of my father's hand. I wanted him to go quickly so that he would not witness my possible failure in this frightening new world. But I also longed for him to stay, to take me home.

"Hello, Mr. Armstrong." I looked up quickly and thankfully; that somebody knew his name was reassuring.

I recoiled. There peering up at my father was the strangest creature I had ever seen. It was covered from head to foot in black robes that formed a solid wall of musty-smelling darkness, like winter coats hanging up to dry. Glancing at the ground I saw two feet shod in gleaming black leather. Then the wall rose in perpendicular folds. No legs. Cautiously, the little girls quite forgotten as I stared in fascination, I reached out for the skirt and touched it gingerly, lifting it slightly to see whether I could discover the missing limbs. Yes, ankles. I lifted it further to see for a brief second two sturdy black calves. Then a hand reached out and deftly seized my hands, ending any further exploration, and I was pulled gently up against her. Somehow I knew that this creature was friendly. My eyes traveled up. Some way above me a black and silver object gleamed. I recognized it from my few visits to church but had never seen such a big one on a person before: Jesus on the cross, I told myself wonderingly. Then I looked up, puzzled, to the face, small and putty-colored. I searched in vain for hair. The voice was deep. Did it belong to a man or a woman? It was explaining things to my father.

"Yes, four o'clock."

"Right, Mother, I'll be there," he said. Mother? A woman, then. I gaped incredulously. I looked up again at the face. There was so little of it that I could see. There was a wart, I noticed, on the top lip. Did all nuns have one?

"Come along, Karen," and I was led away from the alarming din; this friendly "Mother" would interpret the world for me. I was safe with her.

Gradually I learned to adapt to the aggressive and turbulent life of the classroom and the playground. I learned to read very quickly and discovered the joy of losing myself entirely in books without my parents' help. Otherwise work bored me somewhat. As I grew older and was set small tasks for homework, I skipped through them as best I could, relying on my wits to get me through. But during my time in the Junior School two incidents impressed themselves forcibly on me, setting a pattern that would profoundly influence me in the future—my love for a challenge.

The first occurred when I was eight. We had by then moved into Birmingham, and my parents decided that I should learn to swim. Three times a week we went to the strange echo-filled swimming baths where a fearsome lady called Mrs. Brewster gave free instruction. The first stages of swimming were pleasant enough, but at length it was time to learn to dive. I was terrified. The idea of falling head foremost through the air, seeing the glittering water rush to meet me, was appalling. I refused to do it, hating myself for my cowardice. At length Mrs. Brewster had had enough of my evasion. She picked me up in her brawny arms, taking no heed of my frantic kicking and screams for help, and strode to the brink of the pool. "One, two, three!" she called and hurled me head first into the water. I flew dizzily; the sinister blue water dazzled terrifyingly for a moment, and then there was nothing but a confusion of water and sound.

I found myself standing in the pool, dazed, yes, exhausted, but also exhilarated. I had survived. And I had done it. I had done it. From that moment swimming became heaven for me. A chunky child, I was altogether without physical grace, but now the water became my element. And I'd learned that to find freedom from my limitations I had to push myself beyond what I thought I could do.

The second incident centered that same year on an encyclopedia called *A Path to Knowledge.* It was a four-volume work that my father had seen advertised and he urged me to read a little of it every day.

"While your mind is young, you'll learn lots of things that will stay with you all through your life. Knowledge is one of the most important things in the world. It gives you freedom."

The volumes looked important in their dark green binding with gold lettering. Glancing through them I discovered that the best part was definitely Volume IV, where there was a lot about writers and poetry and some history, too, the things that I liked best at school. But I closed that volume firmly. Knowledge was a serious business. I had to start at the beginning and work through to the end. Dipping in here and there was a frivolity. I knew the rules of life: before you were allowed cake for tea you had to eat your bread and butter. Also the title of the work enthralled me. A path lay ahead, down which I would heroically overcome all obstacles, grappling with huge intellectual difficulties until at the end knowledge loomed gloriously. And I would do it alone.

So chapter by chapter, page by page, I dragged myself on through all four volumes. My eyes glazed with boredom, I ploughed my way through the dusty paths of mathematics, science, industry, and commerce. One evening, as I was engaged with a study of the iron and steel trade, my father came into the room.

"Oh, you're reading the encyclopedia, are you?"

I glowed with satisfaction at his pleasure.

"What are you reading now?" he asked, looking over my shoulder, and, ablaze with virtue, I announced:

"Trades."

"Trades?" said my father, surprised. "Do you like that?"

"Well, no, this bit is awfully boring."

My father scratched his head, bewildered. "Then why on earth read it?"

I explained. My father looked at me as though he had spawned a monster and then threw back his head and roared with laughter. Helpless, he staggered to the bed and collapsed, shoulders heaving with mirth. Then, seeing my indignation, he explained to me how to use an encyclopedia. It was a relief to put Volume II back on the shelf and open the enticing Volume IV. But I had a lingering suspicion that I had cheated.

One thing that school did for me in those early years was to introduce me to religion. At home religion was cut down to a minimum. My father was a recent convert to Catholicism and never felt completely at home in the church. When we went to Mass he knelt there, glasses on the end of his nose, peering dubiously at his English translation of the Latin that was being gabbled mechanically at the altar.

It took years for religion to mean much more than this to me —an hour of excruciating boredom on Sunday morning which I longed to be over and done with. "Can't we go to seven o'clock Mass, Mummy?" I'd plead, knowing that we would then be home just after eight and the rest of the day would be my own. Often I got up at six on Sunday mornings and walked to Mass by myself, arriving home just in time to wave off my family who were dutifully setting off for the nine o'clock Mass. I watched them go with a heady sense of freedom.

But gradually religion got through to me. At school we lived the rhythm of the church's year, and that rhythm formed the liturgical background to my own view of life. At Lent the drapings of the altar turned to purple. Gloomy hymns were sung; I listened to the story of Jesus' fight with the devil in the wilderness after his six weeks' fast. Lent became a heroic and arduous pilgrimage. We were taught to make "acts." "What are you giving up for Lent?" we asked one another. Sweets, sugar in tea, watching television? Or, "What are you going to *do* for Lent?" Go to Mass twice, three times a week? Every day? Say the rosary regularly? Make a special effort not to quarrel?

The possibilities were endless, and, for me, Lent became another race with myself. Can I keep it up? Can I go to Mass every day for six solid weeks, through the wet, cold spring mornings? Can I force myself to say the rosary every single evening? Lent grew darker; at Passiontide the statues in the convent were covered in purple drapes and stood there clumsy, bulky, and reproachful. For always by that time I had failed. There would be the morning I slammed down the alarm clock as it pealed heartlessly at six o'clock and turned over for another half-hour in bed. Or the orgy of eating sweets. Failure. But I persevered. Now let's have another go during Passiontide. Only two weeks—you can do it; you can do it. Then Holy Week: the long dramatic services that spoke to me more deeply than I could readily put into words. The long lines of people on Good Friday bending to kiss the feet of the crucified Christ, the aching knees. The church stripped and empty in deep mourning. And then suddenly it was Holy Saturday night. We'd stand outside the church at eleven o'clock while the priest struck a new flame and lit the great Paschal candle. Flame passed then to each of us as we handed the Easter light to one another. And then the procession wove its way into the pitch-black church, the light of Easter piercing the darkness, overcoming it as more and more of us entered the church with our candles.

"The light of Christ!" chanted the priest.

"Thanks be to God!" we replied in unison.

The ancient symbolism spoke to something very deep in me. There was the joy of that moment at midnight when suddenly all the electric lights were switched on, flowers were rushed to the stark altars, the organ—silent during the six weeks of Lent—pealed joyously, and all the congregation took out the bells they had brought and rang them: "Christ is risen." Death is swallowed up in victory.

I must have been just twelve years old when death once again threatened our family. One Sunday afternoon my sister Lindsey, who was then nine, complained of a sore throat. I didn't take much notice.

Lindsey and I rarely got on well together; we were too different. She was an attractive child with huge blue myopic eyes and long, dark plaits. Her beauty threw my own plump toothiness into harsher relief, I felt. So did her charm. She was a charismatic child who, wherever she was, attracted a swarm of friends. I had friends, too, in a quiet sort of way, but not spectacularly like Lindsey. At home I liked to be quiet and I resented Lindsey's constant claims on my time and energy. I wanted to read; Lindsey wanted to play. I hated conflict and quarreling. She, turbulent and dramatic by nature, loved it, goading me into arguments and rows. So on that first afternoon of her illness I glanced briefly from my book as she was shepherded up to bed and smiled to myself at the prospect of a couple of days of peace.

But her temperature soared up and up. After two days she was weeping with the pain in her throat, until finally she could scarcely breathe. I heard people whisper "Diphtheria" darkly, and the house was filled with doctors and muttered consultations. My parents crept about looking pale and stricken and I was left to my own devices. Huddled miserably in a corner of the dining room, I tried to read but couldn't. I could scarcely think. Outside the cold March evening blew wetly. Oh, my God, if she died how would I ever forgive myself? I kept thinking of that afternoon when I had repeatedly refused to play with her, and she had gone to my father and climbed on his knee. "I do love Karen so. Why is she always so horrid to me?" At the time I had been disgusted, wondering how anyone could descend to such a sentimental method of getting her own way. Now, inevitably, the words returned with terrible poignancy. If she died, how would my parents ever be able to forgive me for my rejection of my little sister? And how would I be able to forgive myself? She was so small. Death seemed monstrously unfair.

If God took Lindsey away now, He could take anyone at any time. The world once more seemed a frightening and unpredictable place, as it had after Caroline died and those dragons pursued me over endless hills in my dreams.

In bed that night I thought I should be quite unable to sleep. "Dear God," I prayed before getting into bed, "if you make Lindsey better I'll always be nice to her." Outside I could hear the specialist going downstairs to make a phone call. I heard the door closing behind him, and my ears strained in the darkness trying to catch a sound. Nothing. Death made everything fraught with anxiety. "Dear God," I found myself continuing, "if Lindsey gets better I'll think about being a nun."

I listened to myself in astonishment. Why had I promised that? Never in my wildest moment had I ever considered being a nun. The thought of the renunciation involved took my breath away. I heard the surgeon padding quietly upstairs. I heard my mother's voice, strained and anxious, talking about an ambulance. Just a word here and there. But I didn't hear any tears. My mother despised tears. And then suddenly I dropped off to sleep.

In the morning Lindsey was better. She had had a huge inflammation in her throat, and the surgeon had been just about to perform a tracheotomy when the poisonous thing broke and she could breathe again. We could all breathe again, but now once more the world seemed ringed round with a threat. I had forgotten how insubstantial life really was; Caroline's death had been so long ago. There would be many times in the next three or four years when I would forget this again, but Lindsey's illness had scarred my trust in life, and from time to time I would taste again that frightening emptiness of the world I lived in.

I kept remembering the promise I'd made to God. It almost seemed as though someone else had made it for me while I was off guard. Who? God? Had He been trying to tell me something? I turned away from that idea; it was full of disturbing implications, but time and again in the years to come I would flinch at the memory uneasily. Now I tried to salve my conscience. I only said I'd *think* about it, I reassured myself. I didn't say I'd actually do it.

2 · POINTERS
1956-1961

"Children! I have something very wonderful to tell you!" Mother Katherine, my headmistress, stood on the raised dais in the school hall, presiding over the morning assembly. I was in the Senior School now and at twelve was still slightly in awe of the formality and the size of my new surroundings. We stood in alphabetical order in lines of classes. Mine, the First Form, by the wall. Mother's eyes were shining with enthusiasm; her hands, draped in the long, black ceremonial sleeves, were clasped together with suppressed emotion.

I shifted from foot to foot uneasily. These ecstatic announcements were frequent and never seemed to me to occasion much rejoicing.

"You all know Miss Jackson," she continued. "Some of you, the older girls, will know her very well indeed." What can she have done? I thought to myself. Miss Jackson taught A-level physics to a handful of girls in the Sixth Form. She was a pale, colorless figure. Sometimes I glanced at her as she strode round the school with her white overall flapping round her short legs, her frizzy hair gripped back from a bony face. I glanced at her and mentally dismissed her. Perhaps she's got married, I thought with a flicker of interest. Then I shrugged. Unlikely.

"Well, Miss Jackson has decided to give her life to God," Mother Katherine's deep voice rang out dramatically. "She has decided to become a nun."

I gasped. I had always known in theory that nuns were ordinary people once, but in reality they had seemed a separate species. I looked at Mother Katherine with new eyes and for the first time noticed that she was a lovely-looking woman. No, perhaps *woman* was the wrong word. I couldn't imagine her in ordinary clothes, with hair and legs.

Not quite. But her face was lovely.

We filed out of the school hall, each one of us dropping a curtsey to Mother Katherine as we passed the dais.

"Fancy that!" I whispered to my friend Diana. It seemed a terrible fate.

"More fool her!" Diana replied. "I can't think of anything worse, can you?"

I shook my head.

"And never getting married!" Diana sounded aghast. "Imagine —actually choosing not to get married and not to have children. I'm going to get married as soon as I leave this dump!" She looked contemptuously at the cream walls of the corridor, punctuated here and there with bulletin boards. "And I'm going to have masses of children—seven at least. Aren't you?"

I nodded. I had always assumed that I'd get married. After all, everybody did. But suddenly getting married seemed rather less attractive. It was so predictable. We entered the classroom and began scrabbling in our desks for our French textbooks.

"Still," Diana went on, "I don't suppose Miss Jackson would ever have gotten married, do you? She was pretty ugly, really. And old."

"No," I agreed with Diana, "I don't suppose anyone would have married her."

"Well, then, it's probably all for the best. Anything's better than being an old maid. I'd die if I wasn't married before I was twenty. It'd be so embarrassing!"

During the morning I forgot about Miss Jackson. During the lunch hour, however, I noticed a photograph on the bulletin board that hadn't been there that morning. It was, I realized with a shock, Miss Jackson. I looked closely at it. She was wearing a long black dress, a little cape, and a short, floppy white veil. Her hair was drawn back tightly from her face and she looked out at the camera with an expression of—what was it?—yes, surprise. Even Diana was impressed.

"I wonder what it's like," she muttered. "Golly! Doesn't she look ghastly!"

We both involuntarily looked down the corridor to the baize door that separated the school from the enclosure where the nuns ate, slept, and prayed. We were never allowed to go through that door.

"She'll know now what they do all the time," I said, staring at the photograph, fascinated.

I remained at the bulletin board, studying Miss Jackson's expression. What had she seen to make her look so surprised? It was an intriguing thought. I looked at her face. She seemed so ordinary. But, really, I thought, she couldn't have been ordinary at all.

"You seem very interested in that photograph, Karen." I spun on my heel and found myself looking up at Mother Katherine. I was in awe of her. She swept round the school, remote in her exalted position. But when you had a chance to talk to her on her own, it was easy. She was smiling now, looking down at me questioningly.

"Yes, Mother," I said feebly. It was that kind of obvious statement that grown-ups often made, expecting you to reply significantly. I could never think how to go on.

"What does it make you think?"

"Well, Mother, why she did it! I just can't think why anyone would want to be a nun!"

"Why not?"

"Well, it must be terrible!" I said and then blushed. That wasn't very polite of me. "I'm sorry," I said hastily, "I don't mean to be rude, but . . ."

"What seems to you to be the hardest thing about it?"

I thought. There were so many horrors. But then I thought of the happiest moments of my life—the holidays. The first day of the holidays filled me with a pleasure that almost hurt.

"Well, never being able to do what you want to do. I'd hate not to have some time to myself when I'm free to do whatever I want. You know, sleep late, read—and be able to go on reading all day if I want to!"

"You mean freedom?" Mother Katherine said. She smiled. "But no one is really free much of the time, Karen. Think of your mother, any mother of a family. She's not really free to do what she wants either."

I was silenced. It was absolutely true. I thought of my mother endlessly running from chore to chore—shopping, cleaning, cooking, mending, washing, ironing.

"But my mother has fun sometimes," I said. "A nun can't really enjoy herself, can she? It must be like Lent all the year round."

Mother Katherine laughed. "Well," she said, "a nun doesn't enjoy herself in quite the same way as people in the world do. Of course not. But that doesn't mean she isn't happy."

"Happy?" I wrinkled my nose.

"Have you ever seen an unhappy nun?"

Again I was silent. No. I thought of the nuns' smiling faces, unlined and peaceful. I looked up at Mother Katherine. Her eyes were smiling at me and behind the smile there was a peace and a stability. When she was talking to me, she wasn't like other grown-ups I knew. Their minds weren't ever with me one hundred percent. The anxious lines around their mouths, the flickering moments of worry in their eyes showed that their minds were teeming with a dozen preoccupations. But Mother Katherine's mind was uncluttered.

"No, you all seem happy enough," I said grudgingly.

"Why do you say it like that?"

"Well, Mother, I can't really imagine how God can make you happy. Really happy, that is. I know He ought to, but it's very difficult to believe."

"Why?" Mother Katherine spoke quietly as though she were thinking over something precious and secret. Nuns often did that, I noticed. They smiled with amusement when you talked to them about God as though they knew something nice that you didn't.

"Well, it's hard sometimes to believe that God is a real person."

"Of course He is," she laughed.

"But what about other people!" I said, rather dismayed. "Don't you ever get lonely? Or fed up with having a hard life? You know, not going to the theatre or watching television."

She gave me a long look. "When you're in love the things you do with the person you love are always exciting and wonderful—even when they're difficult."

"And are you in love with God?" I said, amazed. "Love" was a fairly abstract idea for me, but I knew what being "in love" was. It made the heroines in films and plays rush about, sing, do incredi-

24

bly difficult dances, surmount all kinds of difficulties. "Are you in love?" I asked again.

Mother Katherine nodded. "Yes," she said very quietly. "There's the bell! You'd better hurry along to class." She turned on her heel and started off down the corridor. She never really walked anywhere, I realized; she seemed to swoop and float—not so difficult from those film stars after all, perhaps. As she reached the foot of the stairs leading to her room she turned round.

"Come and talk to me about this again, won't you, Karen?"

I was reminded sharply of Miss Jackson a few weeks later on my grandfather's birthday. It was 20 October 1956, a cold autumn day, and the family, gathered together for a celebration, were sitting together round the fire, which as usual was banked up far too high and roared dangerously up the chimney.

"Good God, Madge," said my father irritably, "that fire's positively lethal!" Whenever we got together like this with my grandparents there was tension, I thought. Why? I followed my father's eyes and looked at Granny, standing by the window pouring sherry into a glass. Her hand, I noticed, trembled slightly, and the drink splashed onto the crocheted white cloth. I felt protective of her. Tiny, skinny, her spectacles perched perilously on the end of her nose, she looked so frail. In a family of giants the two of us were the odd ones out, united by our small stature and the growing complicity of our minds.

My mother was sitting near me by the fire. She was smiling.

"What are you drinking?" she asked pleasantly, but with a heavy edge of significance. "Gin?"

"Gin!" Granny was horrified. "Gin! I hate gin, *hate* it," she repeated emphatically. "No, I'm having a little sherry." She held up her tiny glass, in which a thimbleful of amber liquid glowed in the angry firelight. "I *never* drink gin."

I felt my parents' eyes meeting over my head. Granny had taken her glasses off and her eyes flickered round the room. They looked frightened and alone.

"I'd better go and look at the dinner," she said.

"Karen! Go and help Granny," said my mother, prodding me urgently in the back.

I got up and followed her out into the kitchen, which was filled with a savory smell from the oven. Vegetables bubbled busily on the hobs of the old gas stove. It was a steamy, comfortable place. I perched myself on the formica-topped table and sat there, legs swinging, while she jabbed the potatoes with a fork.

"Nearly done," said Granny. "It'll be another quarter of an hour, I think. When I was at school," and her voice was softened with memory, "I'd have been expelled for knowing what a potato looked like before it was cooked! A lady didn't do this kind of thing then!"

We laughed comfortably, at ease together. This was familiar ground. Granny had been at a convent school in Liverpool run by the same order of nuns that taught at my own school. That had been an important factor in my parents' choice of a school for me.

"You liked school, didn't you?" I asked.

"Yes," she was smiling quietly to herself. Then suddenly she coughed loudly. "Sorry," she apologized. "I've got a bit of a tickle in my throat." She turned her back to me, and, with a nervous glance in the direction of the living room, she went to the tray beside the stove, which contained a large array of cooking bottles: vinegar, oil, brown sauce, and one squat green bottle. She filled a generous glassful of a clear liquid like water and, coughing markedly at me, knocked back the draught in one swift action.

"Hmm," she cleared her throat. "That's better. It's a nuisance, this cough."

I turned my eyes resolutely away from the green bottle and deliberately closed a shutter in my mind. This, I knew instinctively, was something that I mustn't know about.

"Can I do anything to help, Mummy?" my mother called suddenly.

We both froze and looked guiltily at one another.

"No, thank you, dear!" Granny called back, "Karen's doing a great job out here. We'll be back presently. Help yourself to another drink!"

"All right!" My mother's voice was deliberately casual.

Granny went on, dreamily. "I was terribly naughty at school! I remember once a priest came to give us a retreat. 'In Heaven,' he said, 'you'll be singing "Glory be to God!" forever and ever!' and

I whispered to the girl next to me, 'How boring! I don't think I want to go to Heaven.' "

"I know what you mean," I said. "It sounds awful, doesn't it? Glory be to God forever and ever." But if you didn't want to go to Heaven there was only one alternative. I shuddered. It was a dilemma.

"Unfortunately, the priest heard me whispering, and when he had finished his talk he said, very solemnly, 'Who is the little girl who doesn't want to go to Heaven?' "

"Oh no!" I breathed. "How dreadful! Did you own up?"

"Yes," she smiled slightly and leaned against the wall, her eyes fixed dreamily ahead. "I had my Holy Innocents medal taken away from me as a penance."

"Do you think you'll go to Hell, then?" I masked the fearful import of the question with a giggle.

"Yes!" she laughed. "Oh, yes! I expect the devil's got a nice warm spot for me down there! Do you think those potatoes are done yet?"

I prodded them. "Not quite," I said, preoccupied. Hell terrified me. It seemed so hideously easy to go there. "But you have to commit a mortal sin to go to Hell, don't you?" I asked. "A very serious sin indeed, knowing that you're doing it."

"Yes!" Granny laughed hollowly. "Yes, that seems to be the idea."

I looked at her. She seemed so harmless. And I loved her with a great rush of tenderness.

"Well!" Granny said, looking wistfully at the green bottle. "I think we'd better be getting back to the others. You dish up those potatoes and leave them in the hot drawer, will you? Thanks. I'll just put one or two things away in the larder."

She disappeared into the tiny little room next door, carrying the bottle of Worcestershire sauce and—I saw out of the corner of my eye—the green bottle. Standing at the sink, waiting for her, I saw the darkening garden outside looking misty and sinister in the autumn twilight. The world seemed a puzzling place. "I think you'll have to go to Heaven, you know, Granny," I said. "I don't think you're bad enough for Hell."

My mother's eyes bored into Granny as we entered the room.

I went over and sat close to my mother, smiling up at her, feeling that, in some way I didn't understand, I had been disloyal. Saturated with warmth, I gazed into the flames of the fire.

"Just time for another drink," Granny said briskly. "We ought to leave the meat to stand for a few minutes, don't you think? Is Karen old enough to have a sherry?"

"Oh, yes, I think so," my mother's voice was cheery, consciously filled with the birthday spirit. "Just a small one. Would you like a sherry, Karen?"

"No," I answered promptly, without thinking. The refusal was automatic. For some reason that I would not analyze, it was impossible for me to accept. "No, thank you, Granny."

I watched her walk across the room, replenishing my parents' glasses. As she navigated the coffee table, she stumbled slightly, and my mother's sharp intake of breath cut through me. But as soon as she caught me looking at her, my mother smiled and said, "What were you two gossiping about in the kitchen?"

"Oh, Granny was telling me about her school," I answered. "It still sounds awfully like my school, you know. We do all the same things, have all the same customs."

"Mmm," my mother said vaguely. "You were happy at school weren't you, Mummy? Like Karen." For a moment her eyes were wary as she listened to what she had said, startled. "You like the same things."

"Happiest days of your life, Madge?" asked my father genially.

Granny glanced at my grandfather, who was still quite oblivious to his birthday celebration, and her eyes wandered aimlessly round the room.

"Yes, I expect they were in a way."

"School was?" I said, appalled.

"Yes," Granny said musingly. "You know, you think you hate it while you're there, but lately I've been looking back at those days over and over again. We were happy." She sipped her sherry reflectively.

I looked at Granny in amazement. Surely not. Everybody knew that school was terrible; life began once you had left it behind you. Didn't it?

"I suppose they were," Granny repeated quietly. "You know,"

she smiled inwardly, "when I was just a little older than Karen—oh, I must have been about sixteen or seventeen—I wanted to be a nun. My mother wouldn't let me. You never know," she added obscurely, "it might have made all the difference. . . . Yes, perhaps I should have been a nun."

Seeds had been planted: Lindsey's illness, Miss Jackson's decision, and this conversation with my grandmother were helping me to grow accustomed to an idea: the idea that people like me could become nuns. These incidents raised a question that at the time I preferred not to examine too closely. It was to be some years before the seeds blossomed into a decision.

The year 1960 was an important one for me. I was fifteen and eager to break out of the sheltered world of childhood, but the adult world turned out rather differently from the way I'd expected.

One thing that turned out badly was my friendship with Suzie.

I remember how it all came to a head one hot September afternoon. Suzie and I were sitting in our garden. She was lying sprawled in a deck chair, her skin-tight jeans stretched over her thighs, her breasts peaking provocatively under her orange tee shirt. I glanced down at my own lumpy body. Suzie was formed. She was complete and ready for life. Her lips were coated with orange lipstick; her nails—why would mine never grown that long?—were gleaming orange talons. She had done her best with me. Under her tutelage I was wearing a similar pair of jeans and a grey shirt, and my lips were covered with a chalky pink lipstick. Like Suzie's, my hair was back-combed into a tangled beehive. I should look all right, I reflected sadly. In fact, if I concentrated on my face, I didn't look too bad. My teeth were much too big, of course, but from the neck upward, I would just about pass. My body had nothing to do with my head, however. I could never look finished, all of a piece.

"How can you bear the thought of going into the Sixth Form, Karen?"

"I don't know," I replied untruthfully, "it seems endless." The trouble was, I thought, I *wanted* to do A-levels and go on to college. Suzie—and indeed all my friends—couldn't wait to get into the real world. Suzie herself, having scraped through five O-levels, was leaving school and was about to embark on a secretarial course. The prospect of that just didn't appeal to me. It was no good; I was just different from her. But I did so want to belong to her world.

"You really ought to get out more," she said, "you know, drink a bit, smoke a bit, find a boyfriend. You're really not a bluestocking, you know, Karen. You can be really good fun once you let yourself go a bit. And you would, once you got a boyfriend!"

"Fat chance!" I muttered gloomily. *Fat*, I thought, looking down at myself, was the word.

"By the way," she asked casually, "is Tony in?"

"Who?" I asked blankly. "Oh, you mean Anthony! Yes, he's here. He's in the sitting room, I think, doing something or other. Why?"

"Just wondered," Suzie replied lazily.

Anthony, my cousin, was staying with us. Two years older than I, he was about to enter the police force, having decided not to carry on doing A-levels at school. Another one.

"It's no good," I said in a burst of honesty. "I'll never be successful with boys like you are! I just don't look right and I can't talk to them."

"Goodness, you don't want to *talk* to them, do you? There are much more interesting things to do with boys than just *talking*, for God's sake!"

I laughed knowingly, hoping that it was convincing. In fact, the whole area of sex was a mystery to me. It seemed hedged round with dangers. It was a wonderful thing, I had been told again and again. But if you did it when you were not married or when you were deliberately preventing a baby from being born (by means of some mysterious devices), it was a mortal sin. And that meant that if you did not truly repent you went to Hell for all eternity. And what exactly was "it" anyway? In biology lessons the nun who taught us made us read the chapter on reproduction by ourselves. It seemed to be all about rabbits, and I didn't think I had much in common with a rabbit. The technical details of sex were shrouded in a disturbing obscurity. And then once you got a boyfriend there was all that business about "going too far" or "making yourself cheap."

"Suzie," I asked diffidently, "aren't you ever afraid that you'll get pregnant when you go with boys?"

"Course not!" she laughed confidently, happily ignorant of the fact that in three years' time she would "have to" get married. "There's loads of things you can do before you go that far." I blinked uncertainly. What on earth could she be talking about? And what about those dark masculine urges that I was constantly being warned could not possibly be controlled? But confessing my ignorance would be too humiliating.

"Yes, I know," I lied, "but don't they want to do the whole thing?"

"Oh, yes," she answered complacently, stretching her body in the sun like a contented cat. "But I can always handle them. By the way," she sat up suddenly, "can I go and phone my mother to tell her when I'll be in?" She dusted a few blades of grass off herself.

"Sure," I said, reaching for my book. It was *The Mill on the Floss.* I watched her go into the house and turned back with relief to the ordered world of literature. I'd nearly gotten to the end of the novel. Poor Maggie. I knew just how she'd felt as a child. Ugly, precocious, a misfit. Then she'd become a beauty. Her position was hopeless, but the ugly duckling blossomed into a swan. I read of her drifting down the river with Stephen Guest, conscious of impending disaster.

After a while I glanced at my watch. Good heavens, Suzie'd been gone for a quarter of an hour. Her telephone conversations with her mother were usually brief to the point of rudeness. What could be keeping her? I went in to see.

I walked through the kitchen into the front hall. There, through a crack of the door that had been carelessly left ajar, I saw them.

Suzie was sitting on the hearthrug, her head bent back, her eyes staring blindly at the window. My cousin Anthony leaned over her. One of his hands kneaded her back, the other hand squeezed and paddled in her neck. Even as I watched, their lips joined in what I recognized was a familiar embrace.

I watched the long kiss, mesmerized. Then, shamed, I stole into the kitchen. Sitting there at the table, I reviewed a world made suddenly impossible. Anthony and Suzie must have been laughing at me for suspecting nothing of their relationship. The feeling of exclusion I had experienced in the garden flooded back, more intense. Seeing them like that made all the difference. Hitherto the only kisses I had really seen were on the television screen in plays and films that glamourized them, presenting love as a cataclysmic, all-revealing passion. But this was the real world. I could not go along with it.

This, I told myself in a sudden cold certainty, was not passion. But it was the stuff of which most marriages were made. No one would ever want to do that to me, I knew. But no longer did I want them to. How could Suzie do it? Anthony, with his pimples and his moods—like all his friends.

No! The whole thing was certainly not for me.

With a shock I heard the front door opening. My mother was back from the hairdresser's. Guiltily, I stole into the garden and picked up my book.

"I don't mind! Really, Anthony! I don't mind for myself. But with Suzie! . . . She's such a little slut! . . . She's having such a bad influence on Karen!" I heard snatches of my mother's fury.

Suddenly the idea of being a bride of Christ seemed enormously attractive. I thought of Anthony. There seemed no comparison. Of course I wasn't going to be a nun, I told myself. The idea was ridiculous. To be as fulfilled as Mother Katherine was a reward for having given up an awful lot. Books, theatre, freedom—until an hour ago I would have added sex. But that no longer seemed any sacrifice at all.

"Karen!" my mother called me. I turned round and squinted up at the house, narrowing my eyes against the sharp glare of the evening sun. My mother was standing at my bedroom window. Her face was tense, and momentarily I compared it to Mother Katherine's, which was always so serene and untroubled. No, marriage was not all it was cracked up to be.

"Come up here a minute!" Her voice had that deliberately casual tone it always took on when she was upset and was trying to pretend that nothing was the matter.

"Just look at yourself," she commanded, turning me round to the mirror, gripping my shoulders as though she were about to take me into custody. "Do you think you look nice?"

I stared at my reflection, but all I could see were my eyes. They looked lost. I dropped my gaze. My mother was angry about Suzie and Anthony. It was more than just her view of Suzie as a slut. She was angry with me, too, though she didn't quite know why.

Sex was the matter, I thought suddenly. She wants to save me from sex.

32

"Well!" my mother demanded. "Do you?"

With a start I jerked my mind back to her question. It was an irrelevance. That was not what we were really talking about. *I* hadn't been kissing Anthony in the sitting room, but, obscurely, my mother and I both felt that I had. I felt ashamed and guilty.

"No," I said dully. What else was there to say?

"You look cheap! You look like a tart!" And with that she picked up my hairbrush and with savage tugs dragged it painfully through the beehive, smoothing it flat. Then she picked up my damp washcloth and scrubbed my face, her fingers jabbing into the tender flesh round my eyes. She breathed in shallow, agitated gasps. Neither of us said a word.

"There!" she said. "That's better!"

I looked at the schoolgirl in the mirror.

"You look like yourself now," my mother insisted.

I nodded slowly. My brief flirtation with beauty was over. She had expressed the simple truth.

So, giving up hope in the body, I began to develop my mind. That first year in the Sixth Form was in one way intoxicating. Pitting myself against more and more difficult ideas, I discovered I could fly. My body might well be clumsy and unformed for love, but my mind was graceful. It could have been a very happy year.

But things were changing at home. They were changing silently because, as a family, we never talked about the really momentous things. Yet again I wanted to shield my parents from a knowledge of something *they* were anxious to keep from *me*. And the easiest way to do that was not to let myself realize what was happening.

For one thing my parents had reversed roles. After years of housework my mother had started to go out to work. This was unusual in 1960. Nobody else's mother worked; mothers were supposed to be chained to the kitchen, a constant welcoming presence in the home. I liked the change. I was proud of the distinction of my mother—her new alertness and interest in the world of the university. She came in anxious, harassed by having too many things to do, but alive in a new way with a challenging breadth of understanding. It was good for her. When we got in from school it was my father who was there with the tea ready, the inexpertly cut bread and butter. For he was at home all day.

What was it? I asked myself and then quickly turned away from the dangerous topic. I watched my father drifting aimlessly about the house, carefully doing the small tasks that my mother set him. His pride and gaiety had all gone. He seemed snuffed out. When our eyes met, he hastily looked away. Every morning he walked the dog in the park and sat sometimes for hours on a bench, gazing blankly at the lake.

But nothing was said. The misery of my father, and my mother's worry about him, ran silently through every conversation. I thought of my grandmother, still drinking gin in the larder. What kind of a world was this when people shut themselves up with some unhappy secret, unable to communicate it to anybody? And how many other secrets surrounded me?

At school things were better, and more and more I found myself watching the nuns walking round the grounds, their hands hidden in their sleeves, their eyes bent on the ground as they glided under the shade of the huge cedar trees on the lawn. Sometimes, at midday, we saw them having recreation, sitting in a huge circle under the cedars, sewing and laughing together, their laughter harmonious and innocent. It seemed to me a vision of sisterly unity. They would have no secrets from one another, living together in such a close, loving community. And what conversations they must be having, I thought enviously, looking at that closed little circle. Excluding all trivia from their lives, filled with the joy of seeking God, they must have so much in common and so many wonderful discoveries of the mind and spirit to share. "Such happiness," Mother Katherine had said.

One morning in late summer I went into the Sixth Form classroom and overheard a conversation I would never forget. Charlotte was standing in the center of a tight little knot of girls. I stood by the door, frozen with unhappiness, as I realized they were talking about me.

"She shouldn't be at the school, you know."

"Why not?"

"Because her father has gone bankrupt."

"It happened at the beginning of the year, and she's just deceitfully gone on pretending that everything's normal! She's a hypocrite!"

"That's right," another girl agreed. "This school is for people who can pay the fees. Not for people who can't."

I felt winded with shock. If my father was bankrupt, how on earth were my fees getting paid? And then what kind of attitude was theirs? Yes, it was a fee-paying school, and in a sense they were right. If my fees weren't being paid then I shouldn't be here. But stronger than all this was amazement. They seemed to have no hearts at all, no compassion.

I took a deep breath and made my presence known. I didn't feel in the least tearful, thank goodness. This was something too fundamental for tears.

"Well," I said quietly, "so what? What has it got to do with you?" They wheeled round to face me sharply.

"It has, you know." Charlotte's reply was almost saucy.

"Why?" I asked. What else had they got in store for me?

"Because our fathers are paying your fees!"

"What *do* you mean?"

"Your father's a Catenian, isn't he?" I nodded. The Catenians were a Catholic society exclusively for men, the Catholic form of freemasonry. "Well, the Catenians—and therefore our fathers—are paying your fees. Didn't you know?" My expression must have told them that I didn't, despite my belated attempt at a nonchalant shrug. I felt deeply humiliated. To be living on other people's charity was bad enough, but what would my father feel if he found out what was being said at school? He must feel bad enough anyway.

"No," I said, with as much dignity as I could muster, "I didn't know that. But that's because my father didn't want me to know. And I still think," I added, my voice gaining conviction as I went on, "that it has nothing to do with you."

I turned on my heel and walked out.

I was still shocked that they would reject me for such a reason. I found myself walking in the direction of the chapel. I wanted to be by myself, to think, and that was the only place in the teeming building that guaranteed privacy. The chapel was a modern one, all pale shiny wood and cream walls. There was a faint smell of incense, and here and there nuns knelt, black lumps in the sunlight, their heads buried in their hands.

I sat down, finding that I was trembling. I could never tell my parents about this, I knew. It would hurt them, and I'd feel so feeble running home and saying that the others were being horrid to me. It seemed so unfair. My father had had a tough enough struggle to get where he was. He and my mother seemed so brave in their lonely struggle with disaster. I remembered a cocktail party I had gone to with them a few weeks ago. It had been one of those Sunday morning affairs; the room was filled with cigarette smoke and loud, frenetic talking. Everybody had been to Mass that morning and priests filled the room. They were standing in groups, florid with gin and tobacco, worldly, disillusioning. My parents and I had squeezed into a relatively secular corner.

"The church here in full force, I see," muttered my father sarcastically as we studied the guests.

"Who on earth is that?" I asked. My eye had been caught by a man wearing a green uniform with epaulettes, a thick leather belt, and a sword. He looked like a cross between Prince Charming and Buttons the clown.

"Ssh!" hissed my mother, giggling. "Don't talk so loudly! It's Sidney Foster."

"Yes, but what's he doing dressed up like that?"

"He's a Knight of St. Gregory." My mother was on the verge of laughter and my father snorted with amusement.

"Him," he said bitterly, "he's a shark in business. An absolute bloody shark! He'd sell his own grandmother."

"Shut up!" my mother laughed helplessly, "he's coming this way. Hello, Sidney!"

His dress sword brushed against me, laddering my stocking.

"I was just admiring your uniform," I said innocently, ignoring the poke my mother gave me. "What is a Knight of St. Gregory?"

He took a slug of brandy and swirled it in his mouth. "It's a special order," he said complacently, "given by the Pope."

"Gracious!" I said, winking at my father, who earnestly studied the olive in his martini. "What a marvelous person you must be. What's it given for?"

"Well," he said modestly, "it's given in recognition of charitable works." There was a splutter from my father, who had transferred his attention to a potted plant. His shoulders were heaving strangely. He coughed.

"Haven't seen you for some time, have we?" my father said, and

I noted an ironic edge to his voice. "You were always popping in and out at one time. Not so long ago, either." Sidney Foster looked momentarily confused and cleared his throat. "Still, I expect you've been too busy getting on with your charitable works," said my father genially. "Well," he finished, clapping Foster jovially on the shoulder as he determinedly set off in another direction, "be seeing you, no doubt."

As we forced our way through the chattering crowds, I looked back at the Knight who, red in the face, was talking animatedly to a monsignor about the funds for a local church roof.

"I was damn useful to Sidney in business once," my father said caustically. "Interesting that we never see him now, isn't it?"

"It's Birmingham," my mother replied shortly. "All they ever think about is money."

And now, sitting in the peaceful chapel, I saw what she had meant. What had that very Catholic party with its materialistic values—values that even my "friends" seemed to share—to do with Christ? My readings of the Gospels over the years had built Christ up for me as a dynamic figure. He stalked across my mind, vivid and challenging, driving the money lenders out of the Temple, inveighing angrily against the hypocrisy of His day, overturning all the conventions with the unpredictable nature of His love. He had mixed with prostitutes and sinners, not hypocritical Knights of St. Gregory, and had frightened His hearers with His shattering commands. Leave all you have and come, follow Me.

Follow Me. Suddenly the familiar invitation leaped out at me with a new force. Leave all that you have. Really, what was there in the world that was worthwhile? You couldn't count on anything the world had to offer. Friendship could be destroyed in a moment because people valued what you had, not what you were, whereas God's love was perfect. Human love just couldn't measure up to it. I thought of Suzie and Anthony. I wanted more than that. Even the most perfect love would ultimately be destroyed by death. In fact, when you came to think about it, death was the only thing in life that you could be absolutely certain of. It was inescapable and made everything but God seem empty and hollow.

Follow Me. How much more satisfying to leave all the emptiness of the world and follow Christ! A nun in the bench in front of me got up, genuflected gracefully in the aisle, and quietly left the church. Her face was serene. It was as though she had tapped some hidden store of strength before plunging into the melee of afternoon school. I looked up at the crucifix. That was what sustained her. The cross turned all human values upside down; they just weren't worth worrying about. And the cross showed the greatness of God's love. As I looked at the tabernacle, which contained the Real Presence of Christ, I felt a pull toward Him that was almost physical in its intensity. I'd thought a few minutes ago that death was the only certainty. Now I saw clearly that the only way to achieve life was by leaving the world behind and looking for God Who was there for the seeking. Absolute power, goodness, and love.

As I knelt there I knew that something very important had happened. I wanted to find God so that He would fill my life, and that meant giving my life back to Him. I wanted Him with a desire that was frightening in its urgency. And I knew that looking for God had to be a full-time job; no half-measures would do. The cross showed that clearly. But how satisfying such a search would be. Far more satisfying than pursuing the chimeras of the world, which could only lead to disappointment and death.

Silently I made the sign of the cross and left the chapel. I had made up my mind.

Once my decision was made, the world with all its confusions seemed to fall into place. Second place. The strange pull I had experienced in the chapel stayed with me and I knew that I must act upon it soon. That was why I found myself some weeks afterward standing outside Mother Katherine's room one afternoon. I have to do something about this, I was telling myself. Until then it won't be real. "Come in!" I heard Mother Katherine call. I glanced down at myself, straightened my school skirt, and, seizing the brass doorknob, burst into my headmistress' office.

"I want to be a nun!"

The words were out now and, startled, I listened to them in the ensuing silence, turning them over and examining them. Yes, they fit. But how strange to hear them spoken aloud for the first time, after hearing them lumbering round in my mind as a possibility that was almost too momentous to believe in.

"Sit down, Karen."

I looked at Mother Katherine. For a moment I had almost

forgotten about her, I had been so intent on speaking the words, spilling them outside myself.

"Come on!" she urged kindly. My hair fell over my eyes in two sweeping curtains, but shaking these aside I looked at her intently, shifting from foot to foot, my plump adolescent body self-conscious and uneasy at being the object of close scrutiny. "Come on!" Mother Katherine repeated. "Don't stand on one leg like a restless stork. Sit down!" and she gestured dramatically at the small wicker armchair opposite her desk.

Everything Mother Katherine did was dramatic. Rumor had it that she had been an actress before she became a nun. She was certainly beautiful enough. Her smooth olive skin was slightly touched now by middle age, but the lines spoke of character and strength. Her regular, generous features were enhanced by the severe wimple, and her blue eyes looked out challengingly on the world—frightening, passionate eyes.

I sank into the chair and looked at her apprehensively. What was she going to say? How was she going to react? It suddenly seemed an impertinent announcement to have made so impetuously. "What, *you*!" she would say. "You! What makes you think you have it in you?" No, she wouldn't say that. She'd be kind and tactful. But wouldn't that be even more humiliating?

"Say it again," she said quietly, her face for a moment alight with attention before she continued sorting through the untidy pile of papers on her desk. "I'm listening to you, but it will probably help you to talk if I don't look at you, won't it?"

"I want to be a nun." Less of an eruption this time. More calmly spoken.

"I'm not in the least surprised," she said, still leafing through the pile of bills. "It's a wonderful life."

We sat there silently, at peace.

"Why?" she asked suddenly, her eyes watchful.

"Well," I sought round helplessly for a second as the reasons swarmed round me. Which one should I pick out as the most important? "Well, really, Mother, I want to find God."

"Yes?" she pushed her papers to one side and leaned her chin on her hands. "Go on."

"I want to know more about Him," I plunged on. "The more I think about Him the more other things and other people fade into insignificance. He seems so passionate and generous with no time for compromise and sloppiness. And I want to get to know Him better."

"Then why become a nun?" Mother Katherine probed. "You don't have to enter the religious life to get to know Him better. Couldn't you do that just as well in the world?"

"No," I said quickly. I was really in my stride now. "Not so well. Not for me anyway. I mean, He said that if you wanted to follow Him you had to be prepared to give up everything. After all, He gave up everything for us."

"Are you prepared to give up everything?" Mother interposed swiftly and, seeing me about to rush on, said, "No, wait. What about your family? Are you prepared to leave them?"

I thought for a moment. Yes, it was hard. I'd often felt that leaving one's family was one of the hardest things about the religious life. But there was no option.

"It's awful to think about it," I said slowly, "leaving home for good. Nuns never go back home again, do they—even for a visit?"

"Some orders don't," Mother nodded. "We don't."

"After all, nobody knows you as well as your family does. And no one ever will—not in the same way. I feel bound to my family —closely tied up with them in all sorts of ways. It's almost a physical bond."

"Yes," she said quietly, her eyes watching me carefully. "St. Teresa said that when she entered her convent and left her family she felt as though she were being pulled apart, limb from limb."

I remembered.

"Would you be prepared for that kind of suffering?"

"There really isn't any choice, is there, and in a way it'll be even worse for them."

We looked at one another. "Yes," Mother Katherine said, "I know. My mother lost three of her children to the religious life."

I nodded soberly. "You've got two brothers who are priests, haven't you?" We'd seen them at the school when they came to visit her. "It must have been so hard for your parents. At least I'll have chosen this, but my parents won't have. It'll just be pushed on them."

"Yes," she smiled at me, her eyes still boring into mine, watching my every reaction. "Your parents will share your sacrifice, but

40

they'll also share your joy eventually. I know my mother says that she'd never have it any different. But there are other things, too. What about marriage, children? Are you prepared to give up all that natural fulfillment?"

This was easier.

"I used to think that I wanted to be married," I said, trying to choose my words carefully. "But lately I've not been so sure. For me it isn't the answer to everything. You know, 'The Prince married the Princess and they lived happily ever after.' "

"Go on, think it out carefully. You can't go rushing into this without thinking over all the pros and cons. It wouldn't be right."

"Well," I said, "can any one person fill all your needs? Every single one of them? A husband's not like God Who is perfect, Who isn't limited, and Who knows you through and through. You said that marriage is our *natural* fulfillment . . . "

"Yes," Mother Katherine said, "for most women it is. Do you think it is for you?"

"It's hard to tell," I shrugged slightly. "How could one be *sure*? But even if I didn't want to be a nun I'm not certain, really, that I'd want to get married. Husbands, babies—all that. I don't think I'd be completely fulfilled being a wife and mother."

"But even so, that doesn't mean that you have to be a nun," she insisted.

"No," I said, "but I was going to say that even if—and it's a big *if*—marriage does fulfill most women naturally, there's a *supernatural* part to all of us. Nuns are brides of Christ, aren't they?"

She nodded and glanced down at the ring, shaped like a crucifix, on the third finger of her right hand. Her wedding ring. For a while she said nothing, twisting her ring round and round her finger, and for a moment I thought I saw a flicker of pain on her face. Then she looked up and smiled.

"You've thought it all out very carefully, haven't you, dear?" she said quietly. "Good." There was a pause. Then, "Is there anything else in the world that you think you might miss? You know, parties, high life, all that." She gestured extravagantly with a wide sweep of her hand as if conjuring up a vista of glittering social occasions. We laughed easily together.

"Not really. When I go to parties often everything seems so empty, so pointless. People caring about their appearance, money,

41

and so on. I mean, once you've seen that God exists, everything else —all these other things—seem much less important."

"Yes, I know. It *is* a waste of time—and energy."

"People get so worked up about all that!"

"Karen." There was a warning in her voice. "It's hard, you know. Christ's way is the way of the cross."

"Of course it's hard," I returned energetically. "It's a challenge!"

She laughed. "You're a great one for a challenge, aren't you?" she said. "The harder something is, the better you like it. You've been like that ever since I've known you. Ever since the first year!"

I thought for a moment. "Yes, I suppose I have."

"But becoming a nun is like signing a blank check," Mother Katherine said. Her voice was a mixture of affection and concern as she looked keenly at me. "Tell me," she went on. "How long have you been thinking about this?"

I thought for a long time. I could, I found, pinpoint certain events that had all pointed to my decision, a series of steps that, when I looked at them now, had started a long time back.

"I don't know." I pushed my hair out of my eyes and squinted across at her in the brilliant afternoon sun.

"Is the sun in your eyes?" she asked. I nodded, and she drew the blue curtains slightly, filling the room with dim, cool shade. I watched her quick, vital movements. For a long time I had admired her. Everything she did she flung herself into wholeheartedly. Everywhere she looked she found beauty; everything she touched she found significant. She'd given up the world for God and He had given it all back to her a hundredfold.

"I haven't had a vision or anything like that. But gradually things have pointed that way. Step by step. It seems as though God's been there always, giving me the odd nudge in this direction."

"Yes, I think you have a true vocation. Thank God." Mother Katherine spoke gently with a certain awe. From the playing fields the whistle sounded. Everything so ordinary. Just another afternoon at school. But for me the start of a new life.

"Have you got a lesson now?" She looked at the clock. Twenty-five to three.

"Yes, history," I said and smiled.

"You like history, don't you? Do you like it better than English now?"

"I don't think so." I paused for a moment. "I can't stand the ins and outs of the wool trade!" We laughed. "And literature—books, reading—are very important to me, always have been."

Mother Katherine looked hard at me for a moment. I wondered at the concern—almost fear—that passed over her face. Then casually she asked, "Which order do you want to join?"

"Yours." The reply came instantly.

"Why?"

"Well, it seems meant, somehow. I've been at school here for eleven years, ever since I was five. I've gotten to know you all. I've gotten to know the Order well. It's a teaching order; I like the idea of teaching. It all fits in. It seems natural."

"And when do you want to enter? I mean, you'll have to finish the Sixth Form; you're not old enough yet. You're a year young for your class anyway. Aren't you still only sixteen?"

"Yes, seventeen in November," I answered. "Another year at school. A-levels this time next year. And then I'd like to enter straight after that."

"You don't want to go to college first?"

"No," I shook my head emphatically. "What's the point? Now that I've made up my mind, why waste three years mucking about?"

"Yes, I think you're right. After all, if you persevere in your vocation the Order will probably—though only probably; you can't bank on it—send you to college after your religious training. To prepare you for teaching." She thought hard. "Yes, I think you have a vocation. I think it's for next year. September 1962. I think you should go to the Provincial House in Tripton then. You'll be a postulant for nine months, a novice for two years. Then, if you stay, please God, you'll make your vows. Up to then you can leave at any time, or we can send you home if you're not suitable!" She smiled confidently. "But I don't think we'll do that. Then once you've made your vows, it'll be for life."

The bell rang and I got up to go.

"God bless you, dear." Her voice was affectionate, almost tender. I walked to the door.

"Karen," she said suddenly. I turned to look at her. Her face was solemn now and her eyes steadily commanded full attention. "Karen," her voice was quiet. "Remember that blank check, won't you?"

For a long, long moment there was silence. Mother Katherine was looking hard at me, trying to find the words—for what? I waited, looking at the apprehension in her face, wondering what was in her mind. Finally she spoke.

"It's a very austere order, you know."

"I want to be a nun." Once more the words were out. But this time they fell into no welcoming acceptance. My parents froze with horror.

It was the summer holidays. We were sitting in the living room waiting for supper. Outside the hot sun blazed through the thin silvery curtains that softly muted its glare. My parents each had a drink.

"Have a sherry, Karen!" my father said. I refused emphatically. I could never be persuaded to drink. My ideas about Granny were more clearly formulated now. I was too like her ever to dare to take one fatal step down the liquid path to alcoholism. She had ruined her life by not becoming a nun, I thought. That too was a factor in my decision.

I had not intended to broach the subject that evening. We had been discussing my future. My mother asked me whether I was still thinking of staying on at school an extra term after taking my A-levels.

I knew only too well how much my parents longed for me to go to Oxford. Nobody in my family had ever gone there before and it seemed a paradise to them, a fairytale world of intellectual perfection.

"No," I said slowly. It was no good allowing them to cling to this hope. I felt their disappointment sharply fill the room. "No, I don't think I want to do that now."

"But what do you want to do?" my father asked unhappily.

"I want to be a nun."

In the silence that followed, I sat, trembling slightly, feeling sick and excited. I had dreaded telling my parents, but now, for good or ill, the die was cast.

"But why?" asked my mother. The question came out in a bewildered wail.

"I want to give my life to God," I answered shakily. These answers had seemed quite in place in Mother Katherine's study, but here they seemed thin and unreal.

"But you can do that quite as well in the world!" snapped my mother briskly. She had obviously decided on the no-nonsense approach.

"No, you can't," I said, "not really. I mean, honestly, how much time do we all have for God at the moment? Oh, I know we're good Catholics and all that. We go to Mass every Sunday, we don't eat meat on Friday, we go to Confession twice a month. But that's not enough for me. We fit God into our lives but they're crowded with other things."

"But there's nothing to stop you from going to Mass every morning if you want to," my mother said. "You often do, anyway." My father just sat there, turning his glass round and round.

"But even that's not really enough," I said. "Seeking God has got to be a full-time commitment. A profession, if you like. He's too important for half-measures."

"But why not think about it again after you have been to Oxford?" asked my father miserably. "You'll be a bit older then, you'll have had a chance to look around a bit and see . . . " he trailed off.

"See whether it is convenient for me to enter a convent," I finished for him. "Put the world first and give God second option." I was determined to counter this approach. It seemed so reasonable but was, I felt, quite wrong.

"If you've got a true vocation it will last a few years," said my mother rather crossly. I could tell she was feeling that she was losing control of me. I had never really argued with her before. She was so firm and definite in her views and needed so much to impose them on me so that I should be exactly what she wanted. If I argued with her, such an uncomfortable atmosphere ensued that it just wasn't worth it. She was astonished and hurt, I could tell, by my obstinacy.

"Not necessarily," I said. "You can throw a vocation away, you know, just like everything else. I might get to like the world too much to want to put God first." I could see that happening. Once

I was at Oxford the world would beckon with all its seductive wiles. I could not imagine what these might be. The world seemed futile and trivial now, but human nature was weak. I could easily persuade myself that the sacrifice I had decided on was not for me. "After all," I added cunningly, "look what happened to Granny."

It was a direct hit. My mother gave a start and looked moodily at the fireplace. My father shifted in his chair, which squeaked uncomfortably.

"But you can't mean to go now," my mother said despairingly. "You're much too young. You're only sixteen."

"No, but I can go next year when I'm seventeen," I replied firmly.

"It's ridiculous," said my mother hotly, "quite ridiculous. A child of seventeen—oh, I know you don't think you're still a child, but you are. Anyway, it's quite out of the question. They'd never accept you as young as that."

"Mother Katherine said they would," I replied, watching them carefully. It was another hit. They both stiffened. They respected Mother Katherine. I knew that. They were also just a tiny bit in awe of her. Whenever my mother protested against school policy she had been gently and with considerable charm put firmly in her place. Mother Katherine was the only person I knew who could do that to her.

"You've already talked to her, then, have you?" asked my mother. I could tell that she was hurt. "How long have you been thinking about this, then?"

"Oh! quite a time now," I replied vaguely. It was true. The decision had been quietly growing for years, now that I looked back over my life.

"Why didn't you tell us sooner?" asked my father. "Did you think that we'd be so much against it?" He sounded aggrieved.

"Well, you are against it, aren't you?" I countered.

Impasse. My mother waved her empty glass at my father, who, glad of something to do, leaped up and busied himself with the ice; he poured out large measures of gin, I noticed. I was sorry for them. They seemed out of their depth.

"You don't know what you're doing," my mother said impatiently. "What about all the things you're going to miss—the theatre, books? How the hell do you think you're going to adapt to community life? You haven't even been to boarding school. Believe me, I know what I'm talking about. Life in the forces was hell. Endlessly cooped up with other people—all their annoying little habits get on your nerves till you could scream." Her voice had risen now as the objections came tumbling out.

"Look," I said quietly, amazed at my calm. "I'm not saying it's going to be easy. Of course it isn't. Mother Katherine has told me how hard it will be sometimes. But if it's God's will for me to become a nun, then my whole life will be ruined if I don't. God has a special plan for each one of us. You don't want me to mess up my whole life, do you?"

There was another pause. My mother nervously lit a cigarette. My father kept silent. Since the bankruptcy he had become more and more withdrawn. He had lost confidence in his ability to run his family life. I knew how much I was hurting them both, but there was no going back now.

"After all," I said again into the dead silence, "you believe in God, don't you? You believe that the religious life is the highest human vocation. Well then, how can you possibly refuse to allow me to enter?"

I could almost hear my parents' thoughts crackling through the room. I could feel them struggling with the dilemma they were in.

"Of course we believe that," my mother stubbed out her cigarette. Her voice was quieter now. "But that doesn't mean that we can believe you are ready to take such a big step. I still think," her voice rang out confidently now—once she took her mind off the disturbing thought of God and His will, I noticed wryly, she became much more sure of herself, but God was the whole point; He couldn't just be ignored—"I still think," she repeated, "that you are much too young. You don't know anything about the world that you are going to give up. Don't you think so, John?"

"Absolutely, dear, absolutely," muttered my father gloomily. He was looking at me with astonishment. "Do you really want to give us up?" he asked, his voice trembling slightly. "Don't you see how much we'll miss you?"

I sat there, fighting a lump in my throat. I could barely trust myself to speak. Don't let them turn on the emotion, I prayed silently. I can't cope with that.

"Of course I'll miss you," I said huskily.

47

Once again we sat in silence. The cars on the main road outside swept by with a carefree swishing sound. I wanted this to be over. But I knew too that while I was at home it would never be over. The convent was there now, splitting the bond between us. Things would never be the same again.

"The meat must be nearly ready," said my mother weakly. "John, will you carve? And call Lindsey . . . " she gestured helplessly toward the kitchen.

"Look," I said, "it's pointless going on with this. I'll never be able to convince you. To you I'm just a little girl. I always will be, as far as you're concerned, even when I'm"—I paused, searching frantically for an age of suitable antiquity—"thirty! Why don't you go and see Mother Katherine? She told me that she'd be very willing to talk to you about it. After all, she's the professional. You know about life and the world. But she knows about life and the world and the convent. She's known me ever since I was five—almost as long as you have. Why don't you go and see her?"

"And if she doesn't make us change our minds, then will you promise to go to college before you think about becoming a nun?" asked my mother quickly. She was already setting her shoulders squarely, ready to do battle.

I had every confidence in Mother Katherine. "Yes, I promise," I said.

From odd things my parents said after their momentous interview with Mother Katherine, I could imagine exactly what had happened. My parents had been taken into the convent parlor, a room I knew well. There were a sofa, two or three easy chairs, and rugs placed chastely over the polished floor boards. Fra Angelico prints hung tastefully on the walls, and a restrained flower arrangement adorned a little bureau by the French window. It had been early in the evening, and outside they could still have seen the cedar trees and the graveled terrace. They would have been given coffee and biscuits.

The pleasant surroundings were a consolation. "One good thing about that Order," my mother always said, "is that they have decent taste. No bleeding hearts or anemic madonnas."

"Too bloody aristocratic," my father would quip. "What was it that priest called them? A bunch of society ladies!"

They sat in the parlor, filled with determination not to give in.

48

I was too young; later, if I still wanted to enter, there'd be plenty of time. But they were nervous, too; so much depended on their standing firm.

Then Mother Katherine came in. I could see it all—the lilting walk, the beaming smile of welcome. She shook their hands. Mother Katherine's handshake was a family joke. You'd grasp her hand and it would simply lie in yours like a wet fish, with no answering pressure. And she'd lean away from you archly. That handshake summed up what my parents had often noticed about the nuns.

"They always hold you at arm's length," my mother would say. "They seem to be saying 'Keep off; you can come this far, but no farther.' Oh, I like them very much as an order. At least they're all individuals. Not like the nuns I was at school with—you really couldn't tell one from another; they even looked alike. But for all that, you never really get to know them." On that evening the handshake must have stopped being a joke. How could you argue with someone who never really accepted your presence?

Mother Katherine fussed over them, urged more coffee on them while they eyed her warily, waiting for the battle to begin.

"She's too young," my mother said firmly, stirring sugar into her cup. "Far too young. I mean, I know that a religious vocation is a wonderful thing. We're not questioning that, are we, John?"

"No, indeed," my father agreed politely, but I knew that for him it seemed a terrible life, a rejection of all that made life sweet —love, sex, beauty, travel, fun, freedom—even though the faith told him what he really ought to think about it.

"But Karen's just not mature enough to make such a huge decision," my mother continued. "She's never known anything else. How can she make a proper choice? And she's very emotional, you know, very intense."

Mother Katherine smiled calmly. "Of course emotion has to be kept in control. But if Karen weren't as sensitive as she is, all her gifts for poetry and art wouldn't exist. She'd be a different person. And a poorer one. And I think she is far more mature than you realize. Of course, you will always see her as a little girl," she laughed kindly. "How can you help that? It's very, very difficult for parents to see their own children objectively."

As she said that, my parents began to feel quite helpless. Mother Katherine always managed to make them feel like children themselves. Those pale blue eyes of hers looked straight through you and seemed to spot all your weak points, things that other people didn't notice. Now she claimed to understand their own daughter better than they did. And how could they argue? Of course they were biased; they were bound to be.

"Now look," Mother Katherine took a fresh tack, "do you agree that the fundamental question here is not whether you or I want Karen to become a nun next year, but whether God wants it? We've all got to empty ourselves of our own limited, human responses. It's what God wants that matters."

And with the mention of God the whole thing became much more frightening. After all, if you believed in God, then of course a religious vocation was a wonderful thing. It must have made them wonder, in a sudden guilty moment, whether they were selfishly opposing God's will. Who could tell? Once God came into it the solid ground of common sense started crumbling away under you.

"But how can we tell what God's will is?"

And then Mother Katherine gave them the acid test of a vocation as defined by the church, a definition I was to hear many times.

"There is only one way of being absolutely sure whether a girl has a true vocation. She has to be accepted by the religious order she wants to join; that is the only criterion that the church accepts as proof. Feelings, prayers, thoughts, ideals—none of these counts for anything beside that. If the Provincial Superior at Tripton accepts Karen, then her decision has the whole force of the church behind it. And the church, we know, is empowered by Christ."

"But let's face it, Mother," my father said ironically, "you don't turn people away. You must need new recruits."

"Indeed, Mr. Armstrong, we do turn people away," was the rather tart rejoinder. "Look at it this way. Somebody without a true vocation would only be a disruptive influence and eventually undermine the Order. We have to be very, very careful whom we admit."

"But what if—I know you won't admit this—but *if*," my mother pleaded, "a mistake is made—surely that's possible. Then at seventeen Karen's whole life will be ruined."

"Not at all," Mother Katherine retorted. "Of course we do admit people into the Order who find later that they haven't got a vocation. But you know, Mrs. Armstrong, I'd hesitate to call that a mistake. If they were accepted by the Order, then God, in His infinite wisdom, called them there for His own special purposes. And this may happen to Karen. She may find after a while that it isn't God's will and she will be free to go, or we shall be free to send her home. Yes, Mr. Armstrong, we do send people home," she laughed, "at any time during the first three years."

Sadly my parents, faced with these cosmic immensities and Divine purposes, realized that their own feelings didn't count for much. Helplessly they felt themselves carried along by the force of Mother Katherine's certainty.

"Believe me, Mrs. Armstrong," Mother Katherine was saying, "if Karen has no vocation she couldn't stay. It's a very careful training, you know. She will be trained as a postulant and novice by people who really know how to look into a girl's heart. There is no way she could *bear* to stay if it weren't God's will. All the other reasons for entering get refined in the noviceship. The only reason for staying is that God wants it."

"And she can leave at any time during the first three years?" my father asked.

"At any time before first vows."

"I suppose," said my mother, voicing for the first time the reason she would use again and again to comfort herself, "that if we stop her now and insist that she go to college, she'll spend the whole time pining for the convent and never really enter into anything properly."

"Yes," said Mother Katherine. "She'd just be marking time."

"Whereas if she goes next year and then leaves, she'll have gotten it out of her system sooner," capped my father.

"Exactly, Mr. Armstrong, but don't bank on that. I think she has a true vocation—thank God—and I don't think she will leave. I must tell you that. And believe me, if Karen doesn't do the will of God, she can never be happy. God makes each of us for a special purpose. If we choose to thwart that purpose, our lives are useless."

My parents must have thought then of my grandmother. Was that where it had all gone wrong for her? Perhaps she was right. Perhaps she should have been a nun.

"Mr. Armstrong, Mrs. Armstrong, will you give her to God?"

I had been waiting nervously on the stairs for them when I heard the key turn in the lock. It was a moment that was to decide my whole life. As soon as I saw their faces, I knew.

"Well?"

They looked so tired.

"You can go, if you really want to."

"Oh! Thank you!" How inadequate to say it, to embrace them. And how inadequate as the expression of the joy that suddenly filled me. There was nothing to stop me now. The road stretched clearly ahead to God.

3 · A NEW LIFE
1962

The little train jolted to a stop. Anxiously I leaned out of the train to read the sign. Tripton. At last, I had finally arrived. But though it was in one sense the end of a journey I knew it was only the beginning of another.

By the time I'd handed in my ticket and started to walk up to the convent I felt already in another world. The country land that led to the village was banked on either side by thick hedges, lush and tall, enclosing the road in a green silence. Birds sang in the bushes and—yes—there was a faint smell of blackberries.

It was a hot day. Very hot. Already I was regretting that I was wearing my winter coat—navy blue, smartly cut with gold reefer buttons. I was sweating as I labored up the hill. "Don't you think it'll be too hot?" I'd asked my mother.

"Oh, I'd take it. This autumn weather is so unpredictable. You might be cold later on." And I could see what she was thinking: *you may leave in the middle of winter and then you'll need it.* Hoping silently. I thought of them now sitting in the theatre, very aware that I wasn't with them and never would be again. And then they would drive home where my bedroom was empty, the sheets folded on the bed.

They had bought me the black suitcase I was carrying. "A black, simple suitcase" I had been told to get. And a black umbrella, a good stout one. I was clutching it in my other hand, a heavy man's umbrella that looked so out of place with my stiletto heels on this brilliantly sunny day. It would have been more sensible to have worn flat shoes, I thought, grimacing as I stumbled on the uneven surface of the country road. Why hadn't I? And why had I applied a last dab of makeup before leaving the train? Vanity, no doubt, I thought ruefully. I couldn't bear somehow not to be looking as nice as possible on my last day in the world. Still, after today, there won't be any more of that. It was a good thought—the future stretched ahead, clearly unencumbered with stupidities of dress.

At the top of the hill I came upon the village. Just one main street. And so pretty, I reflected, looking at the timbered cottages, the quaint little shops, the picturesque pub. A few people were shopping; ladies in expensive tweeds with poodles on leads strolled on the cobbled pavements. A car or two cruised peacefully down High Street. It was like a chocolate-box village.

Two people passed me, and I saw them glancing at my suitcase and umbrella.

"There's another one!" I heard one of them say.

Of course. All the postulants arrived at Tripton on the same day to begin their religious life. In a little village this size, dominated by the imposing convent, the inhabitants must see girls carrying black umbrellas toiling up the hill at about the same time every September. I wondered how many others they had spotted today.

I looked at my watch again. Four thirty-five. I was on time. I had been so afraid of missing the train, of being late. What a terrible start that would have been! The empty place in the line of postulants, the raised eyebrows. They might think I had changed my mind or was having a last minute panic, or even a last fling. There must be girls who wanted a last cigarette or who were bidding their boyfriends a passionate and tearful good-bye. Lots of the saints, I reflected, had fought against their vocation right up to the last second. And of course I could change my mind right now. All I had to do was turn back, catch the next train to London, and arrive home. How delighted everybody would be! But I didn't want to do that. I was excited. Already I was impatient to begin, to tear off these worldly clothes, to start the new life at once. The mental numbness was wearing off and I was feeling slightly sick with anticipation, a bit nervous, and very shy. But glad.

Suddenly on my left I saw the tall convent wall stretching austerely far down the street. And there was the huge gatehouse arching medievally over the heavy iron gate. You couldn't see the convent from the road. Only a mass of trees down a long drive. The gates were flung back invitingly. The road from one world to another. I suppose I ought to take my last look at the world, I thought, but it seemed theatrical and unreal. What had I to do with that sleepy village?

I walked through quickly without a backward glance.

Turning the corner, I saw the convent. Tranquil and silent, it lay before me. Even the little village street seemed noisy by comparison. There on the left stood the old buildings. I remembered what I knew about Tripton. Before the Reformation it had been the palace of an eminent ecclesiastic. A hundred years ago, in 1863, the Foundress of the Order had brought the little girls in their nearby boarding school here on a picnic. They had their lunch in the palace ruins, just a mass of broken grey stone, save for three huge arches that had once towered over the banquet hall. Now the arches reared triumphantly over the Bedfordshire meadow, the second largest of their kind in Europe. The Foundress had determined then and there to restore the palace to its former beauty and win it back for the church. She had sent her nuns in pairs all over Europe to beg from the Catholic aristocracies who were eagerly watching the Catholic revival in England. And they had raised the money, and the building stood again, noble and majestic. There was the old banquet hall, which was now the convent church, with its tall, sloping roof, its flying buttresses, and its high, arched windows. And just to the left of that was the squat fourteenth-century tower with a rose window and crenellated battlements. A flag floated gracefully on its summit, the white and gold Papal arms in honor of the feast day. That tower, I knew, was now part of the Noviceship, and if I moved to the extreme right of the drive I would see—yes, there it was—the low modern building that was the Postulantship, skillfully hidden so as not to disturb the view. A little to the left of the main building was an old wellhouse. The grey buildings spoke of another world. To the right, hidden slightly now by the arms of an old cedar, but growing clearer all the time as I walked up the long drive, Victorian buildings cavorted crazily, a medieval fantasy in red brick of towers, turrets, mighty windows, and domes, stretching on and on, which housed the boarding school.

From somewhere a clock broke the silence, a sonorous but restrained chiming. Quarter to five.

I pulled at the bell rope hanging over the front door and heard it clanging and then fading back into echoing silence.

Strictly speaking, the nuns of the Order I joined are not really nuns at all. The term "nun" originally applied to enclosed orders of women who remained in their convents through their lives, never venturing out, devoting their lives to prayer and contemplation. It was St. Vincent de Paul who in the last century founded a quite different kind of female religious: the Sister of Charity who went out of her convent to work in the world among the poor. The Catholic church—always hot on red tape—objected. Female religious—nuns—had to be enclosed. Vincent's reply was that the Sisters of Charity were not nuns at all but "religious sisters," and the distinction, I believe, is still adhered to by canon law. Following the Sisters of Charity a spate of similar religious orders sprang up in the nineteenth century. The sisters were, of course, referred to as nuns for convenience' sake, and they took simple vows of poverty, chastity, and obedience and devoted themselves to prayer and good works.

My Order was one of these. It had been founded in the 1840s to meet a specific need. The Catholic revival in England was under way. The great Catholic boys' schools at Stonyhurst and Downside were reestablished and the Catholic gentry dispatched their sons there. It was felt that their daughters needed a similar type of boarding school, and it was for this purpose that the Foundress was invited to open her first convent at Derby. The number of nuns and schools increased rapidly and by 1962 the Order boasted some seventeen convent schools in England, a substantial number of convents in the American province, missions in West Africa, and odd convents in Ireland, France, and Rome, which held the Mother House. Like many of the orders founded at the time, it had adopted very largely the Jesuit rule, and the prayer life of the nuns was founded on St. Ignatius' *Spiritual Exercises.*

When the Order had been founded the nuns had worn a simple black dress, in the style of Victorian women, a cape and a veil. The idea was that they should look unobtrusive. In the outside world fashions changed drastically but the habit of the Order did not. Similarly many of the rules and customs were based on the conduct considered appropriate for Victorian women. The religious life in the Order was originally intended to be an extension of their normal lives, not a complete divorce from everything they had known before. Many other religious orders of nuns were in a similar state: the

anachronism of their lives, which had developed by a type of historical accident, had become endowed over the years with a weighty
religious significance.

As I walked up the path that day in 1962 I had no idea that I
would be one of the very last postulants to be trained along the old
lines of severe Victorian discipline. Pope John XXIII had already
summoned the Second Vatican Council, and a few weeks later bishops from all over the world were to congregate in Rome to begin
Pope John's work of *aggiornamento,* of renewal. The Council, as it
was originally conceived, did not mean to initiate new measures but
to restore primitive simplicity and fervor to the Church in the modern world. One of its tasks was to renew the religious orders in the
light of John's vision, which, sadly for the church, he did not live to
see through. A year or two after the opening of the Council the
bishops published a document in which, among other things, they
urged religious orders of women to go back to the original spirit of
their founders and discard the weight of unessential customs and
practices to bring themselves more in tune with the world around
them. Already Cardinal Suenens in Belgium was preparing his book
The Nun in the Modern World, in which he was to urge nuns to discard
their traditional habits and return to a simpler style of dress. The
modern girl, he said, was too often stifled in the religious life by
unessential practices that had developed many years ago. You could
not train girls of the 1960s to be Victorian women.

But that afternoon no one had any idea that all this would
happen. And I had no idea of what I would have to face before the
convent, confident in its long-established rituals and secluded from
the modern world, did at long last move out of the Victorian era.

"And here's Karen!" A tall, angular nun bore down upon me.
I caught a glimpse of a long, beaky nose, thick spectacles, and a
wide, thinlipped mouth. Then I was enveloped in black serge as she
pulled me to her in the ceremonial embrace of the Order. Her
fingers jabbed into my shoulders, gripping them tightly, and her
hard, smooth cheeks pressed themselves abruptly and fiercely
against mine. One press per side. Then I was pushed away and held
at arm's length.

"Splendid!" she said, her voice deep and rich. "Did you have a good journey?" and then, not pausing for an answer, she rushed on. "She's arrived exactly on time! What a splendid start! A model of religious punctuality already!"

A little gust of laughter rose around her. Nuns' laughter. I recognized it. A quiet, controlled trill that fell on a descending scale and then died away. I glanced at the black-robed presences surrounding her and then looked back up at the sharp face that beamed down at me. It was the Provincial. She ruled the twenty or so convents of the English Province of the Order and had been responsible for admitting me to its ranks.

"Did you leave your parents well?" she asked.

"Yes, thank you, Reverend Mother," I smiled back at her. Well, yes, but happy . . . ?

"Splendid!" she said again. "And now you must meet Mother Albert, the Postulant Mistress."

A shorter, round-faced nun with glasses bobbed up to me. She seemed to be bubbling inside, laughing at some private joke. Once more my cheeks were struck with hers in a gesture of welcome and affection.

Then other names were called and I gave up registering them. The members of the Provincial Council, the superior of the convent, and other dignitaries of the Order embraced me. Dazed and drowning in their musty blackness I submitted to their arms, turning my cheeks obediently to meet theirs, my hands hanging awkwardly at my sides. Often their cheeks never actually met mine and I felt myself poked in the eye, in the mouth by the starched borders of their wimples. Their lips, carefully avoiding all contact, moved in embarrassed little messages of greeting: "So glad, dear!" "Welcome to Tripton!"

"Ah! I remember Karen!" one of them said jauntily, as she held me away from her. "Do you remember me?"

I looked blankly at her crumpled white face, the mouth that seemed to move independently of the rest of her, the shrewd, rueful black eyes. A kind face. I thought frantically. *I can't start off with a lie, even a white one,* I told myself in the silence.

"Of course she remembers Mother Greta!" Reverend Mother Provincial came to my rescue. And just then, I did remember her. She had come to Birmingham years ago for a term. She had taught me Latin. I remembered that her hands had been shaking while she tried to write the principal parts of *diligo* on the board. A gentle, birdlike nun with a sharp mind. I smiled at her in relief. "Mother Greta will teach you theology," Mother Provincial explained. "But not yet. Not until the second year of your noviceship."

"Oh no!" someone said, laughing. "There's a lot to go through before she gets to theology!"

Again that gust of laughter, teasing now, withholding something from me. What? I wondered shiveringly, feeling outside the little circle.

"Now, Mother," Reverend Mother Provincial's voice was firm and commanding as she turned to Mother Albert. "I think the others are all ready and we can go in to tea. Come along, Karen; you must come and meet your brothers."

"Brothers?" I muttered, bewildered, as the nuns swept out of the hall, following their superior in a cloud of billowing veils. I turned to Mother Albert, who was walking beside me.

"Oh!" she threw back her head, laughing silently, her shoulders shivering in little eddies of mirth. "Well, in the religious life, Karen, we are all sisters, but in this Order we call the people we enter with, the people who are trained with us in the postulantship and noviceship, our 'brothers.' Your brothers have all arrived and you're going to meet them now while you have tea."

We entered a large parlor, rather dark, with heavily paneled walls and a dark red carpet on the floor. In the middle of the room was a round table, around which some nine or ten girls were sitting. They fell awkwardly silent as the procession of nuns filed into the room.

"Well, here's Karen," said Mother Provincial as she took her seat between two girls, who looked at her nervously. "Karen comes to us from Birmingham. Is there a chair for her, Mother? Ah yes, there you are; now on your right is Marie from Bristol and on your left is Edna who comes from Dublin."

Other names were called—Adèle, Joan, Margaret, Irene, Nessa, Pia, Teresa. I blinked dazedly but could not take it all in. I registered Teresa's dark Nigerian face: "Our first Nigerian postulant!" Mother Provincial had announced proudly, and I looked with respect at the young, plump, giggly girl who had dared to come to another civilization to search for Christ. Then my eye was caught by Marie's green nail varnish. I turned to look at her. Marie, I recognized with a slight shock, was another Suzie. Her tight skirt was pulled tautly over her knees; her hair was dark and curly, her face sharply pretty. She was at home with the world outside. What had brought her to abandon it? I wondered.

It was a sobering thought. Helping myself to a piece of cake that Mother Greta smilingly offered me, I stole a guarded look at my "brethren." I had been so absorbed in getting myself here that it had never really occurred to me that other girls were going over similar hurdles. Now here we all were together in this convent parlor. And we would remain together in close proximity for the next three years. What a motley assortment we were. A Nigerian, an Irish girl, a Suzie, and that dark, dignified girl over there—Adèle—who was obviously French. Those were just the superficial differences. Heaven only knew what inner differences there were. Would we have anything in common?

"And now you must all eat a good tea!" Mother Provincial said jovially. "Some of you aren't eating anything. They'd better eat up, hadn't they?" she appealed to the other nuns who were standing round the table, pouring tea into china cups. "They don't know when they'll be eating again." She laughed, and the other nuns again joined in that teasing laugh of exclusive knowledge.

Mother Provincial wheeled back to Teresa, turning not just her head but her whole body in an urgent, swooping movement. "Do you think you'll have any meals in the religious life, Teresa?"

Teresa shook her head and turned her eyes down so that she crouched low over her plate. Her body was convulsed in silent laughter. Silence. She raised her eyes eventually to look at us all and was then caught in the grips of another paroxysm. "I don't know, Reverend Mother," she finally brought out in a low, trembling whisper.

It's not *that* funny, I thought as the nuns again trilled into a chime of laughter.

We all watched Mother Provincial tensely, smilingly obedient to her mood, which swept us dutifully along in her wake. Eventually she took pity on us. "What do you think, Mother?" she barked at Mother Albert.

"Oh, I expect so, Reverend Mother," she said, her round face friendly. "Just a little," she added in the exaggerated tones of deliberate teasing, "just a little supper as it's the first night."

60

"Sadists!" muttered Marie under cover of the dutiful laughter that completed this exchange.

I jumped and turned to look at her again. I had been thinking much the same thing but I would never have dared to voice it like that. Marie grimaced at me.

"Oh! I think they're only trying to jolly us through," I said defensively. "I don't think they mean to make us feel worse."

"No, I suppose not, but it's still pretty tactless, isn't it? I mean, for all we know we may *not* have any supper tonight. We don't know anything that goes on behind the locked enclosure door, do we?"

"No," I nodded apprehensively. It was amazing, now that I came to think of it, how little Mother Katherine had actually told me. There had been hints at hardship but no details had been given at all.

"Did they tell you anything?" Marie asked with interest.

I shook my head. "No, just that it was a very austere order." Now that I was actually on the brink of this strange new world Mother Katherine's words struck a pang of fear through me. What had they actually meant? She had obviously been warning me to be prepared for anything, and it was one thing to be that when the convent was still a year away, but quite another now. How many people, I wondered, looking round the table at the chattering nuns and girls, would embark on such an important commitment knowing so little of what was in store for them? Still, I told myself firmly, there can't be any half-measures with God. You have to be ready to sign that blank check. I steeled myself and cast a surreptitious glance at my watch. Five forty-five. Any time now we'd go through the enclosure door and start our religious lives properly. I wished we could get on with it. The reflections Marie had inspired filled me with a fluttery sense of anticipation, but there was a quiet excitement there too.

Marie was speaking to me. "Mother Louise told me that too, that it was a strict order, I mean."

"Was she your headmistress?" I asked.

"No, just a nun in the school. She taught me history."

"How old are you?"

"Seventeen. Seventeen and never been kissed," Marie quoted, simpering affectedly, and then gave me a deliberately vulgar wink. "I *don't* think!" she added, smiling at me rouguishly.

"So am I, seventeen I mean," I said. And we laughed companionably, drawn together by the shared joke. I liked Marie, I decided; she was fun. Still, I was curious to know what on earth had made her decide to enter. She looked quite different from the rest of us. I decided to ask her. She wouldn't mind.

"What brings you here?" I asked, as though we'd met accidentally at a street corner.

"Well, it's such a beautiful life," Marie said. Her black eyes, which usually glinted in her face like shiny currants, misted over dreamily. "You know, the habit. It's lovely, isn't it?" I smiled vaguely. I'd never given it much thought. "And at school the nuns sing so beautifully. It's such a pure life—being a bride of Christ, giving up the world and all that. And then my best friend Angela entered last year."

"Is she still here?" I asked.

"Yes, she's a first-year novice. I can't wait to see her again. Well, I went to her clothing last July. That convinced me. I had to come here. And I've not looked back since."

I smiled vaguely. I felt something was wrong somewhere. Where did God fit into all this? Still, I reasoned, you didn't start spouting about God to someone you'd only just met. I'd certainly feel a bit awkward amidst the teacups and the bread and butter.

"Wish I had a fag!" Marie whispered. "I smoked my last one on the train. My last cigarette!" she added, dramatically throwing her head back in a studied pose and closing her eyes. They were thickly coated with emerald green eyeshadow that was not quite the same color as her pearlized nails. "Still," she sprang out of this and grabbed a piece of shortbread. "Eat up, my girl! If we can't smoke, we might as well eat!"

"Honestly!" Edna muttered on my other side. "I don't know how they can do it. I can't eat a thing."

I nodded at her sympathetically. I want this to be over, I told myself urgently. At the moment I felt as though I were suspended between two worlds. The feeling was accentuated by the fact that the nuns around us were not eating themselves. I had never seen a nun eat. "Why won't you eat with us?" we had asked the nuns on picnics and outings.

"Because we are separate," Mother Katherine had explained. "Nuns live apart from the world. Eating with somebody implies a sharing of values, a common outlook. We don't eat with seculars—people who are not religious—because we have turned our back on the world. You must always respect a nun's separateness."

And here we were now, come from all over the globe to share their lives.

As if she were answering my unspoken wish to begin the new life properly, Mother Albert now spoke.

"Reverend Mother," she said respectfully to the Provincial, "I think as the hooding is at six-thirty we'd better be going along now."

"Ah yes! Splendid!" said Mother Provincial. "Yes. Well, you'll go along now with Mother Albert to the Postulantship," she said, smiling at us. "There the second-year novices will help you to change into the postulants' dress. Then at half-past six we have the hooding ceremony." She paused and her voice swelled out. "You will come into the church and you will receive the postulants' hood, the short white veil you will wear during these first nine months. It will be your formal reception into the community. Shall we say grace together?" Shuffling, we all stood up.

We went back into the garden where the sunlight was almost blinding after the darkness of the parlor, a straggling little procession headed by Mother Albert, who walked with an odd springing step, seeming to dance on the ball of her right foot. We limped along behind, tight skirts, orlon sweaters, one or two neat suits. I felt weak with relief.

Mother Albert smiled at us. "Well," she said, "this is it. The moment you've been thinking about for months. You've been imagining what it was like, I expect, wondering what you'd feel. And now you probably don't feel anything very much at all."

In a way that was true. After the heady excitement of a few minutes ago, that cut-off feeling seemed to be descending again, so that I seemed to be watching myself go through these momentous steps.

"Here we are," Mother said. "We'll go in the back way, through the sacristy, because you're not religious yet," she smiled, "not until after the hooding, so you should go through as little of the enclosure now as possible."

A big heavy door swung back. The sacristy, heavy with the pungent smell of incense and candles. A brief glimpse of a cloister stretching away ahead of us, with rust and yellow tiles gleaming dimly in the dusky light that filtered through the stained glass windows. A quick look at a huge *pietà* at the corner of the cloister. Jesus, life-sized, stretched out broken and dead in his Mother's arms. Mary staring ahead in agony, blank and serene.

Then through another massive door with heavy iron hinges and a large latch that clinked hollowly in the silence. "This," Mother said, "is the door to the Postulantship." The door swung open noiselessly.

Wooden, uncarpeted stairs. A smell of cleanliness and polish. Our high heels clattered thunderously. Already they seemed out of place.

And at last the dormitory. A low, modern room containing twelve beds, draped in white. Light poured in and house martins swooped and chattered in the eaves. The floor shone. It seemed a place of purity and innocence. We stood clustered clumsily in the doorway.

"This is your cell, Karen," Mother Albert said. "You're lucky! You've got a nice corner cell near the radiator. But don't get too attached to it," she smiled. "I change you all round every few months, so that you don't come to regard this as 'your' cell. In the religious life we don't own anything."

My cell, I thought with a strange thrill. It sounded so monastic. I thought again of the lives of the saints, of nuns and monks wrestling with God and the devil in the bare stone cell. This wasn't stone, of course, but it showed that I had finally arrived where I wanted to be.

Sister Rebecca came to show me what to do. My first sight of a novice. She stood looking down at me, her eyes alight with excitement. But she was controlled, calm. She was tall and dressed in the full religious habit, except that she had a long white veil. Her face was utterly at peace, completely beautiful. It was the face, I thought, of a Boticelli madonna, serene and remote. That, I thought, is exactly how I want to be.

"Hello, Sister," she said. Sister! I registered it confusedly and then felt a thrill of satisfaction. At last! "Here are your clothes," Sister Rebecca was saying, her voice scarcely more than a whisper. And calm. So calm. "I'll get you some hot water, because I expect you'd like to wash." She took an enamel jug from under the bed. "And now, you draw the curtains round your cell. Here."

I pulled the stiff calico curtains, bleached and coarse, round the bed; they were pleated rigidly and were suspended from a railing. Drawn, they shut my cell off from the rest of the dormitory. I looked round it. It was tiny. Just large enough to stand up and turn round carefully. On the floor was a piece of hairy matting and beside the bed there was a little washstand, painted white, with a cold marble top. It supported a large porcelain basin and a china jug containing cold water. On the wooden chair rested my suitcase, and I took out my wash bag and the pair of shoes I had brought with me. Flat black lace-up shoes with rubber soles.

Sister Rebecca appeared again with a jug of hot water, which she poured into the basin. "Have you got soap, Sister?" she asked. She seemed so kind, so gentle, and, above all, so assured. I nodded, desperately anxious to get on with it. "Right, then, I'll leave you to get dressed and be back again soon."

"Thank you, Sister," I grinned back at her and her face suddenly lit up with an answering smile.

I tore off my clothes and then, remembering where I was, folded them neatly on the chair. It seemed as though I were shedding the world, shedding the whole of my past life with its untidy confusions, its degrading fears, its pettiness. I scrubbed the makeup off my face harshly, splashed vigorously in the hot, soapy water. I wanted to go forward into my new life absolutely clean. Not just the grime of British Rail, but the grime of the world, scrubbed away and flushed down the sink.

Then I turned to the clothes. From all sides of the dormitory, stifled, nervous giggles were erupting excitedly. I pulled on the black woolen stockings and turned to the underclothes. Long airtex bloomers that reached my knees, an airtex tunic that had long sleeves (a trifle too long, they flopped over my fingers, and I folded them back bulkily over my wrists) and that fell over the bloomers, ending just above my knees. And then an ankle-length serge petticoat. All the clothes, I noticed, were marked with a number, *276*; that must be *my* number. Somewhere in that throng of unknown nuns I had a definite place. I was two hundred seventy-sixth in the line! And then came a black cotton blouse, a long pleated black serge skirt that came just below my ankles, and on top of all this a prim cape, open in the front, braided round the edges, which flapped jauntily about my elbows. It had a flat, linen Peter Pan collar. I looked down at myself nervously, feeling as though I were in a fancy costume. Or dressing up for a play. But, I realized with a pang of apprehension, I knew neither the role nor the lines.

"Goodness! You're quick!" Sister Rebecca entered my cell, gliding in noiselessly. I turned to face her self-consciously. She studied me and, with a grave and decisive nod, looked satisfied. "Good! Now let's find you a cap."

She seized my black hairbrush and pulled my hair severely off my face, fastening it back with hair grips. Then she produced a white linen cap and pulled it on, surveyed me, and shook her head. "Too tight," she pronounced. Eventually she found one that appeared to fit, pulled up the drawstring at the back and tied it in a firm knot under my chin. "Yes!" she said. The cap fit tightly round my face, showing just a little hair in front. Then she vanished, leaving me feeling like a skinned grape, and reappeared with a white semicircular piece of linen that she pinned round the cap, so that the little veil hung round my shoulders. "See?" she said. "I'm putting in one pin at the top and one on each side. Is that comfortable?"

Her voice sounded muffled. *Is this what it always feels like in a habit?* I wondered. All sounds coming from a long way off, closing you in a world of personal silence with God. Forever. I turned my head uncertainly and the starched linen rustled and crackled alarmingly through my head like the roaring of an angry sea.

"Good," Sister said. Then she untied the cap and veil. And the world rushed back again, noisy, clear, and sharply focused.

"Now during the hooding," Sister explained quietly and reassuringly, "Reverend Mother Provincial will place the hood on your head. Like this, see?" she demonstrated. "What you have to do is take the strings that are hanging down in the front. Like that. Yes, that's right, tie them under your chin at the side. No, here. Yes, that's it, tie a good strong bow . . . yes . . . good. Then what you've got is an untidy mess of strings hanging down. So you then have to twiddle them round—the strings—like this, until you've got a sort of twisted rope, and then you tuck it into your cap at the side out of sight. Now, you try all over again."

I tried, fumblingly.

"That's right." She grinned at me suddenly. "All the rest of your life you'll have to be careful of that, of not letting your strings show. Look!" She pulled at her own cap and they hung there, absurdly incongruous, from the severe wimple and her beautiful face. She giggled. "We call it 'having a beard,' " she said, tucking them back. "I pin mine safely in position. You might like to do the same."

Then she took off the cap with its veil, pinned on it a label that read "Karen," and glided off to give it to Mother Albert.

I looked round the dormitory. On all sides girls were appearing from their cells, with scrubbed, childish faces, awkward but already transformed. The superficial differences of hairstyle and clothes carefully chosen to express personality were all thrown away. We emerged now, all identical, no longer of the world. We eyed one another surreptitiously, caught one another's eyes, and grinned, smirking at our mirror images.

"Is everybody ready?" Mother Albert called. "Good. We're just in time. You can go, Sisters," she said, waving dismissively in the direction of the novices, who vanished silently, eyes cast down, white veils floating.

Mother Albert looked at us all critically, walking down the line we had formed, adjusting a collar, pulling a cape, tugging at a skirt.

"This," she said, "is your formal introduction to the Order. After the hooding you will be religious sisters. It's a short and very simple ceremony. Reverend Mother Provincial will read some prayers. Try and listen to them; take in what you can. They're beautiful prayers asking God for what you will need to be good nuns. You probably don't feel much like praying," she smiled ruefully. "You probably feel very confused and numb. But don't worry about that. It's quite normal. You've all had a very tiring and unusual day."

She then called out a list of our names, which placed us in order of age. "Wherever you go, for the next three years," she explained, "you will walk in line in this order. So try and remember it." I was at the back with Irene in front of me and Marie and Margaret behind. It was a daunting prospect, always walking in rank, your place fixed in it. Like soldiers, I thought. And then I remembered that St. Ignatius, whose rule we largely followed in this Order, had been a soldier. Soldiers of Christ.

"How many of you have got head scarves?" Mother was asking. I went and produced mine and so did one or two others. "Yes, you'll need to cover your heads in church as usual. Anyone who hasn't got a scarf can have a mantilla."

I looked at my scarf. It was red and white, and antique cars in bright colors careered cheerfully all over it. I had never thought anything of it at home. But now, suddenly, it seemed quite out of place. I looked down at my strange, sober clothes, and cringed at making my religious debut with this emblem of frivolity on my head.

"Mother," I said, "I *can't* wear this!"

She looked at it and her face lit up.

"No," she said as she laughed at the absurdity of it. "No, you can't possibly wear anything like that ever again!"

Later I learned of my parents' thoughts and feelings that night. They spent the afternoon in the theatre very conscious that I was not with them. It had been odd watching Maria Trapp as a postulant and thinking that I was one too by that time. It was comforting to them that Maria left her order. It nurtured the hope they both shared, even though it was never expressed directly, that I too would prove unsuitable for the life. "Climb every mountain till you find your dream!" They could not quite see a member of my Order dismissing me with an aria—more likely it would be a cool, ironic, but well-bred admonition—but how wonderful it would be if I were advised to leave. "Till you find your dream." What *did* I really want that was leading me so far from them spiritually?

Afterward, driving home again down the highway, Lindsey dropped off to sleep, exhausted by the emotion of the day. It was good that they were so tired. They'd planned a full day on purpose, so that when they got home they'd only want to sleep, not think. But inevitably they wondered whether they had done the right thing in letting me go.

"What could we have done?" my mother kept on saying. "How could we have stopped her? If we had stopped her, she'd only have spent the next few years pining for the convent." It was the one point in all the welter of religious confusion that she kept coming back to.

Again and again on that sad journey home my parents tried to make sense of what had happened. Looking at my sister in the back seat, my mother tried to puzzle out how she had managed to produce two such different children. Already Lindsey's fourteen-year-old body was seductive as she lay asleep, her long, shapely legs sprawled across the seat, her mane of hair tumbling over her shoulders. "Lindsey couldn't be more different," my mother said. "Extrovert from the word go and loads of friends. Any time now we'll be fending off the boyfriends, I expect."

My father agreed. Lindsey, he felt, was more like his side of the family. He could understand her better than me, somehow. She had straightforward emotions and a streak of Irish sentimentality that he shared, whereas I was an unknown quantity with thoughts that I'd never share with anyone. "Why are they so different?" he asked. "They were brought up exactly the same."

"Genes," said my mother drily. "Karen's got Hastings genes. She's exactly like my mother. She looks like her, she's small like her when all the rest of us are such giants, and she's got her sense of humor, too."

"And she always wanted to be a nun, or so she says now," my father said. "Who knows? It may be there that it all started to go wrong for her. This 'will of God' business again."

The lights were beginning to prick the darkness at the side of the motorway. Outside the car the world looked concrete and very bleak to my parents. How had they managed to produce a child who would want to deny all they loved and valued most? They had tried everything in that last year to make me change my mind. I had been subjected to an onslaught of parties and official Catholic functions that had filled me with horror and excruciating boredom. If this was the world and all its works and pomps, they could keep it. The boys from Stonyhurst and Downside ferried me round the dance floor, unable to meet my eyes while we tried to engage in social conversation. My shoes hurt, my dress felt like armor plating, and I longed for the friendly solitude of my own bedroom. "They're such nice boys," my mother protested. Perhaps that was exactly what was wrong with them. Nothing was going to make me change my mind about the convent.

"I've never seen her so stubborn," my mother said now as the car took them farther and farther away from me. "It was strange. It seemed as though God really was supporting her in some way."

That, I sensed, was what baffled my parents most. I had always been a meek child, dreading conflict of any kind, and had always preferred to give in rather than risk a row. Nothing had really

seemed worth such an expense of energy and dignity. But in this
matter I had known I was right and with a strength I hadn't known
I possessed I had calmly stuck to my point, blandly refusing to
argue. After all, I was doing God's will and, kindly, I had to make
my parents see it. I had at least made them uneasy enough to prefer
not to risk encountering God's disapproval. We never spoke of this.
My parents did not talk easily about the more personal and emotional aspects of religion. Once, however, I'd heard my mother say:
"If you believe in God, then as a Catholic you've got to believe that
He calls some people to become nuns. So, logically, why shouldn't
it be your own daughter?"

They fell silent as they neared Birmingham. When God was a
factor, you couldn't win. And you shouldn't want to, either. Yet they
still felt trapped and uneasy.

"When can we go and see her?" my father asked.

"At Christmas; that's not so bad, is it? Then, after that, we're
allowed to go only once every six months."

My father remembered those jovial nuns in *The Sound of Music.*
"How do you solve a problem like Maria?" and cheery songs about
whiskers on kittens with the Abbess. They had made the training of
a postulant seem like a game. Would it be like that at Tripton?
Somehow he wasn't convinced that it would be so normal, but he
couldn't begin to imagine what it was really like behind the enclosure door. Hopefully he turned his attention back to Maria.

"Do you think she'll stick it out?" he asked.

"I don't know. Mother Katherine said that the noviceship was
the most difficult part, especially the first year. If she survives that
she'll probably stay."

Silently they turned into the familiar drive and braced themselves to go into the house without me.

We entered the church for the hooding. At the back an organ
was playing. Row upon row of black, praying nuns filled the pews,
their heads bent at the same angle, their faces hidden in their hands.
In front of them were three rows of white-veiled novices.

I glanced up at the roof. There, lost in the dim shadows, the
three arches towered above us; having survived centuries of perse-
cution and dissolution they were now triumphant again and breath-
takingly beautiful. The austere grey stone of the walls was softened

to a faint pink as the evening sun shone obliquely through the tall windows of clouded glass.

The organ played on peacefully.

We walked down the aisle behind Mother Albert. We seemed to make so much noise. All my life I had moved freely, never thinking how to place my feet so that they wouldn't clatter. We seemed to be tramping like vandals into this holy place, bringing the tumult of the world right into the stillness and prayer of the convent church.

Above the altar hung a large, fourteenth-century crucifix. The painted Byzantine Christ hung there suffering but victorious, lost in His own vision of glory.

Mother Albert ushered us in our long straggling line to kneel around the wrought iron altar rail. I looked at the tabernacle, which housed the hidden presence of Christ. *I've come to find You,* I thought. *I've done it. Here I am.* The tabernacle, lit by two candles, glimmered back at me.

From behind I heard Reverend Mother Provincial's voice. "In the name of the Father and of the Son and of the Holy Ghost, Amen," and there was—not a rustle exactly—but a movement of clothing, soft, whispering, as the seventy women behind me crossed themselves. Mother Provincial's voice, which had sounded too large and full in the crowded parlor, ill-attuned to the casualness of a social event, now swelled into the vast church, finding here its true medium. Divorced from the sharp face, it was a beautiful thing.

Concentrate. I tried to push my mind along with the prayer she was reading. She read a petition and then the community answered her, praying with us, for us: "We beseech Thee to hear us."

"Grant, O God, I humbly beseech Thee, that I may bring with me into this state of Holy Religion a mind humble and obedient, a heart tender with compunction, and a body the apt and docile instrument of my soul."

All at once my body froze and panic raced through me, causing my heart to pound. What had I done? What on earth was I doing? I listened to the huge demands that the prayer was making. How did I think I was going to manage this? What was I doing here with these women whose hearts melted with sorrow for their sins, whose minds were supple with entire obedience to God's will, whose bodies were no longer clamoring for satisfaction but were tools of a pure soul

that burned with unwavering love of God? I glanced up in terror at
the crucifix and wanted to run away from this broken and suffering
Christ who hung there triumphant over His hideous pain. I wanted
to run through the little village street, back to the station. Back to
the world I knew, where I could manage some, at least, of the
demands. I wanted out. But my legs felt weak as water.

Then the organ began to play from the back of the church. I
recognized the hymn *Ave Maris Stella,* with its sweet wooing cadences. "Hail, Star of the Sea" it called out to Mary, Mother of God
and all men. I thought of my own mother, back home, tidying my
bedroom, carefully avoiding looking at my clothes hanging limp and
useless. I ached with the hollowness inside me. For me now there
could be no simple natural love, no ease of companionship, only the
horror of that breaking, endless crucifixion.

"Show yourself to be a mother to us," the community sang.
"Monstra te esse matrem." I recalled Mother Katherine's words, "Our
Lord makes it all up to us." The tearing bereavement I was feeling,
ripped away as I was from everybody I had known and loved, would
be replaced by something far more satisfying. Already God had
provided me with His own Mother. The beauty of the chant flowed
through me consolingly, making my heart swell at the promise of
perfection that the music implied. I felt the hood descending over
my head, muffling the music, blocking out the world, the flesh, and
the devil, and shutting me inside my own head to begin my long
struggle with God.

Then from the back of the church, a long, long way off, a voice
prayed, "O most sweet Jesus," and the community prayed the
prayer of the Order in unison. They whispered the words lovingly,
knowing to a hair's breadth of a second when to pause, how long
to pause, when to breathe, when to speak. A familiar prayer. I had
heard it so often at school. I listened, comforted, afraid to join in.
They spoke as one person, a corporate identity. For twelve years I
had listened to that prayer but now I belonged for the first time. I
too would learn how to say it so that my voice disappeared and
melted into the single voice of the community.

This, I thought with awe, is my new family. I will learn the
rhythms of that prayer of the life of this community. I will become
a part of this close-knit family, burning with love for God. At peace.

4 · TRIPTON

"Yes, it was terrible. Last year they locked me up for a month."

"Locked you up!" I was aghast.

"But yes. Last year I should have entered. It was all arranged. I had my suitcase packed, my ticket was booked for the boat. My parents, they were not speaking to me, but *que voulez-vous?* I was not expecting them to. There had been scenes for months—terrible scenes!" Adèle was silent, her elegant face heavy with remembered horror. "Well, I went upstairs to pack and then went to open the door of my room. It was locked."

"What did you do?" I asked, enthralled.

"Well, I banged on the door for a little while. But I knew that it was useless. So I sat down to wait."

"How did you feel? I'd have gone *mad*!" I said emphatically.

Adèle shrugged. "What would have been the good? It would have done nothing. No, I knew that I just had to endure—how do you say it—stick it out."

I looked at her with respect. What control! But then Adèle was very controlled. Her face was calm and beautiful in a dark, French way. She held herself very straight and her movements were very slight as she spoke. Beside her I felt all flailing arms and limbs. She had been in her postulant's dress for only half an hour but she looked as though she had been born in it. Mine felt uncomfortable —all flaps—and not being able to hear very well made me feel disoriented and rather giddy. But perhaps that was just excitement.

We were sitting in the postulants' community room half an hour after the hooding. Mother Albert had led us back here through a maze of corridors and cloisters and had left us to go to supper.

73

Sister Rebecca, the second-year novice who had helped me to get dressed, had been left with us, and she would take us along to what they called "second-table supper" at eight o'clock. For some reason postulants did not eat with the professed nuns and the novices.

The community room was long and austere. A table stretched down the centre of the room with ten chairs round it, one for each of us. There was no carpet and the old wooden floorboards gleamed a deep brown in the electric light that glared from shadeless bulbs. Around the walls of the room, facing toward the centre, were ten old desks—each with a seat combined. One for each of us arranged in order of age. Sister Rebecca, who was looking at us all benignly, had told us to find our desks and that we could talk for a little while. Soon she was going to tell us what to do in the refectory. Adèle, who was the oldest postulant, had a place in the far corner. She was twenty-six. Edna came next and I was right down the far end of the room. There were two postulants younger than I was, Marie and a plump, blonde, dreamy-looking girl called Margaret. Opposite us on the far wall was an old-fashioned press and on top of that was a statue of Our Lady, who was holding the Holy Child. Behind us the large sash windows were uncurtained and the night pressed blackly against them. The windows were like a mirror and it was very hard to resist the temptation to look at ourselves in our new get-ups. I had tried to resist—come on, I said to myself, you've got to give up this vanity business sometime—but I felt my eyes constantly wandering back to my reflection. I could see my face, looking skinned with all my hair scraped back, framed by the billowing shoulder-length hood. My face looked very white and my eyes glittered, huge and dark. But that was just the harsh light, I supposed. I had drifted across to talk to Edna and had come in on Adèle's tale of her escape from her parents.

"And you had to stick it out for a month?" I asked incredulously. It sounded like an exaggerated tale from a novel. "But didn't you try and shout for help from the windows?"

"My room overlooked the garden," Adèle replied tersely, "and if anybody had heard me, who would have come? My parents are old; I am their only child. People told me that I was selfish, that I was needed at home. They were on my parents' side."

"I suppose they were," I said slowly. Yet of course Adèle was right, however much pain she caused her parents.

"Did they give you food and everything?" I asked Adèle.

"But of course! They would not have me die! What would have been the use of that? No. They wanted me living and well and with them always till they died. Each morning my father would bring me my breakfast. And sometimes—oh, it was pitiful—he would give me a treat. A cake that he had made specially for me, perhaps, or a tiny bunch of flowers on the tray. I felt so—how do you say—torn? Yes, torn two ways.

"My father argued that God could not want me to leave my parents. That I had a delusion. You see, the parish priest agreed with them. Oh! He is old. He has known them for years and he is very boring. I think, too, he did not like it that I wanted to join an English order."

"How did you come to know about this Order?"

"A few years ago my parents decided that as I was not to go to the university, I should go abroad just for a year to learn a language. They wanted me to be in a convent because I would be safe—you know, from the wicked English men!" Adèle smiled at me, her rather stern face lighting up for a moment with humor. "So, we got in touch with an agency and they put me in touch with the convent of this Order in Liverpool. I worked there as a kind of *au pair,* you know, and I decided that this was where I wanted to be."

"The same with me," Edna nodded. "I've a sister who's a Sister of Mary, and she's been after me to enter with her for ages. You know, Mammy used to say to me, 'Go on, now, Edna, why don't you? Maureen would be over the moon. The two of you would have such a great time! The two of you together!' But once I'd seen those nuns in Dublin, that was it."

Adèle turned and stared at Edna: "Your mother, she was encouraging you to enter?"

"Yes," Edna drawled. Throughout the conversation her eyes had been fixed on Adèle with a bewilderment that was so extreme that it was comical. "Honestly, I've been listening to the two of you talking and I just can't believe my ears! Can't believe my ears!" she repeated as she was wont to do when moved. "In Ireland it's considered an honor to have your children entering the religious life. Mammy was always saying, 'Come on, now, Edna. Which order is it going to be? Come on, now, make up your mind. Ye're leaving it awfully late.' And I used to say, 'Oh no, Mammy! Ye've got

75

Maureen in the convent down the road and that's enough for you. I'm not entering.' And she used to say, 'You wait and see, my girl! The Lord will get you yet!' And then I hear ye talking about being locked up and your mother in tears. I'm flabbergasted—honestly. I can't believe my ears."

It was now the turn of Adèle and me to look astonished. "And you," Adèle turned politely to me. "Did you have any trouble with your parents?"

"Oh, nothing to speak of," I replied humbly, "nothing like what you had to put up with." How would I have stood up to that? I wondered. Adèle must be so strong, so certain of what she wants to do. "My parents didn't like the idea at all; in fact they were dead against it, but my headmistress talked to them, and finally they gave in."

"Didn't like it!" Again Edna was shaking her head as though she wanted this recalcitrant information to settle in her head so that she could give it the serious consideration it deserved.

"When I think! Mammy is on her knees night and day about Patrick—he's my youngest brother; he's only fourteen. She's set on making him a priest. Michael, my other brother, he's going to get married and Mammy said to God, 'Fine! On condition that you take Patrick instead!' And she'll get her way!" Edna laughed gleefully. "Mark my words."

"But are most people in Ireland like this?" I asked.

"Of course they are. Why ever wouldn't they be? D'ye mean" —a terrible understanding was creeping slowly over Edna's honest face—"that most parents are like yours, or *yours*?" she said, turning finally to Adèle.

"Oh no! not like mine," Adèle laughed quickly.

"But like mine, yes, I should think they are," I added.

Edna swirled round in her seat and rested her elbows on her desk, laying her head wearily upon it as though this had been the last straw in an already exhausting day. "Honestly," she spoke very slowly, and I could almost see the ideas painfully working through her mind. "I always heard that England was different. But I never thought it'd be as different as that! Of course here ye've got all the Protestants, haven't ye? I suppose that makes a difference to all ye Catholics in England."

We left her shaking her head, wide-eyed with wonder over her new disillusionment, and I turned back to Adèle.

"Did your mother ever come to see you while you were shut up there?"

"Never! Not once! Always my father. And always he tells me how ill my mother is and that I am killing her. Sometimes he used to come in and say nothing to me at all. That was easier. It made me angry instead of sad for him. Sometimes, when he used to collect my supper tray, he would lean on my windowsill, looking over the garden, and just chat. He used to tell me who had entered the shop that day and what they had said and how the bread was going. You know, just as if everything were normal. Poor Papa! How he must have hated it all."

"Do you think that if it had been left to him, he'd have let you go?" I asked. Adèle shook her head firmly.

"No. He was not so much against it as my mother, but he was against it all the same."

Down the room I could hear Marie roaring with laughter and just to my right Joan and Pia were having a conversation. How strange it was, sitting and chatting to one another politely. Like getting to know the other people on your crew when you are embarking on a long and dangerous voyage. *Why had I said dangerous?* I asked myself, surprised. No harm was going to come to me here. It was going to be difficult and like a voyage in that it was going to take me somewhere quite different. The new life with God I sensed already was going to be quite outside the limits of my experience. Some people, though, had come so far already. Like Teresa. Or Pia, who also sounded foreign. And look at Adèle, how far she had had to travel emotionally before she got to the starting point. I looked at her humbly, sensing in her a strength and quiet love of God that far surpassed my own. I only hoped that I would have a similar courage for what lay ahead.

"And what happened in the end?" I asked. "What made them let you out?"

"Well, Mama got ill. I could tell she was ill. The doctor came. Visitors came. Papa came to me in tears. He could not leave her. He had to shut the shop; it was all a calamity. So," she shrugged again ironically, "I could not leave them in this state. Mama was really ill.

77

But how far it was only up here," Adèle tapped her forehead, "I do not know. They had won."

"So how did you manage it tonight?"

"Oh, this time I told them nothing. I pretend that I have given up the idea, that I now see my duty is at home and then, pouff! Two days ago, I just walk out. I have no luggage, nothing that will make them suspect. I come only in what I stand up in. It was a lie, but what can you do?"

"Will they know where you are?" I asked, picturing them frantic and defeated. I almost looked out the window expecting to see them striding over the dark Bedfordshire fields.

"I posted a letter this afternoon in London," Adèle said, and suddenly her face twisted in an expression of such pain that I had to turn my eyes away. "Now I have to wait for them to write to me."

"Sisters!" interrupted Sister Rebecca, who had been listening to this story as moved as the rest of us. Her own father, though never resorting to the extreme measures of Adèle's parents, had made her wait three years to be sure of her vocation. She knew the suffering Adèle had gone through. Her gentle voice could hardly be heard in our worldly din. "Sisters! Will you all come and sit round the table, please, in order of age. I want to tell you about the refectory."

In caché order we filed down the cloister. Rust- and cream-colored tiles stretched away before us, gleaming dimly in the yellow light of one lamp until, far away, they became lost in dark shadow. "Postulants and novices may only walk down the left side of the Cloister," Sister Rebecca had told us. "The right side is for the professed nuns, those who have made their vows. Keep as close to the wall as you can, Sisters." Glancing up, I saw the head of the procession disappear through one of the large oak doors on the left into a vast, high-ceilinged room. Tables stretched round three walls; the places were set down only one side of each table so that they all faced into the centre of the room. At the far end of the long room a smaller table was laid for eight people. (That must be top table, I noted to myself, where the superiors of the house sit.) Over this table was a large crucifix and to its left was a heavy oak lectern, built like a pulpit where at first-table meals the reader sat. All meals were taken in silence to the accompaniment of reading—the life of a saint at dinner and a more devotional book at supper, Sister Rebecca had explained. I wondered why we were not eating with the others. The room seemed very empty, rather echoing, and unfriendly. One or two professed nuns sat at one of the side tables but that was all.

Sister Rebecca was leading the way to a long table placed in the centre of the room that was for the novices and postulants. We advanced in line to the end of it, and then, looking up to the crucifix, we bowed low before filing into our places down one side of the table. Then a silent grace was said and we all sat down. I tried to keep my eyes fixed on my plate as Sister Rebecca had directed. She had told us that nuns were not supposed to stare around them all the time; that was distracting and we should always be in a prayerful state, waiting on God. It was an old monastic practice that had the quaint name of "custody of the eyes." I tried to remember all the other directions Sister had given us. Heavens! This was going to be so complicated! Custody of the eyes wasn't too easy either. It had sounded simple enough in the community room. Every time I heard a spoon crashing or somebody walking past, I found myself mechanically looking up. I was dying to see everything that was happening. I glanced guiltily at the two professed nuns eating at one of the side tables opposite us. They did look funny with their napkins pinned under their chins—like solemn penguins. I had to hand it to them, though. They never once raised their eyes from the table, never once looked our way, though surely they must have been curious to see what we were all like.

No, I said firmly; *no more looking about.* I turned my attention to the table. The turn squealed as it swung round and Mother Albert and the novice bustled toward us with steaming metal serving dishes. Taut with concentration, the novice quietly placed a dish in front of me and glided away, her rubber soles squeaking slightly as she hurried over the polished floors. I looked at the food.

Oh, my God! Macaroni cheese!

It lay there, reeking gungily. The stench of the cheese I found nauseating. All my life I had hated macaroni cheese—all cooked cheese, in fact. My mother had tried to get me to eat it, but since I was invariably sick afterward she had abandoned the struggle as being more trouble than it was worth.

"In the religious life," Sister Rebecca had said only a few minutes before, "we eat everything that is set before us. We don't say

'Oh! I don't like—say—carrots. I won't have any!' We eat every-thing."

"Why?" Margaret had asked.

"Well, we're not supposed to pay any attention to our likes and dislikes. It's a way of getting the better of our bodies so that we govern them, not *vice versa.* That's how we become absolutely cen-tered on God's will, instead of our own."

Mortifying the body, putting it to death. I didn't realize then what a problem food was going to be. Hitherto, at home, it had always been a source of pleasure. My father had loved good food and had gone to great trouble to educate our palates, so that we knew exactly what we liked and how it should be eaten. Now meals were going to become a constant battle. Not only did we have to eat everything, we had to have two helpings of at least one dish at every meal. And at every meal we were urged to make one real act of mortification. If you were really set on doing this that meant taking an extra big helping of something you disliked, or, if you liked everything on the table, finding a way to spoil it for yourself: doing without salt, for example. We never had pepper and mustard. Meal-times became a means of making my body die; for me food became associated with that dangerous sensuality that had to be ruthlessly trampled on if my body were ever going to become the slave of my will, which in its turn was the pure vehicle of God's will. It was such a little thing, my stomach, but it became such a big problem. And that in itself was humiliating.

That first night, with an ominous sinking feeling, I eyed the macaroni cheese as an adversary, warily assessing its powers. Still, what had I come for? All that talk about blank checks had been fine. I was ready to scale the heights and depths of religious agony described by the poets. And here I was balking at a plate of macaroni cheese. It was funny, really. *This is it, Lord,* I said; *here goes,* and, inwardly regretting the amount of real heroism involved, I picked up the spoon.

The macaroni slithered onto my plate in a soft mound and then collapsed. Scarcely daring to breathe—*I can't smell it,* I told myself; *another night, Lord, I'll really try and smell it too but tonight all I can do is eat it*—I spooned on another spoonful and another and thankfully passed the dish to Marie. Gripping my fork, I plunged it into the slimy mass, shoveling the horrible stuff into my mouth and, with a gulp of scalding tea, swallowing it whole. Retching, with beads of cold sweat standing out on my forehead, I managed somehow to eat the whole plateful.

At the end of the meal tin bowls containing soapy water and washcloths were carried to each table; with these we were to wash our own things. *Help!* I thought as my plate clanged against the side of the tin and my fork vanished into the soapy depths. When I tried to pile the washed articles neatly on the napkin the pyramid disintegrated with a clatter that seemed to echo sonorously in the high rafters overhead. Red in the face, I looked across at Sister Rebecca. Her face was calm and she completed the whole messy business smoothly with never a sound. My brothers, I noted with a certain comfort, were making just as much of a hash of the whole thing as I was. Awed, I looked back at Sister Rebecca. What had happened to transform her from a girl to a nun in two short years?

Back in the community room, Mother Albert smiled drily at us. "Normally," she said, "we have community recreation for an hour after supper, but tonight I think you ought to go straight to bed. We *never* speak in the dormitory. At nine you'll hear the big bell strike ten times. That's the start of what we call the Great Silence, which lasts until after Mass the next morning. It's a daily retreat, really," she explained, "a time when we lovingly prepare to receive Christ in Holy Communion each day."

I recognized there the beauty of what I had come here for. A life of prayer, a daily search for God.

It was strange to be back in my cell. It seemed ages since I'd been here last. My worldly clothes were hanging up neatly on the rail over my bed, looking like empty husks. There was the strangeness of queuing at the tap for hot water and washing by my bed, overhearing the others' private sounds: personal splashing, the explosion of poppers, the odd cough or grunt. Finally, in my stiff calico nightdress, I eased myself gingerly onto the narrow mattress and lay there trying to fit my body with a modicum of comfort round the lumps. I was also trying to ignore the revolution that was going on in my stomach. *Think of something else,* I thought and tried hard to identify each sound with one of the brethren. It was no good. A few minutes later I was dashing to the lavatory to get rid of the macaroni cheese. Kneeling on the floor, I wiped the beads of perspiration that had gathered on my forehead yet again. The words of the hooding ceremony returned, spoken in Mother Provincial's dramatic voice. "A body the apt and docile instrument of my soul." Plenty of room for improvement there. What could you do to subdue a body that had its own rhythms, that could stage its own "rebellion," never giving the soul so much as a by-your-leave?

I crept back to bed. No doubt I would find out.

When all was still in the dormitory I heard Mother Albert entering. I was lying in that feeble postvomiting state, feeling homesick. At home—surely they'd be back by now—they'd be wondering how I was getting on. And how was I getting on? Being sick had brought it home to me that for the first time in my life I was really functioning as an adult. And I didn't like it. At home whenever I had been sick there had been a certain amount of consoling fuss: a hot water bottle, solicitous inquiries, special cosseting. It was childish to miss it, of course, and I had insisted that I was grown up enough to come here. But here nobody cared whether I was unwell or not. I felt very lonely, suddenly, and the future seemed bleak and impersonal. I heard Mother Albert entering each cell, one by one. What is she doing, I wondered? I didn't wish I was back at home; of course not. I knew I'd feel better in the morning, and I was excited about the new life that was really going to begin in earnest tomorrow. But I did wish I felt less alone.

At last I saw the curtain of my own cell parting silently, and Mother Albert crossed the two paces that took her up to my bed, casting a swift, appraising look at the pile of folded clothes on the chair.

She smiled down at me kindly. Then she reached out the finger that wore the profession ring and made the sign of the cross on my forehead.

"Good night and God bless you," she said quietly.

I turned over after the lights had gone out, comforted, and felt myself sliding into an exhausted sleep. It was going to be all right.

Mass at seven o'clock the next morning was beautiful. Kneeling in the front pew, aware of the novices behind me and behind them the ranks of black-robed nuns, I looked at the altar. I had that fresh feeling of a new beginning. I was starting out, I felt, on an adventure, on a lifelong quest like that of the knights who had sought the Grail. Every single morning of my life I knew I would start my day with Mass, with the reenactment of Christ's sacrifice on Calvary. For the first time I saw the Mass in its true beauty. Instead of being filled with a noisy congregation of obstreperous children bored with a ritual that meant nothing to them, and adults whose worries and preoccupations with business worries or the Sunday roast expressed itself in a reverent fidgeting, the church was absolutely silent. All these women had given their entire lives to God and were here uniting that sacrifice with the one Christ made. It was the central moment of the day, not a duty that had somehow to be fitted in. And in my own way, I felt that I too had given to God everything I'd got. True, I hadn't made my vows yet, but I had left everything else behind and was here entirely at His disposal. After the flurry of yesterday with its crowding of new impressions and experiences, it was a moment of stillness. I watched the sacristan light the candles on the altar, watched the priest stride up the aisle and begin the familiar ritual, heard again the responses of the nuns. Prayer and tranquility filled the church and I felt deeply at one with the community. *This is what it's all about,* I told myself. *Help me not to hold anything back now,* I prayed. When the Communion bell rang I saw the nuns file up silently. Mother Provincial first, then the Provincial Council, the superior of the Tripton house, and the rest of the community. They glided up the aisle, their veils pulled down to cover their faces, hands joined together with the fingers pointing to Heaven, heads bent forward devoutly. When it was my turn to receive Communion I felt a deep peace. I had offered myself to God and, in return, He had given Himself back to me. What more could I want?

When I got to know Mother Albert better and heard her talk about her years as Postulant Mistress, I could imagine what she must have been feeling on that first morning. Each September a new batch of postulants came to her to be transformed into nuns. Each year they arrived with the same look of dazed bewilderment. Every year they made the same predictable mistakes. Postulants forgot so easily. The disciplines she taught were only skin deep, and periodically you'd find someone forgetting she was a religious, whistling while she shook her mop in the garden, running upstairs two steps at a time, swinging her arms while she walked. Then Mother Albert had to be angry, even though nine times out of ten the fault wasn't intentional. But a postulant can't learn too early that the religious

83

life is an hourly waiting on God. Every little thing is an act of the worship of God and a nun can never slacken off, even for a moment.

Some postulants, of course, had made the fundamental mistake of coming to Tripton in the first place. God works in mysterious ways. It might well be a definite part of His plan for a particular girl to spend a few months in a convent. But it was very wearing for the Postulant Mistress. As well as that, we must have seemed a particularly problematic set. Four of us were only seventeen, and in addition to the inevitable strains and stresses of the religious life Mother Albert had to cope with the equally inevitable problems of adolescence. If she had let herself criticize her superiors, she must have wondered what on earth Mother Provincial was thinking of to admit some of us. Mother Greta had apparently seen Marie standing outside the gates of the convent on that first afternoon frantically puffing through the remains of a packet of cigarettes. But then you could never tell. Many of the saints had been tearaways before they'd turned to God—St. Francis, for example, or St. Ignatius himself. The trouble was that one bad egg could infect all the others by damaging the tone of the little community.

It was September, the beginning of the school year. The nuns who worked in the attached boarding school were already bustling about making up the children's beds, checking piles of exercise books, sticking labels on lockers. Six years ago Mother Albert had been a part of all that and had also been headmistress of one of the Order's junior boarding schools at Lyme. She had loved teaching and continued to miss the children. But a nun has to be prepared to give up any loved work, any pet project, at the drop of a hat. In July the whole Order waited for that little list that went up on the notice board every year, announcing the moves that had been planned by the Provincial. The nuns would scan the lists anxiously to see whether their names were there. If your name was not on the list then you could breathe a sigh of relief and continue happily in your present position or grit your teeth for another year's service if you did not like it where you were. Again, happy or unhappy in your work or in your community, you could be sent to another part of England or to Ireland, Africa, or America. A nun is not consulted. She has to wait on the will of God as it is revealed to her through her superiors with absolute detachment. That was what the vow of obedience meant. Not my will but Thine be done.

Later I learned of Mother Albert's horror when she saw that she had been appointed Postulant Mistress. It was not a job that any nun would have wanted. The responsibility was immense: Mother Albert had the future of the Order in her hands and she was a humble person, well aware of her own failings in the religious life. Who was she to turn these young girls into religious, detached from their own desires, wanting only to do God's will?

As she entered the community room and saw us that morning, still looking lost and vague, our hoods awry, our hair untidy, her heart must have sunk to her boots and she must have sent up a quick prayer asking for help in the task she had to begin.

"Good morning," she smiled at us cheerfully, "did you all manage to get some sleep?"

"Oh, Mother!" Edna groaned. "I slept like a log, I was so tired!"

Mother Albert smiled at her with genuine liking and I noticed how closely she was watching our every move, studying the way we spoke, the way we moved, turning to catch slight nuances of tone and expression. Sharply she judged us behind those glinting spectacles and I suddenly realized that for the whole period of training I would be scrutinized like that, watched to see how I was developing, watched every moment of the day. It was a sobering thought.

"Did the rest of you sleep well?" she asked, and her query was met by a chorus of polite murmurs. Suddenly we were all on our best behavior.

"I think the best way of spending the morning," Mother began, "is for me to show you round the Postulantship. There's not much more to see," she said, "but at least it will help you to get your bearings and I can explain things en route."

She led her bedraggled little tribe into the next room. There was an expanse of red tiles, a sink, some doors, and one huge door with a heavy hinge. "This," Mother said with a flourish, "is the lower outer."

"The what?" Nessa exclaimed. The rest of us exchanged bewildered looks. Mother Albert smiled; it was a weary, resigned smile, I noticed.

"Sister," Mother spoke to Nessa in a remote and ironic tone, as if she were distancing herself from the scene. "You don't speak to your superior in that familiar way. You say, 'I beg your pardon, Mother.' "

Nessa blushed and we all avoided looking at her, trying to send out sympathetic thought-waves. How formal it all sounded! In a way that was what I'd expected, but was there to be no room for the casual word in this new life? "The lower outer," Mother was explaining, "is called an outer because it's . . . it's . . . well, it's an outer region," she said, wrestling with the problem of translating terms that were basic in her own mind. "Look, there's the door leading into the postulants' garden." She opened the heavy door and the sunlight fell in a bright golden shaft across the floor. "And it's called the lower outer to distinguish it from the upper outer upstairs. But really *outer* is just a shorthand term in the Order to describe the bathroom and lavatory area.

"Here," she threw back two doors. "You've got two baths." Our jaws dropped when we saw the bathrooms. Two ancient baths with massive claw feet, cold stone floors, and a slatted wooden bath mat. They were so comfortless. Mother Albert didn't miss our looks of dismay. "This isn't the Ritz, you know," she added tartly. "I expect you're used to wall-to-wall carpeting and washbasins and all sorts. But nuns are poor people. We take a vow of poverty as you know, and that means that we do without luxuries."

"Can we have a bath whenever we like, Mother?" Margaret asked innocently.

"Oh, no!" Mother laughed. "No. You can have one bath a week. There's a rota up on the board."

"One bath a week!" Marie voiced the general horror.

"Yes, Sister. And in the religious life we don't object to arrangements that are not to our liking in that insolent way!" Mother spoke sharply, far more sharply than she had spoken to Nessa. "We welcome opportunities to give things up, to mortify ourselves. And we never grumble."

There was a tight, anxious silence.

"And no bath salts or talcum powder," Mother Albert fell back into her usual cool tone. "If any of you have brought anything like that, would you put it on the desk in our room and I'll give it away." She broke off as she saw us exchanging more baffled looks. Which room was "ours"? Weren't they all? "In the religious life," she explained, "we don't own anything. Every single thing you use

86

down to your toothbrush belongs to the community, and to remind us of our vow of poverty we never say 'my' or 'mine.' We say 'ours' instead."

How complicated it all was. The customs, the vocabulary all had to be translated to us at every turn, as though we had started to live among an obscure tribe. But of course that was what we had done really. And these were just the superficial instances. There would be others, far deeper in significance and perhaps more surprising than this. It was a beautiful idea, I thought, sharing everything in common, living a poor, simple life. I turned back to listen to Mother Albert. "Bathing isn't supposed to be a luxurious affair," she explained. "It's a functional exercise. And no singing in the bath!"

We all laughed. Already we seemed miles away from behavior like that. "You may laugh," Mother said grimly, "but it has been known to happen in the past."

"What about soap, Mother?" I asked.

"It's in the cupboard, over there." Mother gestured vaguely.

"Where, Mother? I can't see any."

"How funny. I was certain I put some there yesterday." She peered into the cupboard and looked at me as though I were mad. "There it is! Right in front of you."

We stared awestruck and tongue-tied at the long strips of green carbolic soap, two feet long. "And there's the knife," she pointed to a rusty old blade, "to hack off a piece when you need it." She smiled wryly at our consternation.

"But, pardon me, Mother," Edna said, politely, "isn't that scrubbing soap?"

"No. It's to scrub yourselves with. No more smelly soap for you. Ever. You wash your hair with that too."

"But it'll ruin our skin," Marie bleated.

Mother's lips tightened and I could see her clocking off Marie's failings in her head. "Does that matter, Sister?" she asked coldly. "In the religious life we have abandoned the idea of physical beauty. As long as we're always clean and tidy, it doesn't matter what we look like."

"And here," she pointed to a large wicker basket, "is the laundry basket. Every Saturday night you put your washing in: you can send each week one cap, one hood, and one collar, so that you look nice and fresh on Sunday. Then underwear. Each of you has four pairs of knickers and four tunics. You can send one tunic each week to the laundry. And two pairs of knickers *only*—we don't change our underwear more frequently than that."

She laughed openly at our dismay.

Later that day, Mother Albert took us into the grounds. The Bedfordshire country rolled away interminably—green fields, trees, and in the distance a glimpse of hills.

"Our grounds stretch as far as that signpost there; can you see it?" Mother Albert was saying. I squinted into the distance. "But you should usually stay in the postulants' garden. Every first Sunday of the month, however, we have a retreat and then you can walk all over our fields. But not out in the road, of course. You may not go out of the convent unaccompanied. Every day, after lunch, the novices and postulants have a walk for an hour up that road there. In all weathers," she added firmly, "rain, hail, and snow! It's good exercise."

It all sounded very Spartan, I reflected nervously. Those washing arrangements! That soap! No more Tampax, no more deodorants, and—horror of horrors—only two pairs of knickers a week! Already I was feeling grubby and it was awful to think I'd got another four days to go before I could have a bath. Never mind! I told myself. I've not come here to live an easy life. No doubt I'd get used to it—but still! The flesh is weak, I thought sadly. We'd often speculated about these things at school; now I knew.

We were walking now past the large school buildings. "When are the children coming back, Mother?" I asked.

"Next Sunday," Mother Albert said. "It gets very crowded then, of course. They're all over the place, playing netball, and the church is absolutely jammed. By the way," she said to us all, "you must never speak to the children or to any seculars. Postulants and novices are meant to be kept secluded from the world so that you have a chance to develop a deep, personal relationship with God. The children will probably try to talk to you. But don't let them! They know perfectly well that they're not allowed to!"

Mother Albert was honest and straightforward, I decided, and I enjoyed her ironic sense of humor. Her voice was an unusual one. It wasn't the accent or the pitch that was different, but the tone. She sounded remote and everything she said was without emphasis. It seemed aloof, far beyond the muddle of feelings and the complexities of communication. She used her voice simply to convey information, not to enter into a personal relationship. I found that a bit disconcerting. It frightened me a little. She was my guide in this new world. Without real contact with her, how could I find my way? When she spoke of a deep relationship with God, that must be the main relationship of her life. Did a relationship with God necessarily exclude human closeness, and if it did, would I be able to reach that level of detachment from other people? That would be harder, far harder, than washing with carbolic soap. But then I remembered how she had thought to come in to each one of us last night. The understanding in her eyes, the sign of the cross on my forehead had been a tacit sign of sympathy with the renunciations of the day. No, I decided, that's all right.

"Here's the cemetery," Mother announced. I looked through the latticed fence at the rows of mounds, each marked with a simple wooden cross. "The Novices have just been scrubbing the stones," Mother explained. "That's why they're all so beautifully white!"

I looked at the little mounds. Each housed a nun who had given her life to God, just as I was doing now. Each of them had had a first day in the convent, had struggled with the intricacies of the refectory, had eyed her "brothers" surreptitiously. Each of them had left behind her family and had endured the pangs of homesickness. Each of them had lived here in prayer and renunciation until the end of her life. For some it may have been only a few years. Others had lived in the Order for fifty or sixty years, giving themselves so totally to the life of Christ that they had lost those early uncertainties. All of them had given everything.

"Every day," Mother Albert was saying, "after the walk at midday, you will stop here and pray for the repose of their souls. Let's say a *De Profundis* now."

And softly in unison we began Psalm 129.

"Out of the depths have I cried unto Thee, O Lord; Lord hear my voice. . . . If Thou, O Lord, will observe our iniquities, Lord who could endure it; but with Thee there is merciful forgiveness."

I stared through the fence at the graves. For the first time the absolute nature of my sacrifice had been brought home to me. Would I be buried here? Was I looking at the site of my own grave? All at once the years stretched ahead in a long clear perspective, leading to my death.

5·POSTULANT

The postulantship is a time of testing. An aspiring nun arrives at the convent and for a minimum period of six months canon law insists that she live on probation, observing only specially selected parts of the rule before beginning her real training in the novice-ship. The postulant is asking for the privilege of the habit and for the honor of becoming a novice, and the Order is scrutinizing her carefully to see how strong her vocation is and whether she is really suitable for the religious life. The postulant, on her side, carefully examines her own responses and questions the purity of her intentions. Is it God she is really seeking or just security or escape from an uncongenial world? Is she prepared to deny herself all self-fulfillment by laying aside her own selfish desires to lose them in that close relationship with God to which the nun aspires? The postulant looks at the Order and the Order looks at her. She may leave the convent at any time she chooses; no promises or vows are made. Similarly the Order can send her away if they feel she hasn't a true vocation and isn't progressing as she should. A few years before I entered, it had been decided that girls of the 1950s took longer to adapt to the religious life than their predecessors. We seemed to be more worldly; we'd enjoyed greater freedom and were more reluctant to lose ourselves in the apparent restrictions. So the postulantship had been extended from six to nine months.

It was only a week after our arrival that the first shock hit us: the rule of silence. We were sitting in the community room round the long table in order of age. It was six in the evening. Time for the daily instruction on the religious life. I liked these sessions; we all did. Mother Albert's words pointed so directly toward God. If I can do all that she says, I promised myself, then it will all be simple.

"You are, I expect, used to speaking whenever you want to," Mother was saying. "Now you have to learn to discipline that need to express yourself and communicate with others. We are allowed to talk twice a day—for an hour after the midday meal and an hour after supper in formal recreation. The rest of the time we keep strict silence."

There was a gasp. Looking up, I saw Margaret's china-blue eyes suffused suddenly with tears, her cheeks flushed with shock. There were questions I was dying to ask. But it was not the place of postulants to question the rules of the Order. Our part was to accept it humbly. If there was anything that we found difficult, Mother Albert had told us the day before, that was because we were not yet spiritually mature. As we grew in spiritual insight our difficulties would disappear.

"Obviously," Mother was explaining, "there are times when you have to speak, in the course of your work. But any words spoken then should be few and said in a low voice. You must never prolong any of these necessary conversations in unnecessary chit-chat. You are not here to communicate with one another; you are here to deepen your relationship with God, and for that, silence of the lips and of the heart is absolutely necessary."

I quailed at the words. Not to communicate with other people. Ever. It seemed so bleak. Of course I knew that there was going to be sacrifice, and when I'd looked ahead to my new life, silence had been a part of it. But the actual fact of it and the practicalities had never occurred to me. After all, hadn't Christ said that we could only approach the love of God through loving one another? Solitude seemed difficult to square with those words. But, I told myself firmly, this must be one of those inner criticisms that revealed my spiritual immaturity. I'd see it properly in time; Mother Albert had promised us that.

"And a few further points," Mother said sternly. "Novices and postulants are kept in a particularly strict seclusion. They may not speak at all to seculars. If a secular speaks to you, you must never reply. It is only by severing yourself absolutely from the world that you can begin to shed some of its values. Again no novice or postulant may ever speak to the professed nuns unless she is working with them and those few necessary words are essential for the job. The professed are in contact with the world, and even that indirect contact might seriously damage your spiritual progress."

Margaret was looking more and more distressed, I noticed. Irene, next to her, looked dazed. And I was struggling with conflicting thoughts that I was trying to suppress. All this talk about the world was frightening. It showed that the quest for spiritual perfection was such a frail thing that a mere puff of the world could extinguish it. *Yes,* I pondered, *I know the world is bad—a lot of it—but a lot of it isn't.* I thought of my parents: why did the condemnation of the world have to be so absolute, excluding the good along with the bad? As if answering my thought, Mother Albert went on.

"You have to be absolutely ruthless in your rejection of the world, you know, Sisters. So many of its attitudes, even in really good people, are permeated with selfish values that have nothing at all to do with the self-emptying love of God. You yourselves are riddled with these ideas; you can't help it—it's not your fault. For instance, I expect you feel that you have a duty to yourselves to find self-fulfillment."

I glanced up at her swiftly. That word *self-emptying* had caught my attention. How on earth did you empty yourself of yourself? Would I be myself at the end of it?

"Well," Mother went on, "that is absolute nonsense in supernatural terms. It's only when there's no self left at all that God can fill us entirely with Himself. And silence is just one of the ways that give us a chance to empty out all our useless thoughts and distractions and let God take possession of our minds."

Put like that, it sounded beautiful. A prosaic way of saying what Hopkins said:

> Elected silence, sing to me
> And beat upon my whorlèd ear,
> Pipe me to pastures still and be
> The music that I care to hear.

But the loneliness. Fundamentally I was electing solitary confinement.

"Finally," Mother warned us, "the first-year noviceship is a time when this seclusion from the world is especially emphasized. Postulants, who are still full of the world, are never allowed to speak to any of the first-year novices."

So they were to be kept strictly apart from us lest we contaminate them! I felt a tremor of self-distrust. I'd never seen myself as someone who could corrupt, but now my mere conversation could damage them and hold them back in their progress toward God. I looked at my brothers, sitting there so meekly, with their eyes cast down. Already after only a week we looked a little more like nuns. And yet we were essentially dangerous. It was a frightening thought.

The next opportunity we had to discuss this was during the daily walk that was our midday recreation. Every afternoon in an odd little crocodile we walked primly up the road outside the convent, three by three, turned round, and walked back again. One of the second-year novices always took us. Today it was Sister Rebecca. I was pleased and skipped up to walk on one side of her. Edna was on the other side.

"Phew!" she breathed as we stepped outside the gate. "At last we can talk! Honest to goodness, I thought I'd go clean out of my mind or burst!" she exclaimed.

Sister Rebecca laughed. I was struck again by the serenity and control of everything she did. "It *is* hard at first," she said. "Has Mother Albert given you the rule of silence to keep, then?"

"She certainly has. Honestly, Sister, whoever heard of a silent Irish woman! I'll probably die for lack of a good chat!"

"You look remarkably well," Sister Rebecca returned smoothly with that prim little smile. "You don't look in danger of death to me."

"But doesn't it get awfully lonely sometimes?" I asked. "You know, never being able to share your feelings with anyone? I know God is enough for everybody and once you've got a strong relationship with Him then you couldn't want anything else. But all the same, it must be lonely."

"Yes, it is," she replied matter-of-factly as she stepped down the road, holding her skirt up daintily to prevent its trailing in a puddle. "It's often very lonely. But it's only in this way that we ever realize how much we need God."

I marveled at the confidence in her voice. "Oh, I know," I said quickly. "No, I didn't mean endlessly going round sharing dark secrets with other people. Obviously we've got to keep our deepest feelings for God. I meant more mundane things, like sharing a joke or an interesting idea."

"But you can! You can share them with the community at recreation."

"Yes, but that's usually hours away!" Edna said. "I know what Sister Karen means. By the time you get to recreation your head's so teeming with the things you've saved up that you probably can't think of a thing to say. Like this afternoon. I thought there'd be so many things I was dying to say, but now I'm here I can't remember a single one of them!"

"Some people would say they weren't very important then."

Ironically I now felt very much at ease with Sister Rebecca. I liked her quiet sense of humor and frequently we found ourselves exchanging a look of mutual understanding and amusement. I felt more at home with her than I had with any of my Birmingham acquaintances. What a pity that, just as I was beginning to discover a friendship, I was learning that it was something I could no longer explore fully. *No,* I corrected myself. *I mustn't think that. It's not a pity.*

"Don't let it worry you too much, Sisters," she was saying. "You know, after a while it really gets easier to be silent than to talk!" I looked at her with awe. Would it ever be like that for me?

I longed to achieve that degree of serenity, and in those first few months as a postulant the route seemed so simple. The way to sanctity, Mother told us, lay through strict observance of the rule. As easy as that. If I tried—really tried—to obey every single one of these rules I would find God. Of course in theory I knew that it would take years to make myself a good nun and that I needed God's help every step of the way, but the goal seemed clear and attainable in those early days.

All I had to do was to push myself toward God, never giving in to myself for a moment. Push myself further than I thought I could reasonably go, and finally God would fill me—infinite perfection, infinite love, fulfilling me as no human person could. With His help I could break through the limitations of myself and know real freedom, real peace.

So, energetically I threw myself into the rule of silence. I didn't want anything at all to hold me back from my progress to God, no trivial conversation, no turbulent undisciplined thoughts. This was the first step. Once I'd mastered that I'd go on to greater things, discovering always a deeper level of peace and joy.

But it didn't work out as easily as that. However hard I tried to keep the silence, it was only too easy to slip into a chat with Marie or Edna as we were shaking our mops at the rubbish dump called Job. And as for interior silence—that was the hardest of all.

I had elected Hopkins' silence but it very rarely sang to me. I remember particularly one day when the silence seemed humming with my self-indulgent thoughts. It was 14 November, my birthday and a miserable afternoon. The rain was beating angrily against the window and the sky was so leaden that we had to have the light on. We were sewing. *How I loath sewing!* I thought gloomily. We'd begun to make our first habits, and I squinted crossly at my buttonholes. I'd had to practice them in white cotton on black material until I'd mastered the art of that intricate stitch. The others had all graduated very quickly, but I'd had to do sixty-three on my piece of black serge, and they were still far from perfect. "Sister Karen, what *are* you doing?" Mother asked.

"Still practicing buttonholes, Mother!" And her expression of scorn when I had explained that I just couldn't do them! Stupid things anyway! What did it matter that I couldn't sew? I hadn't come here to learn to be a seamstress. I jabbed the needle savagely into the material and caught my thumb. A tiny jet of red blood plopped onto the black material, where it spread in a rust-colored stain. Damn! I bit my lip to keep the expletive in. I could just hear Mother Albert's voice: "Sister, we don't say 'damn' in the religious life."

I felt so neglected. Nobody even knew that it was my birthday. At home there would be presents, food, love. I would be special today. And here I was miserably homesick. Periodically I found myself feeling weepy. The black serge swam before my eyes. When would I grow up? Self-disgust made me tighten my lips angrily. "Manual work," Mother Albert had explained, "keeps our minds free for God." But manual work was so tedious. How I missed reading! I never thought I'd have to give that up or realized how much I'd miss it. I remember asking Mother Albert whether I could take a copy of Hopkins' poetry out of the library. She was furious.

"Nuns don't waste their time indulging in poetry!" And, it went without saying, no more novels. How much I'd depended on fiction to interpret the world for me! I was like an addict, suffering withdrawal symptoms. I thought wistfully of all the conversations I'd had with Mother Katherine. I suppose I'd pictured the religious life as a series of philosophical conversations sandwiched between prayerful ecstasies. It wasn't turning out a bit like that.

I glanced at my watch. Nearly time for evening prayers and Vespers. I'd wasted an hour when I could have been waiting on God. Interior silence sounded so easy when Mother Albert talked about it. But the great thing about the religious life was that every moment presented a fresh opportunity. No use crying over spilt milk. The best thing I could do now was to try to pray better during Vespers. With determination I reached for my Office Book.

That evening as we gathered for recreation I was feeling less buoyant. Homesickness had again set in and there was a gloomy atmosphere. It was odd how our moods shared confidences when in many ways we scarcely knew one another at all. The ordinary channels for relationships were just not there. And yet our continual physical proximity created a curious empathy. The lights were on in the community room and the uncurtained windows seemed to reflect us all mockingly. Adèle, as the eldest postulant, was moving Mother Albert's chair into the middle of the throng and we were all bringing out our needlework. "A nun is never idle," Mother had explained to us. "You should never sit there doing nothing." And so every evening we met for this formal ritual called recreation. It was growing rather more familiar now but at first it had been difficult to see it as in any way recreational. It seemed like yet another of those communal sewing sessions with the addition of contrived polite conversation. In fact, on the third night after our arrival, Mother Albert had discovered Marie and Margaret sitting in the community room after the evening examination of conscience, chatting happily.

"What on earth do you think you're doing?" she had demanded angrily. "Talking during the Great Silence!"

They had looked up at her blankly. "We're waiting for the others to come for recreation, Mother. It says on the board that there will be recreation every evening," Marie explained.

Mother Albert looked blank in her turn. "But we've *had* recreation!" she said at last. "Have you gone mad or something? We were here having it from eight o'clock to nine."

"Oh!" There was a bewildered silence. "Was that *it*, then?" Marie said. "When you came and talked during sewing? That was recreation?" The genuine astonishment in her voice had made Mother laugh in spite of herself.

I got out the hated piece of black serge and found myself scowling at the grotesque buttonholes. On to number sixty-four, I thought wearily. The white stitches framing the inexpertly cut gashes in the material looked like clowns' mouths grinning their contempt. It was hopeless. A complete waste of time. No, I told myself firmly. We'd been told that the rule said we were to be joyful at recreation, increase the bonds of sisterly unity, and give edification to all. I forced my own mouth to smile serenely back at the terrible buttonholes but still felt simmering inside. It's all very well for the rule to say we had to cultivate a spirit of joy, I thought, but how can you be joyful when you feel miserable and frustrated? You couldn't just switch it on like that, could you?

Irene, who was sitting next to me, broke into my perplexity by nudging me. "Can I borrow your scissors, Sister?" she whispered.

"Mmm," I nodded absently and pushed them over to her.

"What were you talking about, Sister Irene?" Mother asked sternly.

Irene flushed. "I was just asking Sister Karen whether I could borrow her scissors."

"Sister, I've *told* you that you mustn't take part in private conversations during recreation." Really! I was exasperated. You could hardly call that a conversation. This was ridiculous! No. Again I swallowed my sigh of irritation. That was a worldly thought. I forced myself to look contritely up at Mother. "The idea is," she was explaining wearily, "that we should all talk together. Every remark you make should be addressed to me." Poor Mother. I suddenly found I was feeling contrite after all. Recreation can't be much fun for her either, stuck with us all the time. She must be dying to go to the professed recreation. At least there they've got other things to talk about—school, their work. "The proper thing to do," she went on, "is to wait for a pause in the general conversation and say, 'Mother, I wonder whether I could just ask Sister Karen whether I could borrow her scissors.'"

I felt suddenly blank as years of these formal recreations stretched ahead in a deadly vista. It wasn't that I was longing to have closely intimate conversations. We'd always been a reserved family and I didn't easily confide in others. But what kind of a life was it when you couldn't even say "Pass the scissors"? It all seemed so contrived and unreal, like performing in a play the whole time. Up till now if I'd felt happy I'd smiled; if I'd been fed up I'd usually said so in one way or another. But here all that had to go under. Then I remembered what Mother had said the other night—that perfection in the religious life had to be pursued with special vigour during times of depression. That was exactly the time to prove our real love for God, not when the going was easy. Determinedly I smiled again and tried hard, as the rule said, to enter fully into the general spiritual gaiety.

Despite my moods, I still wanted to go on. Mother Albert had promised us that if we observed the rules outwardly it would eventually affect our spirits. If we acted like nuns soon we'd really *be* like nuns. I pressed on eagerly. But often the endless suppression of mood and ideas made me long to do something outrageous. Just for once. To smash the silent formality and get it all out of my system. Often when I was feeling like that the rest of the brethren were too. You could sometimes feel the tension crackling in the air waiting to explode.

It did erupt a few evenings after that recreation when Marie suddenly burst through the façade of religious restraint. We were waiting for instruction. Marie, who was standing next to me, was in charge of the community room. Her eyes, which were less perfectly cast down than ours, glanced up at the large statue of Our Lady opposite us. She groaned and dug me in the ribs.

"Help!" she whispered. "Look at those flowers."

Oh no. A few withered sticks of greenery mocked us in the little vase. And in front of Our Lady! My heart sank. I hated any of the brethren getting into trouble almost as much as when I was in for it myself. Mother's searing words knew just how to hit home hard in all of us. I was always only too well aware that it could have been me. "Another row!" Marie was sighing, and she broke into an excellent imitation of Mother Albert. "Sister, have you no reverence for Our Lady that you leave those flowers like that! Better no flowers at all than dead ones." Scandalized but loving it at the same time, I looked nervously at the door. Mother would be coming in any minute. "When are you going to learn that every little thing matters?" Marie continued. She shouldn't do it, but what a relief it was to have a laugh at the whole thing. I started to giggle, warily at first, but then unreservedly as the pent-up effort of the last few weeks exploded inside me.

"Ssh!" hissed a few virtuous souls at the top of the table.

"Oh, shut up yourselves!" snapped Marie, gloriously abandoning the rules of religious courtesy. Adèle raised her eyebrows in shocked reproof. "I wonder if there's time," I heard Marie say, and before I could see what she meant she stepped onto the table. No! I watched her, mesmerized, feeling the thrill of her rebellion and knife-edged daring. I could hear the others gasping—horrified but enchanted too with the terror and danger of it all. A quick stride carried Marie across the table; she jumped off the other side, seized the vase, and—surely she wasn't coming back the same way? She'd never dare—Marie jumped back onto the table.

"Sister!" we breathed, scandalized.

"What was it you said St. Teresa of Avila did at recreation, Sister?" Marie asked me. I had told her that the sixteenth-century Carmelite had once done flamenco dancing on the table at recreation, crying, "Sisters! Let us dance for joy in the Lord!"

"How about a spot of this at recreation tonight?" Marie stuck a wilting flower between her teeth, handed me the vase, and swirled her skirt, snapping her fingers.

By now we were all helpless with laughter. A spring seemed to have snapped after all those weeks of silent suppression. Terrified but unable to stop laughing, we looked at Marie and then looked back at the door.

"Marie, for God's sake come down!" I pleaded. "Mother will be here at any second!"

"Poor old Albert; can you see her leading us in the flamenco, like St. Teresa?" asked Marie, and with a final wild flourish she struck an attitude: *"Olé!"* she whispered hoarsely and leaped back down into line a split second before Mother made her entrance.

It was never easy to keep silence when working in the refectory. Every day I appeared amid the debris of breakfast, wearing my blue gingham apron, to work there under Sister Brendan's tutelage. The large room echoed strangely with just the two of us rattling round in it. Sister Brendan, a short, stooped, Irish lay sister whose bony face had eyes that glinted humorously, was an inveterate talker.

"Praise be!" she said wryly, the first time I reported for duty. "Another raw postulant! The crosses our Blessed Lord sends me! I don't suppose you've ever swept a floor before, have you?"

"Oh yes, Sister." Then I looked at the vast expanse of gleaming parquet. It was a far cry from the tiny kitchen at home. "But perhaps not quite such a large floor as this!"

"I knew it," she sighed. "I'll have all the trouble of training you, and then, just when I've got you beautifully set up, you'll disappear into the Noviceship and I'll have to start from scratch with another one!" Her smile belied the sternness of her voice. "Tell me, Sister," she said, her eyes sharp behind the gold-rimmed spectacles. "How old are you?"

"Seventeen."

"Lord bless us and save us!" she shook her head. "You're only a baby!"

Sister Brendan showed me how to sweep. "Keep with the grain of the wood, Sister." To plunge my hand into a nauseating mess of wet tea leaves, to squeeze them out—ugh!—and scatter them on the floor to catch all the dust. Privately I found all these trivia a waste of time. I'd come here to seek God, I thought, not to bother my head with these housewifely details. And Sister Brendan chattered. She asked me about my family, my school, how the other postulants were getting along. The lay sisters, I reflected, were quite different from the professed nuns. They were far freer, less buttoned-up. Whenever I passed their community room in the evening after I had finished the washing up, gales of laughter issued from their recreation. Quite different from the starchy recreations back in the Postulantship. Our Foundress, I knew, had fought against the canon law that decreed that the choir sisters and the lay sisters should take separate recreations, but Rome had refused her request. I didn't think the lay sisters minded at all. They seemed to have much more fun on their own!

How was I supposed to keep the silence with Sister Brendan? It was a tricky business. If I refused priggishly to answer her then I would be tacitly rebuking an older nun. And I enjoyed our chats. I felt at home here in the refectory, except for all the awful cleaning.

Once work had gotten under way Sister Brendan started to storm Heaven with a volley of vocal prayer. We went through every prayer in the book—the rosary, the Stations of the Cross, novenas to St. Anthony—and finished up with the Divine Praises. All to the accompaniment of clattering brooms and brushes.

"Hail Mary, full of grace, the Lord is with thee," Sister Brendan would croon, keening her prayers in the manner of the Irish as she pushed chairs back into place with a rattling squeal. "Blessed art thou among women, and blessed—Sister, look at all these crumbs under top table! Glory be to God, have you no eyes in your head! —blessed is the fruit of thy womb, Jesus!" The Holy Name was shouted triumphantly with an emphatic banging of the water jug.

"Sorry, Sister," I would reply, hurrying top table-ward with my broom. Half an hour later we were still at it.

"The Fourth Station: Jesus meets His Blessed Mother on the road to Calvary," Sister Brendan would chant mournfully, her eyes glittering sharply as she examined the newly laid tables. "We praise Thee, O Christ—Sister, will you look at this slop bowl you've missed? You'll never get through before you go to Office—and we bless Thee," the tone dropped again to a lugubrious reverence.

"Because by Thy Holy Cross Thou hast redeemed the world!" I would answer briskly, wringing out a dishcloth into a pail brimming with slop.

"Blessed be God," Sister Brendan would announce firmly. The last lap, the Divine Praises at last. "Blessed be God!" I would repeat cheerfully as together we seized the heavy pail and staggered over to the turn with it.

"Easy does it, Sister," she would mutter, panting with the effort. "Blessed be His Holy Name! Watch out, Sister Karen, ye'll spill it all over yourself and then I'll have to answer to Mother Albert for the state of your skirt."

"Blessed be God in His angels and in His saints!" we would finish triumphantly in unison, flushed with the effort of the morning, surveying a gleaming refectory.

I knocked at Mother Albert's door. It was time for my weekly talk with her. Friday at twelve-thirty. My "happy time," as Marie irreverently termed these sessions. "Come in!" I heard her call, her voice hollow and uninflected.

"Sit down, Sister," she smiled and then sighed as she looked me up and down. "Sister," she said wearily, "you do look untidy! Why is it that you always look like a rag bag?"

I glanced down at myself. My cape was fraying at the edges and there were two streaks of drying candle wax on my skirt left over from this morning's procession. "Is that a tear?" Mother went on, indicating a jagged rent inexpertly pulled together by my amateur attempt at darning.

"Yes, Mother," I said apologetically as I sat down by her desk in the little hard chair.

"How ever did you manage to tear it?"

"It happened last Saturday, Mother." I grinned at the recollection. "Sister Martin was taking the walk and we got lost. We were going to be late and the only way to get quickly back onto the road was to get through a barbed wire fence." I looked brightly up at Mother Albert.

"And you were the only one to tear your skirt, I suppose?"

"Yes, Mother." The others had found it terribly funny. It was always I who split or tore my clothes. I rather enjoyed being the butt of so much good-natured teasing.

"Have you always been untidy, Sister?"

"Oh no, Mother." It was odd, that, now I came to think about it. I had never looked good in my clothes at home but I had never torn or split things the way I did now. "I suppose," I added slowly, "it's because it doesn't matter anymore. You know, Mother, in the world it does matter terribly what you look like. And I minded about that. But here," I smiled happily, "none of that matters anymore; there are so many more important things to worry about."

Mother Albert looked at me and gave a short, sharp sigh of exasperation. Then she leaned forward on her desk, speaking with urgency.

"But it does matter, Sister," she insisted. "It is most important. It matters that you are always tidy, it matters that your sewing is perfect, it matters that you sweep the refectory perfectly. Perfectly, Sister." She struck the desk gently to emphasize her point. "Not as well as you can. But perfectly."

I blinked, bewildered at this sudden attack. "But Mother," I protested, "I'm no good at these things. I can't sew! I just can't do it."

"In the religious life, Sister," Mother Albert's voice had subsided to her usual toneless calm, "there is no such word as *can't.*" She stopped and looked at me quizzically. "It's a new experience for you, isn't it, being bad at something?"

I thought about it for a moment. It was true. Of course there had always been things that I hadn't been able to do. Math, for example. But then I'd never bothered. I'd just concentrated on the things I liked doing. I nodded, suddenly feeling small and humiliated. What a spoiled child I seemed!

"Yes, I thought so," Mother continued mercilessly. "You're intelligent. You've always been good at academic work. And you think that domesticity is beneath you."

As soon as it was put like that I saw that it was true. And how wrong it sounded. I looked speechlessly at her and made a silent gesture of helplessness.

"Why do you think that we are not allowing you to do any academic work at the moment?" Mother asked. "And you know that you won't be doing any until the second year of your noviceship."

I felt more secure now; I knew the answer to that one.

"It's because manual work keeps your mind freer for God. When you're studying or reading you can't have a quietness in your mind and so you can't talk to God or listen to Him. But Mother," I went on, thinking that I might as well voice this query, "I can see that works for some people. But I get so frustrated by the sewing that I get all steamed up, and then I can't think about God at all. If I could do some reading I'm sure that would help me. It always did before."

Mother Albert leaned back in her chair. "Sister," she said quietly, "you're full of pride, aren't you?" I was shocked. Pride was the worst of the seven deadly sins. I knew that. And I wanted to be a nun.

"Why do you think," Mother went on, forcing me to look back at her, "that it is wrong for you to feel frustrated?"

I was bewildered. Surely the answer was self-evident.

"It is good for you to be frustrated, Sister," Mother said flatly. "You have to learn to lay aside your whole will and all your own desires and preferences. Your own self has to be broken, you know, before God can work through you."

I thought about this. I remembered Mother Katherine's warning about the blank check. Of course in theory I had seen that my own desires were unimportant. But somehow . . . "I suppose I never thought that sweeping a floor had anything holy or religious about it. I just thought that it was something to do while you thought about God . . . " I trailed off lamely under Mother's steady gaze.

"Precisely. You felt that these things—cleaning, sewing—didn't matter in themselves. But they do, Sister. Every failure—a badly swept floor, a torn skirt, a bungled hem—is a religious fault. You are failing in the service of God. Whether you are good at these things or not."

"It seems a bit unfair, though," I said. "People like Sister Margaret or Sister Adèle really like sewing and cleaning. They hate studying and reading; they've told me so. For them the service of God is easier, surely?"

"That's just where you are wrong, Sister," Mother replied. "It's easier for *you* because you have a chance to give more in this respect at the moment. Your will and your whole self will be broken sooner. You'll go on and on failing, on and on feeling bored and frustrated, and gradually you'll die to yourself."

I sighed. "And you'll get into trouble about your failings," Mother went on inexorably, "and no one will spare you. It's only when you no longer think for a second about what would be easier or more satisfying that you are starting to live a Christ-centered life."

It was hard. I could scarcely bear to think of it, but somehow, though I had never before turned it to this kind of negative direction, my love of a challenge emerged. It was another push in the swimming pool. Kicking and screaming right up to the brink. But this time annihilation would not be spared you.

"You have to die, Sister, before you can live again," Mother said, and she gestured as a sign that the interview was at an end. "And nothing is too small an opportunity to put yourself to death. Go now and sweep the boot room; make it perfect, however pointless it may seem. That's what God is asking of you. Frustration and death." She smiled suddenly, kindly, as I got up—in a daze, yes, but resolute in my determination to see this thing through. "Go away and think about it. God bless you."

I left Mother's room feeling rather stunned. There I'd been thinking how well I was doing and imagining that God had all sorts of deep spiritual trials ahead when all He wanted me to do was sweep the boot room. Perfectly. God's will had turned out so differently from anything I'd imagined. It just showed how full of the world's values I still was, I thought soberly as I entered the stuffy little boot room in the basement, with its smell of mud and shoe polish. I choked as the clouds of dust went up my nose and irritated the back of my mouth. I battled with my task for an hour. As my shame subsided I felt a new glow of enthusiasm. God had been speaking to me through Mother Albert. This job, so simple in its scope, would bring me closer to Him, closer to my goal. I made a strong resolution to be on the lookout for more worldly views. Mother Albert was right. My confidence in my own view of things was shaken. How easy it was to be mistaken and find yourself on that wide road that leads away from God and ends only in self.

Indeed, as the weeks went by, the old world receded gradually and became an unreal place. We read no newspapers, heard no news bulletins. Nothing from the larger sphere beyond Tripton High Street reached us. Only once, a few weeks after I had entered, did we hear of an international incident. It was a Sunday morning, the feast of Christ the King, the day of the monthly retreat. Every first Sunday of the month we had a day of special silence and prayer when the professed, the novices, and the postulants knelt in prayer before the Blessed Sacrament that was exposed on the altar. That Sunday Mother Albert called us all into the community room. She spoke vaguely of a crisis over Cuba, about Russia and America, about some ships. We were, she told us calmly, on the brink of a nuclear war. No details, just disconnected facts falling strangely on our ears like tidings from another planet. Death suddenly loomed hideously. I was frightened.

"Pray, sisters," Mother Albert was saying. "Prayer, we know, can work wonders. It can move mountains. Pray for peace."

So we prayed. And prayed. A day went by. Then three days, then a week. We had been told not to talk about it among ourselves and we did not. But, I noticed, we all spent much more of our free time in church. Ten days passed. Each morning I woke looking out at the peaceful countryside that looked so enduring, picturing it a charred and barren wasteland, darkened by clouds of radioactive dust. It seemed possible, I thought. *Will it be today?* I wondered, chanting the Divine Praises with Sister Brendan while I waxed the refectory floor. Now it was a fortnight. Surely something had happened by now. For better or worse, something must have happened: they can't still be staring one another out with their fingers poised resolutely over the fatal buttons. Seventeen days. There must be some news. Three weeks!

At last I could bear it no longer. That evening at recreation I looked down with despair at the habit I was sewing. Would I live to wear it?

"Mother," I burst out. I shouldn't be asking, shouldn't be hankering for news of the outside world. I could get into terrible trouble. "Mother, is there any news about Cuba?"

The other postulants were really listening now, agog, needles suspended in midair. Sister Adèle had grasped a handful of material and was squeezing it hard. We waited.

Silence.

Mother looked blank. "Cuba?" she asked, bewildered for a moment.

"Yes," I pressed on. "You know—the international crisis, the ships . . . " I broke off as the puzzlement deepened on her face. Surely she couldn't have forgotten about it; surely she hadn't reached that level of indifference about the world.

Suddenly Mother's face cleared. "Oh, Cuba!" she said and frowned again, astonished. "But that cleared up weeks ago. The Russians moved their ships." She looked round the table at our faces, the truth dawning on her. "Didn't we tell you?" she asked.

We shook our heads.

"Oh!" Mother threw back her head and laughed her characteristic laugh, silent, her shoulders heaving. "We must have forgotten! How terribly funny!"

For once, we didn't join in her laughter. It didn't seem very amusing.

The incident showed me how completely cut off we had become, even in a matter of weeks. When, a few days later, I noticed that Nessa was not in her place at spiritual reading, I didn't give it much thought.

Mother Albert came in and we all sat down.

"Sister Nessa left this morning," she said perfunctorily. "I've just put her on the London train. She decided that she had no vocation." Then without a break in her voice she glanced at Sister

Margaret, whose turn it was to read that morning, and gave her the signal to begin.

Thunderstruck, I looked at my sewing. Nessa gone! The world now seemed so remote that it was difficult to remember that there was anywhere to go to. And how silently she had gone too. No good-byes, no explanations. She had been plucked from our midst. I had never known her and now I never would. It was a strange thought.

Even my family became a distant memory. We got letters once a week, except during Lent and Advent, and they were opened and read first by Mother Albert. In the noviceship, she explained, we would only receive letters once a month. We were allowed to write to our close family on the last Sunday of the month from eleven to eleven forty-five. At first I looked forward to this but gradually it became a chore. "We never write about what happens inside the enclosure," we'd been told, "nor do we ever discuss our private or personal feelings in a letter to a secular." That might be all right, I thought wearily one Sunday when I was sucking my pen in a dearth of inspiration, if you are teaching or engaged in some kind of work that takes you outside, but we never left the Postulantship except to go on the daily walk. I looked gloomily at my letter. What on earth could I write? This was just an account of the changing face of nature, a description of the muddy walks, the picturesque woods, the plants and flowers found along the hedgerows. Here and there, thrown in for good measure, there was a dutiful comment on the Creator of all these wonders. All our letters were supposed to edify our families and inspire them to a greater love of God. Mother Albert read all the letters before they were posted and that was a further inhibition. This letter, I thought, was not a natural letter at all. I was retreating from my family behind a screen of stilted words and phrases. It was so painful.

From across the table Marie suddenly exploded into mirth. Snorting with laughter she scratched out a word.

"Ssh!" hissed Sister Adèle across the table.

I looked at her hopefully. Marie always managed to cheer me up. "Sister," she whispered, still giggling, ignoring the disapproving looks of the brethren: "I wrote, 'At last there are signs of spring. At last the blossoms are bursting out all down the road.'"

I looked at her nonplussed. It sounded as though the sentence had been lifted straight from my own letter. I didn't see anything funny about it.

Marie giggled again. "Sister!" she explained, "I left the *l* out of *blossoms*!"

As the world faded the convent filled the whole horizon. Things like the strange ritual in the refectory, the scratchy hot underwear, the impersonal silence became the only realities. True, I'd often find myself longing for a nice hot soak in the bath, a really good laugh, a good book, but as the months wore on a world where these things were everyday realities instead of impossible and unworthy fantasies seemed to have belonged to me in another life. How trivial it all was after all! As Christmas approached we settled down to the somber penances of Advent. Outside, I reflected with a kind of wonder, they'd be racing round the crowded shops, wasting absurd sums of money, stuffing themselves with food. They'd never give a thought to what Christmas was all about. The convent seemed the sane center of a mad world.

But however alien the outside world with all its standards and values was becoming, I knew I'd have to collide with it when my parents came for their appointed visit. As the date crept nearer I found myself looking forward to it with a certain trepidation. Of course on one level I was longing to see them. How much I'd missed them—my father's way of screwing up his face as though he were in excrutiating agony whenever he ate stewed fruit, my mother's wide anxious smile when she was listening. Little things that made them unique. Above all I missed that simple acceptance of me and all that I was. Of course in a way that wasn't real either, but here, where my faults and idiosyncracies, my loud voice and laugh, my too expressive face, were constantly being criticized and corrected, family life seemed so easy and undemanding.

But really, I thought as I approached the parlor, was I the same person? Would they find me impossibly changed? I had no idea. I felt very much the same and was often miserable at any apparent lack of progress. After all, I'd come here to change myself radically. What would it be like for them to see me in these clothes, in this gloomy setting?

Nervously I pushed open the door and turned to close it carefully and silently as I had been taught to do, easing it into its position and releasing the handle gently, so as not to disturb the prayerful spirit of the house. For the good nun, Mother Albert had said, even opening and shutting a door is an act of the love of God. Then I turned round to face my family.

There they were in the huge library parlor, looking rather lost and diminished by the heavy heights of books that loomed down over them, giving the room a faintly musty smell. My mother was sitting bolt upright in a brocade armchair, straining to catch the first glimpse of me, taut and alert. My father and my cousin Anthony stood over by the fireplace, apparently examining a print with tremendous interest. With assumed nonchalance they turned round casually, as if taken by surprise by my entrance, refusing to let the situation get out of hand. Lindsey was sitting over in the window seat glaring at me mutinously. They looked so familiar, and a part of myself raced forward to them instinctively. But yet how strange to see them in these surroundings and how ill at ease they were. There was a moment's awkwardness while we looked at one another silently, taking in the changed relationship. This was my place, not theirs, and the part of me that instinctively rushed toward them was the part I had to renounce.

Then I went over to kiss my mother, taking care to walk smoothly and modestly.

"How are you, darling?" I heard the worry in her voice. She looked at me in the strange uniform. Perhaps she was feeling nostalgia for that awful beehive and the tight jeans. Then her face cleared. "Gosh, you look well!" she turned to the others. "Doesn't she? I've never seen you with such a healthy color." The rest of the family made polite noises of agreement.

"Are you happy, Karen?" asked my father dubiously as we all sat down.

"Oh yes!" I said emphatically. How could I convince them? And anyway what did the word *happiness* mean? Mother Albert had redefined the concept for us: happiness, she had said, was doing God's will. Nuns didn't enter a convent to be happy; they came to do God's will. Already we were speaking in different languages. "I'm very happy," I repeated. "I've never been happier in my life."

There was a strained silence. What a conversation stopper, I thought. How could anybody follow that? My mother tried bravely. "Well, that's marvelous, isn't it? Yes. I must say you do look happy."

She was searching my face as I smiled steadily back at her. The rules of modesty required us to look peaceful and contented at all times. Now, as I smiled at my family, I could feel myself looking at them blandly just as the nuns at school had smiled at me. It was a habit. In no way did it reflect what was going on inside. "Doesn't she look happy?" my mother sought reassurance. My father and Anthony hastily agreed with noisy enthusiasm. Only Lindsey, who was kicking the table leg, looked sulky and incredulous.

"But Karen," she demanded. "What's it *like*? I mean, what do you *do* all day?"

"Well, sewing and housework mainly." Wryly I thought it made me sound like a daily help. It wasn't a real answer.

"You! Sewing!" gasped my mother. "But you must hate that."

Of course I did. On one level. But that was no longer the truth of the matter. If it was God's will, then it made me happy. But how could I explain all this? "Yes, I was hopeless at it at first. But I've been learning. I'm ever so much better at it now. I don't hate it now." What a skeleton of the truth those words were. My family stared back astonished.

"But isn't this an awful waste of time?" pressed my father. "After all, you've got three good A-levels."

"Oh, well," I said smoothly, "this is part of the training. Books and study would distract us from God. Later I'll probably study again. But I wouldn't want it any different."

I saw Lindsey and Anthony make faces at one another. I didn't blame them. I sounded such a prig. But the words did express the truth of the matter, however clumsily. And the tone, the manner? One part of me knew that I was putting on an act as I had to, behaving as a nun should behave. But it was also true that I couldn't behave differently. It was odd. Like being two people at once.

"How much time do you spend in church?" Anthony asked.

I calculated. Mass, half an hour's meditation, two examinations of conscience, a Rosary, half an hour's evening prayer, spiritual reading, Office. "About five hours, not counting Office."

"What!" Lindsey shrieked in horror. "How terrible." My parents, who were obviously feeling the same, struggled to look reprovingly at her. "How on earth can you go on praying all that long? It must be so *boring*!"

I thought of the long hours. My knees two fireballs of pain and my mind a blank. Longing for the bell to ring. Then the guilt. Trying to get it together again. The sinking lethargy. But also those other times when my mind soared; I could feel God's love. He was almost, almost there.

"It's hard sometimes, of course," I said. "Nobody feels like praying all the time. But then it doesn't matter what you feel like. It's trying that counts." Mother had told us that often we were closest to God when we felt most empty, as long as we went on trying. "You just have to try and keep going," I explained. "It's a prayer in itself just to be where God wants you to be."

"Well, I'm jolly glad he doesn't want me to spend all that time in church," Anthony said in heartfelt tones.

"I don't know how you stick it out," said my mother.

"What time do you get up?" asked Lindsey.

"Six o'clock this year. But after the postulantship it's half-past five every morning."

"God!" Lindsey sounded appalled. Then she blushed and looked round the parlor guiltily as though she expected God to pop out of one of the bookshelves. How she must hate this, I felt with a sudden rush of sympathy. What a way for a fifteen-year-old to spend her holidays. "Every morning! Don't you ever have a rest?"

And so the questions went on. What was the food like? Was I allowed to have a bath? Did I have a lot of friends among the other nuns? All the questions just off-center. And my answers were getting more and more remote from the truth. I couldn't tell them about cheese making me sick, about being miserable and depressed, about the rule, about anything that was really important to me. I could see my parents exchanging glances. I knew that I sounded too good to be true, but more and more I was aware that I had changed. I was beginning to think and speak and act like a nun naturally.

As the afternoon wore on I felt more and more exhausted. After the months of silence all this conversation was unnatural. Words, I was quickly realizing, were not a vehicle for communication at all. They just erected a screen of misunderstanding and separation. My head was bursting with the effort and I felt drained and empty. I was longing, I found, to return to the silent enclosure. Sister Rebecca had been right. After a while, silence did become easier than talking.

"So we can't persuade you to come home?" my father asked.

Beneath the deliberate jocularity I could hear the wistfulness and the pain. I smiled back, maintaining the fiction that this was a joke question, and answered brightly.

"Oh, no! Not likely!" I could see from their expressions that they knew they had lost me in a far more fundamental way than when they had put me on the train at Kings Cross. Was it really only a few months ago? Their pain suddenly stabbed me and we gazed at one another, sadness filling the austere parlor. Being glad to make a sacrifice for myself was one thing; to feel their suffering was quite another. I couldn't bear to let myself think about it too much. The clarity of my decision blurred for a moment and I felt a wrench of loyalties. It wasn't that I seriously considered going home with them for a second, but I didn't want them to feel so bereft and left behind. I went on quickly. "Mother Albert will be coming in to see you for a moment. She'll take you along to tea while I go and have mine. I'll join you in the big parlor."

"Aren't you allowed to have tea with us?" my mother demanded, shocked.

"No," I said as gently as I could. "You know that nuns aren't allowed to eat with—" I was about to use the word *seculars* but bit it back. It was such a distancing word, rubbing salt in their wounds. "With . . . people outside." Oh, God. That was even worse. "We never eat outside the enclosure."

"But we're your own family, for heaven's sake!" She sounded so hurt. This separation at teatime was only highlighting the real gulf between us that the afternoon had revealed so cruelly. *Please don't make a scene,* I pleaded silently. "It's ridiculous!" she snapped.

"Well"—the earlier assurance I had felt was ebbing away fast —"it's just one of those things." I no longer felt like a nun, serene and above human feelings. I felt the pull of my parents' unhappiness tugging me back to my former self, unhappy and confused. I tried silently to communicate the love I felt for them and my real sympathy for what they were going through.

There was a discreet tap on the door and Mother Albert strode in, all smiles.

"Well, how do you think she's looking?" she asked, beaming round the room. My family pulled themselves back into hearty politeness and a muddled chorus of "Fine!" "Very well indeed!" "Marvelous" broke and then fell away silently.

"We couldn't persuade her to come home with us," my father joked, smiling charmingly.

Mother Albert laughed and beamed at me. I joined in and smiled back at her. *Over to you,* I thought, abandoning them to her firm management. "Oh, no!" Mother said. "I don't think she'd want to do that. Do you, Sister?"

We all laughed again.

"No." Mother Albert looked at me with a detached and appraising smile. "No, she seems happy enough. Even with the housework. At first she hardly knew one end of the broom from the other!"

We all smiled obediently. "But," Mother shot me a knowing smile that spoke volumes, "she's learning." Again I felt pulled in two. It was Mother Albert who understood me now, better than anyone else in the room. She was my new mother. But my feelings were dragging me over to my family; they, after all, had created me. I moved over and stood next to Mother Albert.

"How long are we allowed to stay this evening?" asked my father bluntly.

"Until seven or seven-thirty, I think, Mr. Armstrong."

"And then," unconsciously my mother moved nearer to me and her voice was slightly higher than usual. She edged up to me, wanting to touch me but somehow not quite daring to. "We can't see her for another six months? Is that right?"

"I'm afraid that's the rule." Mother nodded. "But I hope you'll be coming to the clothing in July. Now," she said briskly, "Sister has to have her tea. Will you come along with me to the big parlor and have yours with the other visitors?"

Standing in the silent refectory I felt a huge relief. Nuns stood, facing the large crucifix, a cup in one hand, a piece of bread and margarine in the other. The walls were a soothing neutral shade. There was no raw emotion here, tearing and pulling. Steadily we all turned in one direction, toward the crucified God who was showing us the meaning of His love. It seemed so simple. For a while in the parlor I'd felt as though I'd begun to react like a nun. Now I knew how far I was from that pure single-mindedness. My parents were worldly. Their views, their natural way of looking at the world had created the worldly self that I had to lay aside. And that meant laying them aside, too, not falling back into the old easy ways of thought and speech, not allowing my natural feelings of sympathy to hold me back from God but going forward ruthlessly into God's world where supernatural views prevailed. Why was it so hard to be simple in my desires? I wanted to make my parents happy, wanted it so fiercely that I felt torn by the conflict. I knew that this was part of the sacrifice. I had to let my parents suffer and feel the pain myself, but I felt muddled and miserable. Please, I prayed silently to the impassive figure on the cross, help me to be calm in spirit as a nun should be. As I said grace and prepared to rejoin my parents, I made a firm resolution to try even harder to be a good postulant, observing the rules even more strictly, praying more fervently. Only then could I get to that haven of peace that Christ offered and that he said the world couldn't give. A place where I could act simply, calmly, above this conflicting welter of messy feeling.

The atmosphere in the parlor was one of subdued gentility. Everybody was being extremely polite, and I was fresh enough from the world to remember how offputting it was to be eating with an audience of nuns who were not partaking themselves. Two novices and several professed were in the parlor, passing cakes and pouring tea. Anthony, who was miserably crumbling a scone on his plate, offered a carton of processed cheese to a thin, elegant woman sitting next to him. She examined it and wrinkled her nose with refined disgust.
"Cheez Whiz," she read from the label with a slight shudder. "No, thanks so much. I don't really think I will."
Anthony instantly snapped into life: "Cheez Whiz!" he cried. "Not *Cheez Whiz*! Gosh, my favorite! Pass the Cheez Whiz, please. Lindsey, have some Cheez Whiz." He took a large dollop of the thick, sticky substance that I knew he hated and passed it to my sister, who by this time was choking with adolescent giggles. "Aunty Eileen," he cried to my mother, "have some Cheez Whiz!" The superior lady was gazing at him as though he were deranged. The nuns were smiling politely with raised eyebrows. "Karen, are you sure you're not allowed any?" Lindsey asked. "I bet *you* didn't have Cheez Whiz for tea!"
Sweating with embarrassment, I smiled serenely as the parlor

rang with resonant Armstrong voices extolling the virtues of the carton, which was passed with mock enthusiasm from hand to hand. I understood. My family had cracked under the strain and were revolting against those forces that were carrying me away from them.

A few weeks after this Marie beckoned me from the community room. I debated for a moment—should I break the silence?—but curiosity got the better of me. Marie was pale and looked as though she had been crying. Her dark eyes glowed with drama. I followed her into the lower outer and we went into one of the bleak bathrooms and sat on the edge of the bath.

"What is it?" I whispered. Marie, now that she had gotten me, seemed to find it difficult to speak. She stared at the floor and was tugging nervously at her handkerchief. "Have you got into another row?" I pursued. She was always in trouble—for running upstairs, for being late, for breaking the silence, for laughing at the wrong time. It didn't usually upset her, though. Not like this.

She shook her head vehemently. "Sister," she said, "I've got to tell you. I know it's not allowed, but I can't help it. I'm leaving tomorrow."

"Leaving!" I gasped. We sat together in silence. After Nessa two other postulants had left, but Marie had always seemed so happy. "Tomorrow!" I repeated stupidly.

She nodded. "Straight after Mass," she said sadly. "I've got to go up the Cloister as soon as we leave the church, go into the big parlor, change, and have breakfast—I shan't be able to eat a thing! Then Mother Albert's walking me to the station to catch the early train to London."

I looked at her, still stunned. So that was how it was done. I'd often wondered how postulants disappeared so silently. "I just had to say good-bye."

"But Sister," I said and then stopped uncertainly. Marie wasn't really my sister anymore. "You look so miserable about it. Do you want to go home?"

"No," Marie's voice came out in a long wail. "No, I don't! I'd love to stay. Oh! I wish I could!"

"Have you been sent home?" I asked, appalled. We knew it was a constant possibility for any of us. It was one that I dared not think about because, like Marie, I wanted to stay. More than anything else I wanted to go on.

Marie shook her head. "No. But Mother Albert said that if I hadn't decided this myself, she was going to recommend to the Provincial Council that I should be sent away. I haven't got a vocation."

I looked at her pityingly, not knowing what to do to help.

"What made you decide to go?" I asked at last.

"Oh Sister! I'm not like you. You're a born nun—anyone can see that." I listened, amazed that she could think so. "You don't mess around like me. You keep the rules!"

"I'm not keeping them now," I interrupted.

"No!" Marie went on, "that's because of me. Mother Albert says I'm a bad influence on you all. I make you talk and lark around. Oh, I know everybody falls down time and again at first because it's so difficult. You've got real determination. Mother Albert told me that. But me! I understand the rules and all that. I'm just not serious enough about keeping them!"

She sighed. "What made you finally decide?" I asked.

"Oh!" she shrugged angrily. "Well, last week I had a typing lesson with Mother Serena. You don't have typing lessons, do you? Lucky you, is all I can say. That woman is a cow!" I jumped. Already such language had quite faded from my vocabulary. "Anyway I was late for the lesson and she told Mother Albert."

"Well," I prompted.

"Mother Albert said, 'Sister, I hear you were late for your typing lesson.' And I said—more fool me!—'Oh, sorry,' and Albert hit the roof. She said that I just didn't see the seriousness of it all. That I still thought that if I apologized casually it made it okay. And it isn't. 'That was a religious fault, Sister. You failed to keep the rule of punctuality. You have failed in the service of God!' Well, that got me thinking. It's no good, Sister. I can't be doing with all the pettiness and fussing. Oh, I know that's a worldly view, but that's just it. I *am* worldly."

"But Marie, I'm hopeless too!" I said. "Here I am talking to you and not keeping the silence. I'm always distracted when I ought to be praying. Sometimes in meditation in the morning I can hardly keep awake, let alone pray. And I laugh too loudly, walk too noisily. Mother Albert's told me I'm full of intellectual pride. I sneer at those sloppy books we read; I'm always hankering to read poetry or a novel or anything at all . . . "

"No, Sister," Marie interrupted me firmly. "You've changed. If you commit a fault you're really upset. And you've got—oh, deeper somehow. You're always in church if we have a free half-hour. Your face is calmer, more nunlike somehow. But I haven't changed at all. And the thing is, I don't want to."

"But if it's not for you, why are you so sad to go?" I asked.

Her eyes filled with tears. "Because I think it's the most beautiful life in the world. What could be better than this, really? Just being free to love God full-time. I look at the novices, you know, and their calm, beautiful faces. Oh, I was so looking forward to the noviceship. And I love the habit and the singing and the beautiful services. I wish I could be a nun. But I just can't."

"I'll miss you," I said slowly. It was true. Marie had been the nearest thing I'd had to a friend here.

"I'll miss you too. And, of course, if I wrote to you Mother Albert wouldn't give you my letters. I'll never see you again."

I swallowed a lump in my throat. It was another final good-bye.

"Look, Sister," Marie said. "Don't forget me!" The bell tinkled outside. Second-table supper. Marie pressed a holy picture into my hand. "Keep this if they let you. I know how you miss poetry so I've written that out for you on the back. Pray for me, won't you?" and then she bolted. I looked down at the picture in my hand and turned it over. On the back Marie had copied out Hopkins' "Haven Heaven: A Nun Takes the Veil."

> I have desired to go
> Where springs not fail,
> To fields where flies no sharp and sided hail
> And a few lilies blow.
>
> And I have asked to be
> Where no storms come,
> Where the green swell is in the havens dumb
> And out of the swing of the sea.

The next morning after Mass, I watched Marie begin her journey back to the world. I was crying and I could see that she was too.

I watched her walk up the Cloister with the jaunty stride that she had never lost, knowing that I was saying good-bye to my last friend. Marie had been my friend only because she wasn't suitable to be a nun.

Her departure made me examine my own position. Everything she had said about the beauty of the life I agreed with absolutely. The idea of pushing further and further into a spiritual adventure thrilled me. It was hard, terribly hard. But I wanted to do it.

One thing that separated me from Marie, however, was that I was not longing for the noviceship. The prospect frightened me. As the months moved on toward 2 July, the day that had been fixed for our clothing in the religious habit, I grew increasingly apprehensive at the thought of what lay ahead. Mother Albert had told us that the noviceship was the time when we would be finally broken in. And that would be painful. "You wait," she said, smiling wryly. "The postulantship is nothing. You wait." And waiting was hard. The door of the Noviceship led from the postulants' corridor. I looked at the huge oak door and wondered what lay behind it. When we marched in procession into church for formal spiritual duties, we waited in line in the corridor for the novices to lead us in. We would hear heavy bolts being drawn aside and the huge key turning in the lock—for the Noviceship was always locked against the world. And then the novices emerged one by one, their eyes cast down, their expressions enclosed and prayerful. Often one or two of them had been crying; their eyes were swollen and puffy, their faces white and drawn with purple scars of sleeplessness.

And then there was the Novice Mistress. Mother Walter was an extremely tall woman, well over six feet. Her head was small and pear-shaped, her face stern with thin lips, tightly pressed. She strode down the Cloister like a great bat, prowling, her eyes constantly fixed on the novices, watching their every move. It was she who would be responsible for making me a selfless instrument of God. I wondered apprehensively how I would fare. She looked so strong and spiritual.

One day I was kneeling on the stairs in the Postulantship, cleaning the black marks left by our rubber-soled shoes. It was a task that required a lot of elbow grease and a lot of bending. I was hot and sticky, utterly absorbed in my task, so absorbed that I did not hear the heavy footsteps behind me.

"Excuse me, Sister." I jumped, startled, and flattened myself against the wall, looking up at Mother Walter, who towered above me. She bowed gravely and then lifted her arm. I watched, mesmerized; Mother's hand swiftly approached my cheek; her face was stern. In the quick defensive reflex of a second I averted my face and flung my arm up as if to ward off a blow.

There was a silence. "You've got a beard, Sister," Mother Walter said mildly. But her eyes were shocked. She indicated the tapes that in my hard work had fallen out of my cap and hung down grotesquely from my chin. She had been going to tuck them in. We looked hard at one another. I was horrified. Why had I imagined she was going to hit me? Such a thing was unthinkable. A long silence, and then Mother Walter went on up the stairs and turned down the corridor.

A few nights later, Edna, Adèle, and I washed up in the nuns' pantry and went into church to pay the quick visit of obligation to the Blessed Sacrament before we joined the other postulants for recreation. I loved the church at night. The darkness was relieved only by a sharp, white floodlight on the great crucifix over the altar, and strange dramatic shadows were thrown on the grey stone walls. Bats flapped eerily up among the rafters high overhead. And it was so silent.

But tonight there was singing coming from somewhere. After a second or so I located it. The novices had an Oratory with a huge window that looked onto the high altar. For some reason they were missing recreation and having an extra choir practice there. I recognized the motet. It was one that we had sung at benediction last Sunday. The Latin words crept through the dark church. I closed my eyes and let the prayer flush through me. Suddenly the mood was shattered. Somebody was screaming in a furious voice that echoed through the church and bounced violently off the great arches in an incoherent babble of wrath. And then the slamming started. A fist was beating against the leaded Oratory window, rhythmically angry.

"Jesu, Salvator Mundi."

Crash, Crash, Crash. More screaming. It was Mother Walter.

"Tuis famulis subveni."

The beautiful words speaking of solace and comfort never faltered, but they were overlaid with the terrible echoing fury. I could feel Adèle next to me trembling with hysterical laughter. Soon all three of us, our faces buried in our hands, were shaking with convulsive mirth. It was funny, in a way, that terrible counterpoint. But not that funny. My throat ached with pent-up hysteria.

"Quos pretioso sanguine redemisti."

Suddenly I looked up at the floodlit crucifix: Christ, the blood streaming from His hands, gazed out impassively in His suffering through the dark church, looking straight into that scene in the Oratory. My laughter died as suddenly as it had begun as I looked up at the dying God who was asking me to follow Him. What lay in wait for me in the Noviceship?

6 · A NUN TAKES THE VEIL

There was one empty place at the community room table. We were in retreat, spending the last eight days of our postulantship in total silence and prayer, preparing for our clothing in the religious habit and our formal reception into the noviceship. They were wonderful days. I felt a heady exaltation in the face of the gravity of the step ahead. It had been marvelous when Reverend Mother Provincial had come into the Postulantship to tell us that the Provincial Council had accepted us for clothing. There were only six of us left now of the original ten—Adèle, Edna, Joan, Teresa, Margaret, and me.

This evening we were gathering in the community room for an instruction with Mother Albert. We were going through next Tuesday's ceremony with her, thinking through the beautiful words of the prayers, considering all their implications. At these sessions, the sense of having been specially chosen by God for a relationship of particular closeness with Him made me feel happy and humble at the same time. I knew there would be hard times ahead, though I had no idea what their precise nature would be. But now I felt sure that God would bring me through. After all, He had brought me this far.

For some reason, I did not like to look at the gap at the top of the table next to Mother Albert; there was something too disturbing to think of here. Mother came into the room and together we turned toward the statue of Our Lady and knelt as usual, praying for guidance. Then we sat down.

"Sisters, I have some very sad news for you tonight." I held my breath, not daring to think of what was coming. "Sister Adèle left us this afternoon to go home to her parents in France."

Disbelief. Adèle had been so happy these last few weeks. Her habit had been completed for Tuesday's ceremony and was hanging up in the sewing room next door, pressed and ready. She had been given her new religious name—Sister Bernarde. Her bridal dress, which she had looked so lovely in, her dark, dignified face against the white gauze and silk, was hanging alongside ours upstairs. I was used to people leaving by now. I had been sad when Marie had left, but only sad for myself: I could see objectively that she had made the right decision. Adèle's leaving seemed different for Mother Albert also. She never prefaced the news of a departure with sadness and regret. What had happened? I listened, stunned, to what she was saying.

"As I think most of you know, her parents were very much against her entering with us. All during her postulantship she has had terrible letters from them which upset her very much. Too much, really."

Mother paused, frowning slightly as if she were trying to see her own way through this.

"Sister Adèle isn't the only postulant I have known who has had a lot of upsetting trouble with her parents. In the noviceship at the moment I can think of one or two novices who are suffering on that account. Anyway," she spoke briskly now; pure facts were easier, "Adèle received a telegram last week from an aunt telling her that her mother was very ill. This has happened before, as some of you may know. It has been impossible to find out exactly how ill she is and how essential it is for Adèle to go back and nurse her. She decided to go."

There was a silence. How brave Adèle had been, I thought; no one had known. She had even started to make the retreat, as though she wanted to get as far as she could.

"Do any of you want to ask anything?" Mother Albert said unexpectedly. "As you know, we don't usually have questions at instruction, but this is bound to be a shock to you and I don't want it distracting you during the retreat." She looked round the table at the dazed, sad faces.

"Mother," I asked, "you know you told us that because the

Order had accepted us for clothing it was an infallible sign that God wanted us to go into the noviceship . . . "

"Yes, Sister," Mother said encouragingly as I groped to find the right words to say a harsh thing.

"Well, does that mean Adèle has given up her vocation, then? Did she do wrong in going home?"

Mother Albert sighed. "I wouldn't like to make any judgment about that, Sister. How can any of us know? Yes, I thought, and so did the Provincial Council, that Adèle had a strong vocation and that God wanted her here."

"But she couldn't help her mother getting ill," Joan put in. No. How complicated it all was.

"But Mother, what happens if Adèle's mother isn't really as ill as all that? Could she come back and try again?" I asked.

"Of course she could, Sister. But then she'd have to decide whether she really was going to stick it out this time. After all, if this can happen once it can happen again. And a commitment to the religious life must be forever, whatever the difficulties."

I sat silently thinking it all over. How terrible if Adèle had thrown away her vocation just because she couldn't bear to leave her parents.

"Anyway," Mother Albert said at last, "this can help you all to prize your own vocations even more highly. Pray that you may never lose them through your own fault."

That evening in the church I thought of Adèle, who must now be on a train, rushing through the darkness away from everything she had wanted. I looked up again at the crucifix. The message was clear: you had to be prepared for the cross. *Help me not to fail,* I prayed silently.

The night before the clothing ceremony passed in a frantic flurry of preparations. At seven-fifteen Mother Albert called us into the community room.

"Look, Sisters," she said wryly, "tomorrow afternoon you've all got to process down the aisle in your bridal dresses, wearing white high-heeled shoes. It's a good nine months since any of you have worn that kind of shoe and I don't want anybody," she eyed me sternly as the most likely culprit, "to fall flat on her face!"

We laughed delightedly. The past eight days with their intense silent preparation had left me feeling extraordinarily keyed up. The searching of my soul, going right down into the depths of my selfishness as St. Ignatius recommended in his *Spiritual Exercises,* the general confession of all the sins of my past life, and the final arriving at a decision, under the guidance of the Jesuit who was preaching the retreat, to give my whole life to God had left me weak and light-headed. It was a wonderful relief to release that pent-up intensity in legitimate laughter.

"So," Mother Albert went on, "while we are all at first-table supper I want you to put on those shoes and practice walking up and down the aisle and genuflecting to prevent any possible disasters. I'm sorry," she added, sighing, "to make you spend the last evening of the retreat like this, but I'm afraid it's necessary. Don't break the silence, of course, that goes without saying, and try to let it distract you as little as possible."

The shoes that had been given us for the ceremony tomorrow were an extraordinary collection. They were kept in a special cupboard precisely for this annual event and consisted of any white shoes that previous postulants had worn when they arrived at the convent; consequently, they were of diverse vintages and fashions. Sister Edna had a very strange pair of forties shoes with a strap across the high instep fastened by a little lace; Sister Teresa was wearing a pair of chisel toes left by some postulant in the late fifties. I had been allotted a pointy-toed pair with high, spindly stiletto heels.

Trying to avoid one another's eyes, we teetered down the steps of the Postulantship and entered the chapel. One or two children were kneeling in church, their devotions shattered by the sight of five postulants wearing thick black stockings and white shoes that made their feet look enormous and Minnie Mouse-like. It was amazing how odd high heels felt after all that time. I wobbled precariously up the aisle, feeling my ankles trembling convulsively, attempted a genuflection, and staggered wildly, my arms flailing in a vain attempt to regain balance. Sister Teresa, who had never worn high heels in her life, looked a picture of dismay as she attempted to reconcile her rolling Nigerian stride with the mincing steps dictated by Bond Street. From her pedestal the wooden statue of Our Lady looked down disapprovingly at our antics. Presently we were all hysterical, clinging weakly to the pews, doubled up in laughter.

And that night in the dormitory things were no better. "You'll have to curl your hair, Sisters," Mother Albert had said apologetically. "You'll look like scarecrows otherwise," and she put a huge box of rollers and setting lotion in the middle of the dormitory, telling us to do the best we could with ourselves. "Your families will want you to be looking nice," she said to our astonished faces. The idea of curling my hair again in these strange surroundings seemed quite incongruous. "It's the last thing you can really do for them, letting them have a nice memory of you all looking—pretty," she ended, looking dubiously at us all as we again dissolved into laughter.

With a pile of rollers and hairgrips I retreated to my cell, peering into the small handbag mirror that had been specially provided for the occasion. It was months since I'd given my hair a second thought. *Heavens!* I said to myself, horrified as I looked at the wild bush that greeted my startled reflection. What on earth am I to do with that? We had been told to keep trimming our hair as it grew, because too much hair under our tight little caps was inconvenient and unhealthy. I had given the odd half-hearted snip now and again as a stray lock caught my attention, but cutting your hair with huge rusty scissors and no mirror was an impossible task. Nine months of being without light, getting filled with starch from my cap, and being washed with carbolic soap had hardly improved the texture of my hair. I attempted a last-minute rescue job, marveling at how quickly I had lost the knack of winding chunks of hair round prickly fluorescent rollers. I jabbed my skull with sharp hairpins and pulled strands of hair liberally coated with setting lotion so tightly round the rollers that it seemed as though they would come out at the roots. Periodically a stifled gasp of pain told me that the brethren were suffering equally, and gradually, as a strong smell of lotion transformed the atmosphere of our prim little dormitory into that of a hairdresser's, we got more and more giggly.

Eventually, hot and flushed from my exertions and with my arms aching cruelly, I went to collect my cold water for the morning. At the tap Sister Teresa was filling her jug ahead of me, and I waited quietly, feeling the prickles jabbing into my skull. Eventually she finished. I eyed her tight woolly curls enviously. She hadn't had to bother with any of this business. Serenely she turned round, looked at me, and gave a stifled shriek, dropping her jug of water onto the tiled floor. Her brown eyes rolled wildly until they recognized me. Then a huge smile broke across her face and she began her convulsive, gasping laugh. "Oh, my goodness me," she breathed. *Of course!* I suddenly realized. She'd probably never seen anyone in rollers before. The humor of the situation struck me anew and the two of us rolled around the outer, tears of laughter pouring down our cheeks.

For the last few months I had been given the job of ringing the great convent bell to call the community to prayer. This, I reflected the following morning, would be the last time I would do it. This evening I would be a first-year novice, and in their first year the novices led an entirely enclosed life, never leaving the Noviceship. I walked through the garden until I came to the bell tower with its winding spiral staircase. I wondered what I'd be like next time I came here. By that time I would know the worst. I would be over the worst. I reached the top of the stairs where the bell rope hung: thin, taut, and shiny with age and use. I grinned at it companionably. We had gone through a long tussle together before I became proficient in the mysteries of bell ringing. You had to grasp the rope and pull it at a certain level and then learn how to release it gently, otherwise it clanged uncontrollably. The tight rope hurt, too, and made white weals in your hand. *Well,* I thought, *here goes! Here's to the end of our partnership together. Wish me luck.* I pulled violently to give a final celebratory ring.

There was a cacophonous jangle of clashing metal, a wild discord of chimes, and then a terrible silence. The bell rope hung slackly in my hand.

Oh, no! This afternoon as the bishop walked up the aisle there should be forty firm chimes to welcome him and to mark the beginning of the solemn ceremony. It *would* happen to me, I thought despairingly. Whenever we broke anything we had to report ourselves at once to Mother Albert. What would she say?

I watched Mother Albert walking down the Cloister, getting steadily nearer. Her eyes were cast down and she looked the picture of peace and calm, but I knew her well enough to guess that her mind was teeming with the hundred and one things that had to be done that morning. She had to examine all of us and make sure that we were all looking tidy enough for when our parents came. She had to check that the dormitory was ready for the hair-cutting operation that took place there during the clothing ceremony. Then, with the help of a couple of novices, she had to fold all our new habits onto trays—an intricate job that took hours, she had told us —and put them on the altar to be blessed that afternoon by the bishop. She was going to have to pop in and greet all the visiting families in the parlor that morning, arrange lunch for our parents, and supervise us all while we were putting on our bridal dresses. It was the worst possible moment to break the news about the bell. I quailed at the thought of her scalding rebuke.

She looked up at me as I opened the door of the Postulantship for her. I gulped and opened my mouth, and she looked impatient. She shook her head crossly and swept past me down the corridor.

"Mother . . . " I began, hearing my voice quaver nervously.

"I can't stop now, Sister," she said firmly. "I'm terribly busy." Oh, no! I thought, hurrying behind her lamely. Mercifully she turned back. "Is it anything urgent?" she asked warily.

"Well, yes it is, Mother." The relief of being able to get this off my chest made my voice rise in a triumphant crescendo. "I've broken the bell!"

Mother Albert stopped in her tracks and leaned weakly against the wall. I eyed her curiously. She didn't look angry. "What did you say?" she asked faintly.

"I've broken the bell," I said, more quietly this time, but still watching her nervously for the moment when the appalling nature of my crime hit her and the storm finally broke. "When I went to ring the Angelus this morning I broke it. Didn't you hear it? I'm terribly sorry, Mother. I know it's the worst possible day for this to happen. I must have pulled the rope too hard. I'm so sorry . . . " I trailed off in bewilderment. Mother Albert was laughing helplessly.

"Oh, Sister!" she said at last, recovering herself slightly and wiping her eyes. "You would, wouldn't you? You just would! The way you said it," she went on, laughing again, "you sounded so pleased with yourself: 'I've broken the bell!' " She mimicked my ringing tones. "It sounded as though it was the triumph of your postulantship!" Shaking her head mirthfully she started up the stairs to her room. "Oh, Sister!" she said over her shoulder. "For goodness' sake get yourself tidy before you go to the parlor this morning."

For a second time I looked bewildered. "Don't I look all right, Mother?" I asked, looking down at myself. "I spent ages yesterday . . ."

She was laughing again. "Your collar's coming off! True to type right to the last, Sister!"

That afternoon the great convent church was full of people. There were parents and family of the postulants being clothed, some children from the boarding school, and a party of children from the Birmingham convent who had come to see me clothed. The candles glimmered palely on the altar in the bright summer sunshine, and a mass of delphiniums shimmered in a cloudy blue haze in honor of Our Lady, whose feast day it was. The organ was softly playing Bach in the background. The atmosphere was tense and expectant, the beauty of the surroundings mingling with the poignancy of what was to come.

Suddenly the organ stopped in midphrase. There was a pause. The congregation rustled and looked round to the back of the church expectantly. Then the silence intensified. With a mighty chord the organist began to play the "Magnificat," Mary's great hymn praising God's mercy, and the choir of novices at the back of the church burst into song.

"My soul glorifies the Lord and my spirit rejoices in God my Saviour, because He has looked down on the lowliness of His handmaiden and behold, all generations shall call me blessed."

It was wonderfully apt. On each one of the postulants who had been called here this afternoon God had looked down with favor, and He had called each one to Himself. Then down the aisle proceeded the long line of professed nuns, singing this hymn, giving thanks for their own vocation as they slowly filled the church with their black presences and with a crescendo of sound. The procession was headed by the Postulant Mistress, who carried a tall crucifix. The nuns and the postulants who were advancing to the altar were coming here for no ordinary fulfillment. It was an altar of sacrifice, and wherever they went throughout their lives they would follow the sign of the cross and all that it stood for.

The congregation waited breathlessly. Then right at the back of the procession a single file of five young girls entered the church dressed as brides. Each of them carried a candle. The sunlight shone through the tall windows, catching the prim white dresses and making the gauzy veils seem like diaphanous halos. Their un-made-up faces looked young and vulnerable. Each of them looked steadily at the altar where her Bridegroom was waiting for her. Invisible, but present to the eyes of faith.

Each family had eyes only for its own daughter, who was now flanked by these austere black presences and was moving forward to commit her whole life into the hands of God. In the minds of all the families the implied comparison with a secular wedding was present. That was an event they had all looked forward to, and here the tugging at the heartstrings and the dampening of eyes that a bride always conjures up was intensified by the renunciation they were making. This was their formal farewell to their daughters. They were finally giving them up today—and giving them up to a life that most of them could not imagine.

Each postulant entered the sanctuary in turn and knelt at the bishop's feet.

"What do you seek, my daughter?" he asked.

"The grace of God and the habit of holy religion."

That was all. None of them could ever claim that God had disappointed them. They were seeking only God's grace, union with God—not happiness, not satisfaction, not love, not success or companionship. It was God alone.

"And do you intend to persevere faithfully in all the rules and constitutions of this Order?" the interrogation went on.

"With the help of Divine grace, I do intend to and thus hope to persevere."

There was one more formal question, to make sure. "And do you truly desire to enter the state of holy religion?" And the final reply: *"Ex corde volo."* I desire it with all my heart.

"What God has begun in you," said the bishop, making the sign of the cross over me, "may He Himself make perfect." A sober reminder. It is God Who is the origin of every vocation. Only He can enable the nun to live up to His demands. Her job is to open herself entirely to Him, holding nothing back.

After the blessing of the habits the brides slowly left the church. Their parents craned their necks for a last glimpse of their daughters as they had always known them. Then the heavy enclosure door clanged behind them.

In the dormitory all was bustle and hurry. Mother Katherine, who had been allowed to come to Tripton for the ceremony, was waiting for me in my cell. My bridal dress was torn off, and she bent over me, hacking off my hair roughly, ruthlessly cropping it. I watched the curly locks piling up on the bed. *There it goes!* I thought detachedly. *A woman's crowning glory.* Any beauty I had claim to was being torn from me—another thing that had to go. Then Mother pulled the long black habit over my head and I watched as my pale, girlish limbs disappeared under folds of the heavy black serge. I was now a nun. Finally came the wimple, over which my postulant's hood had been clumsily pinned. I shook myself uneasily in the strange heavy clothes. How odd the wimple was! It cut off my vision sharply on either side. As a nun, I could only look straight ahead, then, not glancing distractedly from side to side, but straight ahead, directly to my goal.

We reentered the church. I could feel my parents' eyes boring through the folds of material, trying to see what on earth I looked like in my habit, trying to recognize me in those strange clothes.

Once again each postulant entered the sanctuary to receive the veil from the bishop. And with the veil she got a new name. This was a new life, a new identity. Her old life was discarded now as completely as her hair, which would shortly burn up in the convent incinerator.

"Receive, Sister Martha," the bishop said to me, "the veil of holy religion. By this you may be known to have despised the world and given yourself forever as a bride to Jesus Christ." Again that stress on the renunciation involved, and again my parents would be feeling the pain of rejection. Their daughter was now symbolically set apart, recognized as a consecrated virgin forever, waiting on God for her fulfillment. How had it happened? they asked themselves. And then came the cincture, the belt with its long tails that symbolized obedience. "When you were younger," said the bishop as I kissed the cincture, quoting the words of Jesus to Peter after the Resurrection, "you girded yourself and walked wherever you wished, but now another shall gird you and lead you where you do not wish to go." The words were stern. The bishop does not quote the next sentence of the Gospel: "By these words Jesus was speaking to Peter of the death he was to die," but they were strongly present

132

in my mind. I knew I was kissing the rod that would bring me to the death of all that I was and all that I loved.

And finally the new novices stood up in their long black habits and their white novices' veils, while the choir sang their song, the haunting "Regnum Mundi":

"I have despised the kingdom of the world and all worldly happiness for the sake of my lord Jesus Christ, Whom I have seen, Whom I loved, in Whom I have believed, and in Whom I have delighted."

That, of course, was the meaning of what they had done. They knew it and their parents tried to understand it. They were seeking sacrifice and death not for their own sakes but as a means to union with Christ.

It was a glorious afternoon. The sun was shining brilliantly on the lawn, and behind that the austere convent buildings looked picturesque and idyllic. My parents looked at me. They had been absolutely unable to imagine what I would look like in the habit and now here I was, my face looking oddly familiar in the wimple.

"What does it feel like?" Lindsey asked.

I smiled happily. "Very heavy at the moment—not uncomfortable exactly—but strange. It's odd to have to turn your head right round if you want to see something at the side. And this veil weighs a ton. We were warned about that; apparently you get used to it very quickly."

"You look beautiful," said my mother. And she meant it. I was no beauty—she was not deluding herself there—but this afternoon I looked happy. Of course that ceremony had been perfect, but sad, terribly sad for them. Yet if I really were as happy as I looked, how could they stand in my way? After all, they must have told themselves for the umpteenth time that day, if there is a God—and of course there was—then I had chosen a wonderful thing to do.

"Do you like my new name?" I asked.

My father grunted. That new name was another sign that his daughter was becoming a different person, lost to him.

"Did you choose it?" he asked.

"Yes. I've had to learn that practical things are much more

important than I'd realized before. And Martha is a very practical saint—you remember, she was the one who was busy about the house while Mary, her sister, sat at Jesus' feet listening to him. Poor Martha. I've always had a soft spot for her; she's so human and indignant. It must have been really galling when Jesus said all that about Mary choosing the better part!"

They all laughed.

"Wasn't the ceremony beautiful?" I kept on saying. "Aren't you glad about it all now?"

And they knew they ought to be.

At six o'clock that evening we were back in the Postulantship outside the great door that led into the Noviceship. Mother Albert was busy straightening our veils, adjusting our large rosaries that had been put on in such haste earlier.

"Tidy at last!" she grinned at me as she surveyed me critically. "I wonder how long that will last."

I looked at the Noviceship door. Still buoyed up by the ceremony, I felt less apprehensive than I had expected to. The clothing had bathed the suffering entailed in my sacrifice in a noble and glorious symbolism. God would help me, I felt sure.

The clock in the Cloister struck six. And then suddenly the bolts on the other side of the door were drawn back, one by one. How strange to be locked up there, I thought, and an icy shiver of apprehension fluttered through me. My new confidence was foundering. Of course there was no going back now, and I didn't for a second want to turn back. I touched my new cincture. "Another shall lead you where you do not wish to go." The death I was to die. Into what desolate and frightening places would I be led now?

The key turned in the door, which swung back silently.

And then one by one we walked through.

Karen with her parents

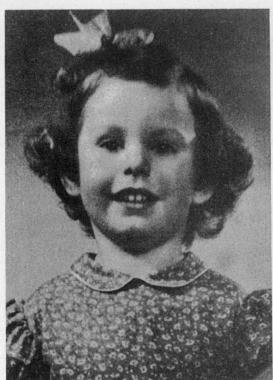

Karen in early years
(she is at far right in the group photo)

After the ceremony in which she
became a bride of Christ

Karen celebrating her veiling
with friends and family

Karen as a young postulant

Karen as she appeared on a
vacation trip to Samarkand in 1979

7 · "THE DEATH I HAVE TO DIE"

When I walked through the door of the Noviceship the first thing I saw was a text on the wall, the saying of a saint: "I would grind myself to powder if by doing so I could accomplish God's will." And that is the purpose of the noviceship: it is a two-year period of training that enables the young nun to make that text her own. She must be prepared in this period of intensive training to be pulverized, allowing her self-love and all her own will to crumble away by a slow process of attrition until there remains only a little heap of powder that God can refashion for His own purposes. The Bible tells us that man, as originally fashioned by God, was formed from the dust of the earth, into which God breathed the spirit of life. After the Fall man needs to be created anew by God so that he comes as near as possible to God's original design for him.

The novice is given the whole of the rule of her order to practice now, not just selected parts as she was given in the postulantship. She is totally isolated from the world so that nothing can distract her from the mammoth task she has undertaken. She is trained in prayer, in the virtues of the religious life: in humility, poverty, chastity, and obedience. But through all this training she is to be broken down. Only when her old worldly self has been smashed to pieces can God build up from the rubble a new, Christ-centered individual.

It is a process rather like the twelve labors of Hercules. Hardships and trials are specially laid on to help the novice overcome herself, and if at the end she is found worthy, she is allowed to make vows of poverty, chastity, and obedience and to begin her life as a nun. People leave during the noviceship, but not in such large numbers as during the postulantship where, although the life is less austere, it is carefully formed to weed out individuals who are not really suitable for the religious life.

During her first year the novice never leaves the noviceship except to go into church for formal spiritual duties or to the refectory for meals. Then there is the midday walk down the road in a procession. The rest of her day is spent in strict seclusion. She is living the life of an enclosed nun so that she can deepen her relationship with God. She reads no books other than those spiritual books that are chosen for her by the Novice Mistress, and she spends her day in prayer and in manual work. She is locked into the Noviceship to wrestle with God, her jealous and demanding Lover.

In the second year the seclusion is relaxed a little. The second-year novice is permitted to study theology, scripture, and church history. Like the postulants, she can be employed outside the Noviceship in the convent refectory and sacristy. If she is a qualified teacher she may sometimes be allowed to do a little teaching in the school. But always the emphasis is on this stripping and breaking down of her selfhood.

Any novice who is going to be a good nun will have a terrible time in the noviceship. In fact, we were told that if we were not finding it unbearably hard then that was a pretty good indication that we weren't trying hard enough. But no two novices will have an identical experience. For each one the things that need breaking down will be different. The most difficult thing is to come to terms with yourself. I had never fully realized how much the world outside the convent shields an individual from having to endure any great degree of unpleasant self-knowledge. We are expected to be social animals and to seek company; most of us have to work with other people. There is marriage, where one's partner can try to build up an ego that is in danger of crumbling. In the twentieth century there are any number of easy ways to escape from yourself—television, cinema, endless noise on the radio, rush, bustle, socializing. In the convent there are just acres of time with yourself and God.

I had never had a particularly high opinion of myself. I knew that I had faults, but they didn't seem much worse than anyone else's. I had a reasonable number of talents—nothing very spectacular—to counterbalance the things I couldn't do. Nothing in my past life had prepared me for this intensely intimate knowledge of myself. However hard I tried to keep the rule, however hard I tried to pray, to practice humility, charity, and the rest of it, however hard I tried to change myself, I failed. Intimate, petty little failures. My meditation became an hour of messy, self-indulgent fantasy; the silent times of recollection were filled with trivial self-pitying thoughts. Whenever I tried to be particularly kind or humble I'd find my thoughts seething proudly. When I tried, as I had to try, not to need people's love and affection anymore, I found myself yearning for it. And feeling so disgustingly sorry for myself. It all seemed so simple when you read the rule. It finished with a quotation from Isaiah: "This is the way; walk ye in it." As easy as that. But I couldn't do it. I couldn't change myself. Oh yes, I could conform outwardly and make a pretty good job of that, but inwardly I remained the same: worldly and full of self. Theologians tell us that Hell is not the popular vision of a pit filled with fire. It is far more terrible than that. It is the endurance of oneself forever and ever with no alleviation at all. It is logical. You've chosen yourself instead of God, so God gives you yourself. But this time without anything or anyone to distract you. Just you on your own.

I remember very clearly the first time this self-disgust hit me. It was on the occasion of my first chapter of faults. Ever since we had been told about this I had dreaded it. It seemed such an undignified, humiliating procedure—to confess your faults in public. But I was not prepared for quite the horror it turned out to be.

After evening prayer one Friday we filed out of church into the Noviceship community room. This was a huge room, far bigger than the postulants' community room, but with the same basic set-up. Desks faced inward round the room and a long table stretched down the middle with Mother Walter's desk at the top. Behind that was a life-sized statue on a heavy pedestal of Our Lady holding the Holy Child. It was a modern room and three of the walls consisted almost entirely of windows.

That evening as I walked in, the first thing that struck me was that the curtains had been drawn and that the room was in total darkness except for one light over the far end of the table, which fell in a harsh yellow spotlight. Our chairs had been pulled back from the table, and in complete silence we went to them, standing in two long lines in order of age—the second years at the top next

137

to Mother Walter, and me, the second-youngest novice, right down at the far end. The Noviceship was always quiet, but tonight the silence vibrated with tension. I found that I was trembling slightly. *It's silly to be so nervous,* I told myself sensibly. *After all, nothing is going to happen to you—it's just a question of making a brief list of the faults you've committed during the past week.*

We had been carefully instructed on how to select these faults. No interior faults could be confessed: I couldn't accuse myself, for instance, of having had uncharitable thoughts. This was due to an edict from Rome. During the seventeenth century apparently there had been a scandal because many Mother Superiors were forcing the consciences of their subjects, forcing them to confess their sins to them, listening in on their Confessions and thus coming between the private conscience and God. To protect the nuns, the Pope had declared that no such probing of conscience was allowed and that public accusation must confine itself to external matters, things that my sisters would have noticed in me and that therefore brought down the standard of piety in the community. *It won't be that bad,* I promised myself. It would be awful if I had to accuse myself of all the countless times this week that I've prayed badly or felt sorry for myself. But this, this was no more really than a public apology to my sisters for all the "disedification," as it was called, that I had given.

But however rational I tried to be, I still found myself terrified. It was the darkness. And more than that the impersonality. Each novice had her hands hidden in her sleeves and her eyes cast down to the ground. Each face was remote and expressionless. And these were the people whom I ate and slept with, whose bodily habits I knew as well as my own. Perfect strangers. Even the brethren. I stole a glance at Edna, who was Sister Griselda. Her face was unrecognizable in the darkness. Withdrawn into herself.

Down the corridor I heard the sound of heavy footsteps and braced myself. Mother Walter and Mother Albert, who was the Assistant Novice Mistress as well as being Postulant Mistress, entered the room. How odd it was to see her, my former superior, under obedience herself! I watched Mother Walter's feet as they passed through my line of vision, massive and gleaming in their outsized shoes. When she reached the top of the table we all dropped to our knees.

"Come Holy Spirit, fill the hearts of Thy faithful and kindle within them the fire of Thy love," Mother Walter began. She said the words deliberately but tonelessly, putting nothing of herself in it. We made the responses and our voices seemed faint and expressionless too. Then we all sat down. Silence. Then,

"Will you begin your accusation, Sister?" Mother spoke as though she were reading the part from a script. And in a sense that was what it was, I suddenly realized. For a hundred years the nuns in this Order had been meeting for this duty following the same pattern, the same script. But the accusations were not written for you, I thought, as a cold feeling settled in the pit of my stomach. Those were dragged out of every single nun's personal struggle every single week.

Sister Margaret, now Sister Jeremy, who was the youngest novice, got up, walked to the end of the table, and knelt in the yellow spotlight. My heart was beating for her. How awful to be the first one, I thought. She began in the formula:

"I accuse myself to you, dear Mother, and to you all, my dear Sisters . . . "

How unnatural that sounded. We never called each other "dear" usually. They did a hundred years ago address each other like that, of course, but we didn't now. It was as though Sister Jeremy were not really speaking to us at all. When she began her list of faults I found myself not wanting to listen. This wasn't Margaret, and if it were I shouldn't be hearing this list of private failures. But I knew that I had to listen and let this confession of weaknesses in. Then quickly, too quickly, the accusation ended and it was my turn. I walked and knelt in the spotlight, which blocked me off from the rest of the room. Outside there in the dark silence were my sisters in Christ, but I couldn't see or hear them. They had quite receded. I cleared my throat and began:

"I accuse myself to you, dear Mother, and to you all, my dear Sisters . . ." but it seemed as though I were speaking into a vacuum. This was an apology, but I wasn't making it to anybody. Usually when I apologized, however painful the experience was, there was contact, touching of eyes, faces reacting, and finally restored contact between me and the other person. Here I was alone, shut off in my own guilt.

" . . . of having committed many faults against charity by showing impatience to a sister;

"of many faults against humility, especially by expressing my own opinion too strongly at recreation and being oversensitive when corrected by a superior;

"of a fault against obedience by criticising an arrangement."

As I rushed toward the end of my accusation, my voice wobbling and out of control, I saw exactly why the room had been set up like that. I was on my own. All my faults screamed of self, self, self. My opinions, my criticism, my impatience. How petty I was, locked in my limitations all the time, thinking of nothing but my puny little ego and my feelings and ideas. What a terrible picture of triviality I presented—no grand faults, no titanic struggles like the saints had. Just me. Boring, indulgent, and futile.

" . . . of a fault against charity by smiling unkindly when another sister made a mistake and by thoughtlessly excluding a sister from a conversation during the walk;

"of a fault against humility and religious reverence by answering my superior back when she was kindly correcting me and by attempting to justify myself."

Self, self. Nor could I even keep the simplest of rules.

" . . . of very many faults against religious modesty by failing to keep custody of the eyes and many faults against silence, particularly silence of action by walking noisily."

I had finished.

I waited shakily. There was a silence that seemed to go on and on. Then Mother Walter spoke coldly and impersonally.

"Sit down, Sister."

I walked back to my seat. To my mortification I found that I was tearful and a lump had risen to my throat. There was no catharsis in this apology. How could there be and how could I ever have hoped to be a good nun? The very measure of my disgust was a soggy self-indulgence, feeble self-pity. When was I ever going to leave my self behind?

That Christmas week of 1963 saw a meeting of the Provincial Chapter. The superiors of all the seventeen houses of the English Province converged on Tripton, each bringing with her a delegate elected by her community. The Birmingham delegate was Mother Katherine, and it was odd to see her walking down the Cloister or to serve her in the refectory without being able to exchange a single word or even a smile. But since the end of the meeting of the chapter fell on the feast of the Epiphany, which was a special day in the Order, the professed were allowed to visit the Noviceship. Mother Katherine came and I was delighted to see her. She gave me the official embrace of the Order, our wimples touching starchily on each side, but her eyes told me of her pleasure at seeing me in the habit. It was difficult in the crowded Noviceship to find a place to talk privately, but at last I discovered an almost empty room. It was the old Noviceship community room, which, because of the recent increase in numbers, had been abandoned. It now yawned emptily. We sat side by side on a broad window seat; other visiting nuns and novices were doing the same. We chatted pleasantly for a while, Mother Katherine giving me news of Birmingham. It was strange to be sitting beside her as a member of her Order, knowing now so many of the things she had never been able to tell me before.

Suddenly her face froze and she sat staring into space, her eyes glazed, her lips parted slightly. I waited anxiously for her to speak.

"This," she said slowly and expressionlessly, "used to be our community room. Mother Gertrude was my Novice Mistress. Have you heard of her?"

I nodded. Mother Gertrude was a legend in the Order. She had been Novice Mistress for twenty years and had trained her novices with exceptional severity.

"She was Mother Walter's Novice Mistress too. Were you in the Noviceship together?"

"Yes." Mother Katherine's voice was flat. "She was a perfect novice. I was always in trouble; I did everything wrong. But afterward Mother Gertrude used to say that Mother Walter was the best novice she had ever trained, the one who absorbed her spirit most thoroughly." For a moment worry flickered across her face and she looked at me searchingly. Since Mother Gertrude's time there had been two other Novice Mistresses; one was Mother Jerome, who had trained Mother Albert, a stern woman, I gathered, but lacking in the ferocity of her predecessor. Then came Mother Leo. A year before I entered, Mother Walter had been appointed.

I noticed that Mother Katherine's face had slowly become

drained of all its normal vitality, turning a muddy grey. Her eyes stared dully ahead at the empty fireplace.

"On that wall," she said, still speaking in that low, dazed voice, "we had a text. We changed it every day. Do you do that?"

"Yes, Mother."

"And over there," she went on, waving in a trancelike manner, "we had cupboards and things."

We sat silently. She was lost in that room of twenty years ago. At last she spoke.

"It was terrible," she said. That was all. She turned and looked at me and our eyes shared a knowledge. "Do you find it terrible too?"

I nodded. It was hard to speak. "I thought you would," she said. "But you're all right, aren't you? You still want to stay?"

"Oh, yes," I said emphatically. "Mother Walter tells us that it's got to be hard—it has to be," and again I noticed her anxiety when I mentioned my Novice Mistress' name.

"What's the hardest thing?" she asked me gently.

"Myself," I said promptly.

"Ah, yes," Mother Katherine nodded. "That's it. That will be with you always, you know. What do you mean exactly, Sister?"

How strange it was to hear her call me Sister. And how strange to be really talking to someone again with affection.

"I just can't get rid of myself," I blurted out. "All the time. I know I've got to die to myself but I can't. Whenever I'm supposed to be praying, whenever I'm told off—"

"And that happens a lot, of course; it always does." Mother Katherine's eyes were reverting to the end of the room where, I guessed, Mother Gertrude's desk had been.

"Yes," I said, sighing at the memory. "Well, I get upset. Sometimes I even cry. And I feel so sorry for myself. It's all so petty, so ordinary."

Mother Katherine's pale blue eyes were looking gravely into mine. "Do you really want to lose yourself?"

"Yes!" I exclaimed. "I can't stand myself. You know, I've been thinking. I always thought I was a special person. Not that I was brilliant or a genius or anything like that. But I was special to myself. Of course, I'd have denied that if I'd been asked. I mean, *rationally,*

I knew there was nothing particularly special about me at all. But
. . ."

"I know," Mother Katherine nodded. "We all think that. And
it's awfully easy to think it in the world. Married people each have
somebody who thinks they are special in some way, and even now,
in my job, I can kid myself that I'm doing something important that
no one else can do. I've always got to keep reminding myself of what
I learned in the Noviceship."

"What was that?" I asked.

"That right at the bottom I'm a selfish, self-obsessed bore!"

We laughed. How good it was to hear someone say this. I could
never have talked to Mother Walter like this. She'd have been so
angry.

"We all are, you know," she said, smiling again now. "Do you
remember what Hopkins said? 'God's most deep decree/Bitter
would have me taste:/My taste was *me.*'"

I nodded. "But Hopkins *was* an extraordinary person," I said.
"Look at his poetry."

Mother Katherine shrugged. "But look at his letters. He was
saying just what we are saying now."

"The thing is," I said, warming to the subject, "in the religious
life there's nothing really to distinguish you from anybody else. You
know, we all wear exactly the same clothes, sleep in dormitories of
identical beds; we can't indulge any of our individual likes and
dislikes—even in food. Nothing different! Oh! I know it's got to be
like that, but often I keep wanting to shout, 'Hey! this is *me* here,
not number 276.' Sometimes I just want somebody to recognize
that, and of course I can't."

"No," Mother Katherine shook her head. "And that's why our
stupid selves get so angry that we can't forget about them for a
minute. And it comes out in all those self-indulgent thoughts."

"But how can I ever get rid of it?" I cried despairingly. "In the
world people are always talking about how they've changed. Or they
say, 'I'm going to work at myself and try to do more'—you know.
I always thought I could change the bits of myself that I didn't like.
But I can't!"

"No, really nobody can change themselves that much," Mother
said. "It's just that not many people have the chance to realize that

as fully as a nun. But, you know, it's important to see how awful we are, otherwise we'd want to hang on to ourselves, instead of letting ourselves die. And we'd start talking about self-fulfillment and all that nonsense."

We looked at one another again. "It's hard, isn't it?" she said. Then, as we joined in a farewell embrace, "Take care. God bless you! I'll be praying for you."

One of the things that had to die was my mind. We were being trained in Ignatian obedience, which aims at breaking down the will and the judgment of a religious so that he unquestioningly accepts the will of God as it is presented to him through his superior. It is the obedience of the professional soldier Ignatius was himself before his conversion: when your commanding officer gives you an order, yours is not to wonder why but to do and die. The superior represents God to a religious: his commands, his orders—"the least sign of his will," as the rule says—are to be taken as a direct message from God. Ignatius says that "all should give themselves up entirely to their superior as a dead body allows itself to be treated in any manner whatever." I had to make myself into that dead body.

And it was so hard. It is not enough for a nun simply to perform her superior's command, while thinking all the time that it is absurd. She must empty her mind of her own judgment and tell herself that this—*whatever it is*—is the best thing she could possibly be doing. But the mind dies hard. To think and judge is a reflex. How do you ever manage to embrace the absurd? During my first year in the Noviceship I had to learn how . . .

The alarm squealed peremptorily and with a stifled groan I heaved myself out of bed onto my knees. I was the caller for that week and it was my job to wake the other novices. Not that there was a chance for any of them to be still asleep. The alarm went on and on, rattling and insistent, and I heard the others tossing restlessly on their beds wishing it would stop. So did I. I knelt on the prickly mat by my bed making my morning offering to God while the alarm rang relentlessly on. I wasn't allowed to switch it off. The only novice who was allowed to touch the sacred clock was the oldest second year, Sister Bartholomew. Swaying with sleepiness I fumbled in the dark for my clothes, pulling my habit over my nightdress,

144

thrusting my feet clumsily into my slippers. The alarm hiccupped and puttered out, mercifully. The silence throbbed blissfully as I put on my veil and wimple and groped my way out of my cell to the light switch.

The room was flooded with harsh light. The long austere dormitory dominated by the fourteenth-century rose window was revealed in its white glare, the fifteen iron bedsteads shrouded in curtains pulled around my sisters, who were trying to savour their last few seconds' rest. I blinked, dazzled, at the clock. Eleven forty-five. It was supposed to be five-thirty A.M. but none of us was allowed to alter the position of the hands, not even Sister Bartholomew. The clock gained or lost erratically every day, and Sister, when she set the alarm, spent ages locked in abstruse calculations in the Cloister gazing at the grandfather clock there with the faulty alarm clock in her hand. Usually she got it right. I shrugged sleepily. The call was always an act of faith.

I set off on my progress down the dormitory, pausing outside each cell, bashing hard on each bed so that the brass bed knobs vibrated: "Blessed be God!" and waiting for the blurred answer, "Now and forever more, Amen!" and then stopping until I heard the novice fall out of bed on her knees. No turning over for another two minutes was allowed. We had to spring out of bed the second we were called, strip our beds, and turn the lumpy mattresses.

"Blessed be God!"

"Now and forever more, Amen!" fifteen times.

Duty discharged and feeling more awake now, I returned to my cell, stripped my own bed, and set off downstairs to tap on Mother Walter's door. "Blessed be God!" I called into the musty darkness and proceeded into the community room to collect the keys that unlocked the various doors of the Noviceship. Glancing mechanically at the clock there I stood rooted to the spot. *Oh, no!*

I darted back up to the dormitory to be greeted by brisk splashing noises and fierce brushing of teeth. "Sisters!" I called urgently, "go back to bed. It's only a quarter past two!"

There was a sudden shocked silence and a few pathetic moans, and Sister Bartholomew emerged from her cell, her wimple askew. Her appalled eyes met mine as I waved the alarm clock at her in frantic dumb show. We gazed at one another helplessly and tumbled out onto the landing. She snatched the clock from me and sat on the stairs, her face puckered with anxious concentration. *This is ridiculous!* I found myself thinking crossly. I couldn't speak, of course; it was the Great Silence. Why on earth couldn't we buy a decent clock? I leaned against the banister and stared at the moon, which seemed to be laughing at us. And if it was against Holy Poverty to buy a new clock, surely Sister Bartholomew could be trusted to set it right without wrecking it entirely. Sister looked up at me, her face contorted and apologetic. What a rotten job! Frequently I saw her emerging from Mother Walter's room, red-eyed, clock inevitably in hand. Mother Walter! I suddenly snapped out of my rebellious reverie. I'd completely forgotten about her. I started down the stairs and stood transfixed as I heard the well-known footsteps. Mother stood before us, watch in hand, and stared at us both in cold fury. I quailed, looking up at her huge bulk. She seemed to look right inside me and see what I had been thinking. A long, angry moment. Then she turned on her heel and went back to her room.

White and shaken, Sister Bartholomew handed me the clock, which I took as gingerly as though it were a time bomb and crept back to my cell, wrapping myself in a blanket. Lying on the thin mattress, I sighed. A fault against obedience. I'd criticized my superior! Yet again. But how could you control your mind's responses at two-fifteen A.M.? It wasn't possible! But that, I knew, was no excuse.

I fared little better a few weeks later with the nailbrush. "Sister!" Mother Walter said pleasantly. "Those steps need a good scrub, the ones leading down to the basement." She stood before me, her skirts tucked up for manual work to reveal skinny ankles and gigantic feet encased in titanic clogs. I found myself staring at them, hypnotized. It was always unfortunate that our eyes had to be lowered when we spoke to persons in authority. I found those feet so distracting. Perhaps, however, it was just as well on this occasion— it stopped me from thinking that I had scrubbed those steps only yesterday and that they were gleaming with cleanliness. Oh, well.

"Yes, Mother," I said brightly and followed her out to the porch.

"You must scrub these steps more regularly, Sister. You haven't scrubbed them for at least a week!" Mother's voice was sharp. "Fidelity in little things! Do you think they look clean?"

I stared dumbly at their pristine whiteness. "No, Mother," I said meekly. *But they do!* I clamored inside. *They look beautiful!* And then the novice in me took over. "Stop it," she said, and, admonished, I peered at the steps, looking for faults. No, perhaps they weren't so clean after all. There *was* a black mark on the corner of the fourth step, and there were two dead leaves, *and* a few crumbs of caked mud where some postulant had trampled with dirty shoes. Mother was right.

"I'm very sorry, Mother," I said again, trying hard not to applaud myself for my perfect obedience. That would cancel it out.

"Right!" she said briskly, "I should think so too. What you need, Sister, is a really good brush. Look, I've got the things all ready for you." She indicated a bucket of steaming water and some scouring powder to our left.

"Oh," I said, startled, "thank you, Mother!" How odd. She didn't usually pamper us like that. "I'll just go and get a brush," I added and started back to the outer.

"No, there's no need, Sister," Mother said mildly. "Here," she delved into her pocket and produced a pink nylon nailbrush. "Here you are."

I looked hard at the brush in her outstretched hand. Slowly I reached out and took it, composed my face into a mask of rigid nonchalance, and glanced up at her. The small blue eyes held mine. They were quite devoid of expression. "Thank you, Mother," I said respectfully. "Thank you very much."

But of course as I worked on, two hours later, it was not enough just to do it. I had to tell myself that this was the best possible way I could scrub the steps. But how could I? I looked at the brush, whose bristles were worn down to useless stubs, and swished the soapy water ineffectually from one side of the step to the other. A job that should have taken half an hour at the outside had taken a full two hours. I looked at the top steps, which were beginning to dry, streaky with tiny little swirls. It was like saying that black was white. And yet, I kept saying firmly, if Mother says it is, then it is white in the eyes of God.

But it isn't! I thought suddenly. *And this is a stupid waste of time!*

I sat back on my heels and sank my head into my hands. Why had God given me a brain if He didn't want me to use it? This was some stupid kind of perversion. I sighed miserably. I knew by faith that this was a worldly point of view. God's view was so superior to my own limited intelligence that I couldn't be expected to understand it. What did it say in Isaiah? "As high as the heavens are above the earth so are My thoughts above your thoughts." To let myself see with God's eyes I had to be prepared to lay aside my own common sense. It was common sense. I had to go above that and let my intelligence die. But while I could see this so clearly, there was another part of me clamoring to be heard. I didn't want to kill my mind. My body I had despaired of years ago. It was clumsy and anarchic. But my mind! I thought back to myself at school, feeling the thrill of following an argument, discovering mental grace and agility. My mind was the best part of me. Why did it have to die?

I shook myself and mechanically went on scrubbing, feeling confused and unhappy. My mind was me. It was the only thing I had that was any good. Oh, I wasn't Einstein or anything like that. But without my mind I'd just be that lumpy indistinguishable body and a welter of muddy emotion. I'd be nothing. *I don't want to be nothing!* I said fiercely to myself. *I don't want to.*

Perhaps—I tried a different tack—perhaps I should just leave Mother Walter out of it. All right. God wanted me to waste my time like this for His own inscrutable purposes. But again something inside me exploded. *Can you really believe,* it said scornfully, *that that Infinite Being can think of nothing better than nailbrushes and faulty alarm clocks? Is He that petty?* And of course I couldn't leave Mother Walter out of it. She stood for me in the place of God. Whenever I spoke to her inside the Noviceship I knelt down to remind myself of the fact. No. It was my faith that was weak. And I was frightened of becoming nothing, of letting that best part of me die.

Wearily I gathered the cleaning implements together. The steps were badly scrubbed, yesterday's work had been ruined, and yet again I had failed in obedience. I lacked courage. I was still hanging on to that part of me that criticized and clung to myself. How feeble I was. Tears blurred my eyes. I wanted so much to think well of myself, to feel that in some respects I had something unique to offer. I wanted to be a good nun, too, but these two desires were irreconcilable. I had to choose. Me and my mind. Or God and that complete fulfillment that somewhere I knew He offered.

With the sewing machine, however, I felt that I was nearer to winning the battle. We spent our mornings in the first year sewing with Mother Albert. My sewing was a little better but still far from the standard expected. Each morning I struggled with a paralyzing sense of inadequacy as the material buckled under my clumsy fingers. It seemed such a long time since I had done anything well. How lovely it would be to get that glow of satisfaction at a job well done. Mother Albert bent over me and inspected the seam that I was overcasting. "Sister!" she groaned despairingly. "Your machining is deplorable! Are you ever going to improve, do you think? You're going to be useless to us if you can't cope with a simple job like that."

That was what worried me. I glanced up at the text of the day pinned over the fireplace: "There are no drones in the beehive of God." Was I going to be a drone all my life, carried by the efforts of others?

"I'm sorry, Mother," I said trying to keep the depression out of my voice. Correction should be accepted with a smile and with real joy that our faults were being pointed out. How else could they be mended?

"Haven't you been practicing your machining?"

"Well, no, Mother," I said startled, looking up at her.

"What!" she shouted, shocking me with the change in her usually quiet, uninflected voice. She sounded at the end of her tether. With me. "Why not?"

There was an old machine that I was supposed to practice on for half an hour a day. "For heaven's sake use that one," Mother Albert had said. "I can't have you wrecking the good machines. Even you can't harm that one!" It seemed such a long time since that morning when she had laughed about the bell. But, of course, that kind of leniency was only for postulants. I was supposed to be stronger now. And I had put the machine out of action, of course I had broken a needle. I had apologized, done a public penance in the refectory for my fault against Holy Poverty, and received a scalding reprimand. The needle had not been replaced. I had timidly reminded Mother Albert of this more than once. "Don't bother me now, Sister!" she always exclaimed. "I'm far too busy to run round after you replacing needles that you're stupid enough to break!"

Now I looked at her helplessly. I struggled to crush the sense of injustice that was rising up in me rebelliously. "There isn't a needle in it, Mother," I said at last, noting with disgust the wobble in my voice.

There was a silence. One part of me knew that Mother Albert had clean forgotten about the needle, but she was angry with me. I waited.

"How dare you!" she said, her quietness now more frightening than her earlier anger. "How dare you answer back like that? Don't you know about humility, Sister? Don't you know that a nun never tries to justify herself when she is reprimanded? No matter what the circumstances. You must never reply to your superior pertly like that."

I got up and knelt down. "I'm sorry, Mother," I said huskily. Another chance gone. Of course I knew about humility.

Mother Albert's voice was icy. "You will go to that machine, Sister, and you will practice on it every day for an hour until I choose to give you a new needle."

A few weeks later Mother Albert looked into the small sewing room and saw me. My feet treadled busily and the machine rattled and whined. But there was something odd about the sound. Quietly Mother stepped a little closer. My hands were folded neatly in front of me, resting beside the machine. My head was bent forward and there was a frown of concentration on my face. Nothing would disturb me—I was miles away.

This is the best thing I can be doing at the moment, I repeated mechanically. *I cannot possibly spend my time more fruitfully.* At first it had been hard. I had felt resentful and frustrated no matter how hard I tried to check it. But now—I'd lost count of the number of weeks I had been doing this—the whining of the machine had lulled something inside me to sleep. *Let go,* I was saying. *Let go.* My stupid mind. What do I know about anything? Anything at all. The machine whirred on. This *was* the best way of using my time. It was God's way. If I let myself be guided all my life by my superiors then I'd always be sure of doing His will. Who would prefer his own limited vision if he could have God's instead? Nothing else mattered. It was so simple, really. Why hadn't I seen it before?

"Sister! What *do* you think you're doing?"

I jumped, shaken rudely out of myself. Mother Albert was looking at me as if she thought I was mad.

"Practicing machining, Mother," I said calmly. I stood up deferentially and looked back at her. She seemed a long way away.

"But there's no needle in that . . . ." Even as she spoke I saw light dawning. She clapped her hand to the back of her head and turned away abruptly, staring out the window, her shoulders shaking silently. *She's forgotten,* I said to myself. It didn't matter at all. My responsibility was simply to obey her perfectly.

Mother turned round, her lips still twitching. She'd been laughing. That was good. I had to make myself a fool for Christ's sake, just as He had clothed Himself in the shame of sinful humanity. I stood and waited.

"Well," she said, her voice remote, "I hope you've profited by all this practicing. And I hope you've learned something about yourself too. You're so full of yourself, aren't you? You know you must never answer your superior back, even if you think she's wrong. Let alone answer as pertly as you did: 'There's no needle in the machine!'" She tossed her head, imitating my defensive manner. "You're full of pride, Sister, full of intellectual pride. You think there's a natural answer to everything, don't you?" She paused interrogatively.

"Yes, Mother, I'm sorry." How good all this was for me. Part of me was hurt and wanted to weep. It even came out in my voice, this treacherous part of myself, but that wasn't important anymore. Beneath all that surface confusion I knew how worthless I really was. What did my hurt feelings matter? Mother could say nothing to this part of me, which would ultimately be filled by God, if I let Him. This surface person, who wept and felt natural feelings, had to die. Mother's harsh words would kill her off all the quicker.

"When are you going to learn to lay aside this wretched critical faculty of yours?" Mother swept on, beating that worldly self into the ground. "You look at things only on the natural level. The world thinks it's so important—the critical faculty, indeed." She wrinkled her nose derisively. "And another thing, Sister," she went on. I knew the form of these reprimands by now. They were a daily occurrence in the noviceship. A tiny incident could reveal so many of your faults, faults that you'd never dreamt you possessed until an unguarded word or action revealed them all. I felt my eyes filling with tears and shook myself impatiently. This wretched, sniveling part of myself had to go.

"Another thing, Sister, you're far too sensitive. Look at you now. Weeping because a superior does you the great kindness of pointing out your faults. What are we going to do about this sensitivity of yours? It will destroy your spirituality and your love of God. You're just a soggy lump of self-pity, Sister. You can think of nothing but yourself. Oh, the world thinks that sensitivity is valuable, but it's pure self-indulgence. Feelings don't count, Sister, so learn that once and for all and get rid of them."

"Yes, Mother." I felt like an executioner, putting this worldly part of myself to death. Dispassionately I felt my tears dry and looked down at the ground, as I should when speaking to persons in authority.

"Right! And mind that machining improves!" Mother Albert stormed toward the door. I rushed to open it for her.

At the end of my first year in the noviceship, during the annual eight days' retreat, I found myself kneeling on the refectory floor waiting to do my special retreat penance. Every fortnight we were expected to do a "refectory penance" during meals for faults against the rule, but during the retreat these penances were more severe. We had to look back over the past year, pick the fault we had failed in most, and publicly accuse ourselves, asking the forgiveness of the community for all the disedification we had given.

With my head bowed I knelt in the long queue waiting for my turn. In front of me a professed nun accused herself of faults against silence and then stretched out her arms in the form of a cross, her big ceremonial sleeves hanging grotesquely, while she began to recite the Lord's Prayer five times. Around us the meal went on as usual: the servers hurried round us indifferently carrying the steaming dishes, plates were passed, eyes were cast down as the nuns ignored the penitents on the floor. I thought over the events of the past year. I seemed to have advanced so little, despite all my grand intentions on my clothing day. I had had no difficulty in selecting the fault I had committed most frequently. Mother Walter had nodded gravely when I knelt at her feet asking for my penance: "For faults against obedience, Sister, you will kiss the feet of all the nuns in the refectory." I was shaken by the extraordinary nature of what

I was ordered to do. But how just it was, really, I told myself. A public act of abasement to remind me of all the times I had proudly clung to my own will.

" . . . but deliver us from evil, Amen." The nun finished her last Our Father, lowered her arms, bowed low to the crucifix, and got stiffly to her feet. My turn now.

"I accuse myself to you, dear Reverend Mother Provincial, and to you all, my dear Sisters, of having committed many faults against the rule since my last retreat, especially against obedience." My voice wobbled treacherously, and then, my cheeks burning with self-consciousness, I got up and began walking slowly up to the superiors' table. Behind me I could hear the next novice in the line striking up, accusing herself of faults against humility. Nobody seemed remotely interested in this act that seemed so momentous to me. Mother Walter I could see was watching me carefully, but the other superior chewed on in apparent ignorance of my proximity. Not so, however. When I fell to my knees and crawled under the table, I found that they had all pulled their skirts up past their ankles and had each pushed one foot out toward me considerately. Sliding along the floor on all fours I kissed foot after foot, crawling carefully round Mother Provincial's footrest, recognizing Mother Walter's unmistakable size ten. "Hurry up, Sister, you haven't got all day," I heard her say as I started scrambling ignominiously toward the next table.

Before entering the Order I had seen Audrey Hepburn in *The Nun's Story* doing what I was doing now. Ironically the scene was very much in my mind. In the film the act had acquired a theatrical dignity and significance, but what the film had not captured, I reflected, was the prosaic nature of the whole penance: the squashed peas under the table, the taste of boot polish, the bunions. I slithered from table to table, dodging the servers as they flew past with dishes of meat and gravy. How hard it was to transcend these banalities and concentrate on the real meaning of the penance. The nonchalance of the refectory to my plight robbed the penance of any exotic glamour, and I was aware only of my aching knees and a splinter in my hand. Suddenly it dawned upon me that the banalities were the whole point. This was where I was supposed to be: down on the ground, the lowest of the low, barely worthy to eat the crumbs that fell from the table. Until I'd learned that, I told myself, as I got up, flushed and giddy, seventy feet later, my spiritual life hadn't begun. Surely I had learned my lesson now for good and all.

But of course it was not really as easy as that. The mind, like the body, has a life of its own. You think you have killed it once and for all, and then it shows, by an instinctive jerk or shudder, that it is still alive and kicking, able to throw all your neat calculations to the ground in a minute.

In the second year, I was allowed to study. Only sacred studies, of course: theology, scripture, and church history. Nothing that would have brought the world to my attention. My studies in theory should only have strengthened my faith, backing up the painfully won relationship with God that I had acquired during the last year. But somehow it didn't work out like that.

The trouble was that when I started to study theology and scripture, the immensity of God and His plans for the world seemed little in accord with the constricted life of the convent. I told myself that this was a matter of intellectual pride and that these critical thoughts did not become one who was ready to sacrifice her whole being, including her mind, to the love of God. What was even more alarming was that even the theology had holes in it that threatened the whole fabric of my life.

One day it all came to a head. I had been put in for a four-year theology diploma and Mother Greta coached me for my first-year exams. I had been set an essay: "Assess the quality of the evidence for the Resurrection." It was part of a course in apologetics, which set out to explain the mysteries of faith by means of reason. But the more I thought about these mysteries, the more unreasonable they seemed. Surely that was the whole point of faith, I argued to myself. If it was perfectly reasonable to believe that Christ had risen from the dead, then faith was unnecessary. Believing in that would be no more difficult than believing in the Battle of Hastings. I had researched the essay carefully, reading all the relevant books of apologetics that seemed to argue that the stone that was rolled away from the tomb was sufficient evidence for any sane person to believe that God had become man, was publicly executed outside Jerusalem, and rose from the dead after three days. *It* can't *be proved,* I worried; *this essay is a sham.* However, since I was working for an examination, I reproduced the mental gymnastics that were expected of me, feeling all the while a sinking loss of integrity. My pen transformed the flimsy, symbolic evidence in the Gospels into weighty, verifiable historical facts. My essay proved clearly, by mental sleights of hand, that anyone who looked at this evidence and failed to believe in the Resurrection was an imbecile. Wearily I laid down my pen and handed in my essay.

The following Tuesday I sat with Mother Greta in a tutorial. She took off her glasses, polished them, and peered at me short-sightedly.

"Yes, Sister," she beamed at me. "This is an excellent essay. You should do very well in the exam." She replaced her glasses.

I looked back at her. Beneath that frail, birdlike body I knew there was an honest mind. I trusted her. I had to ask her about my dilemma. The Resurrection upon which my whole life depended was a miracle, something that the natural order could not account for.

"But Mother," I said quietly, staring at her intently. "It just isn't true, what I've written, is it?"

There was a silence. She sighed, and, thrusting her hand under her wimple in a characteristic gesture, she rubbed her forehead hard. Her voice, when she spoke, was tired.

"No, Sister," she said flatly. "No, it isn't true, but please don't tell the other novices."

She wouldn't say any more than that and I was left floundering intellectually. When I used my mind and sense of logic, then in some obscure and shameful way my conclusions were wrong and could contaminate. The lesson powerfully reinforced what I had learned in my first year: leave your brain alone; it can only harm you.

The conversation with Mother Greta brought back to me an incident in my first year. We had been sitting with Mother Walter at evening recreation and the talk had turned to church music, Mother's favorite topic. The Vatican Council, she told us, had just decreed that more of the vernacular was to be used in the church liturgy and that, in the spirit of this injunction, some priests were introducing guitar music into the services. "They think," she said harshly, "that it's more *relevant.*" The word came near to being a sneer on her lips. "It would be terrible to think of the Gregorian chant disappearing altogether," she added sadly. "Surely there's some form of compromise they can make."

I felt sad too. I had come to love plainsong. I could not sing

at all, but the music, perfectly expressing the words with its haunting cadences, had come to be an integral part of my own prayer,
shaping it with beauty and dignity.

"Mother, what's so wrong about playing the guitar during the
Mass?"

We all gasped as though an obscenity had been uttered. In a
way it had. We turned to look at the speaker, Sister Jocasta, a novice
in the year ahead of us. Her strong, handsome face was concentrated in the grip of an idea. How does she dare to argue with
Mother? I wondered.

Mother frowned. "I should have thought," she said icily, "that
that is something we need not discuss."

Everyone bent their heads over their needlework, disowning
Sister Jocasta. The topic was portentously closed. No one could
pursue it now; it would be a grave fault against obedience.

"But some people," Sister Jocasta persisted to my astonishment, "may come to church initially to enjoy the guitar because they
like that kind of music. I mean," she added hastily, "we've had the
advantage of studying the chant and growing to love it that way. But
a lot of people in the world don't have that opportunity and to a lot
of young people it's quite inaccessible."

Mother was silent, but it was a fearsome silence. I was still
amazed at Sister Jocasta's daring; it was terribly wrong of her, but
somehow—in a way that I was not willing to define—it was vital that
she go on.

At last Mother spoke. "Anyone who needs a guitar to get him
to Mass must have a pretty shaky faith, I should have thought." She
laughed shortly in a way that I had come to dread. It was an angry
bark, and, I knew, it was not worse than her bite.

I looked up at Sister Jocasta through my eyelashes. The other
novices, with frightened faces, were sewing away as though their
very lives depended upon it, apparently concentrating on darning
their stockings or pleating their wimples. *She mustn't go on,* I thought.
She can't, not now, surely. But I felt a certain respect for Sister Jocasta.
My mind seemed so dead and rusty now, and of course that was
good. I couldn't follow through an argument point by point anymore, but in a perverse kind of way I felt thrilled watching someone
else do it.

She did plunge on, her eyes triumphant. "But they might come to church at first just for the music and then find that there is something more. It would give God a chance!"

"Sister!" Mother's voice was thunderous with incredulity. "Do you think God needs a guitar to give Him a chance!"

I looked back intently at Sister Jocasta, no longer trying to conceal my interest. Her face was flushed with a sense of her own daring—or a sense of her fault.

"But surely, Mother, if Christ lived today he would use a guitar!"

"Rubbish," Mother snorted with contempt. "Of course He wouldn't!"

I bent my head to hide a smile. I had suddenly pictured Jesus standing on a soapbox at Hyde Park Corner singing plainsong. He looked pretty silly. Of course He would use a guitar! He would use whatever made sense at the time. But then Mother Walter seemed to have quite a different view of Christ, and she was His representative. Her words were His words; I knew that and was appalled to have found myself disagreeing with them. Was my view of Christ entirely wrong then? The smile faded from my lips. But just too late. She had seen it.

"I'm glad you find this amusing, Sister Martha," she said sarcastically. "I find it very sad."

"I'm sorry, Mother," Sister Jocasta's voice was deflated suddenly. "I haven't really thought much about this. Only . . ."

"No, you've obviously not thought about it at all!" Mother snapped. "And you've committed a severe fault against obedience and a fault against charity by ruining recreation for the rest of the community. Yes!" she said abruptly to Sister Griselda, who was kneeling at her feet. "Yes, you may ring the bell!"

Chastened, we scurried nervously to put away our needlework. Silently we gathered round the statue of Our Lady to sing an evening hymn. Sister Jocasta was giving out the books. As she handed one to me our eyes met and she grinned suddenly. And winked.

That wink, now that I thought about it, was disturbing. It suggested a complicity between us. I liked her, she was fun, but I could see that her mind was dangerous. It was alluring to follow arguments through gracefully, to juggle with ideas, but if I gave my mind the chance it would lead me away from religious obedience, which, the rule told me, was my lifeline to God—the chief Ignatian virtue.

It would also lead me into treacherous areas of the faith. All those books I had read—was it really possible that only Mother Greta and I had seen through them? And if we both felt that what they said was not true, why on earth couldn't I tell the others? Yet Mother Walter had told me so often that my mind would hinder my progress toward God. "Knowing God in prayer has nothing to do with the mind," she said again and again at instruction. "It's a matter of clinging to Him with the will. We have to be prepared to let our own ideas of God die so that He can reveal Himself to us as He is."

But there were other difficulties during that second year. A new set of novices had been clothed in the summer of 1964. They were all much older and more experienced than we were. Shortly after the clothing I found one of them in fits of laughter in the boot room. It was a big feast day and talking was allowed. I looked at Sister David, a woman in her late twenties, Welsh, short, sharp, and independent.

"What are you laughing at, Sister?"

"It's this," she pointed to a notice that was carefully written out in elaborate Gothic lettering above the box containing the shoe-cleaning materials. "Every time I look at it, it just starts me off!" and she was doubled over again in a paroxysm of mirth.

I stared at the notice. It had made me laugh a year ago, and I remembered Mother Walter had been very angry. "How dare you show a flippant disrespect for an official notice, Sister! They all express the will of God!" Now I scarcely registered the notice; it had become an unquestioned part of the environment. I read it again. It gave minute directions about how to clean a shoe: take it up in your left hand, cover it liberally with polish, brush it off and shine it with a soft cloth. The punch line came at the end, I remembered: "Repeat for the other shoe." It was hard to believe that I had found that so funny once. I was now so used to waiting to be told what to do step by step and line by line.

"Repeat for the other shoe!" Sister David breathed ecstatically. "Beautiful! It just sums up the noviceship, doesn't it, Sister? Don't do a thing unless you're told to. Can you imagine! If Mother hadn't had that last sentence printed all the novices would be walking round with one shoe perpetually clean and one dirty!"

It was a ridiculous picture and in spite of myself I found myself smiling. I enjoyed Sister David. She had been an art teacher at one of our schools and had decided to become a Catholic. Then she found that she had a vocation to the Order. The whole world of Catholicism must still seem strange to her, I thought, let alone convent life, and her good-humored response to it all was fresh and alert. Life seemed so solemn always, yet laughter so often showed how worldly and flippant I was. But it was nice to hear laughter again, and there had been a lot more of it since Sister David had come into the Noviceship. Still, Mother Walter had spoken very seriously to us about our responsibilities as second years in helping the first years get the right ideas about the religious life. I found myself parroting her rebuke of last year.

"Sister, you shouldn't really laugh at notices, or at the ideal of obedience behind them." I heard myself sounding awfully pompous, but what else could I do?

"Oh, come on!" Sister David groaned, sitting down on top of the boot lockers. "Really, if we don't laugh sometimes we'll all go mad! Don't be so serious all the time. God knows there's enough to laugh about here!"

"What do you mean?"

"Well! Look at things like the alarm clock—I ask you! I've never heard of anything so ridiculous. Sister, you're a bright girl and you're sensible too. I've got to ask you. Are all these rules absolutely *de rigueur,* or are they just idiocies perpetrated by stupid novices in the past and handed down traditionally?"

"Oh, *no*!" I spoke emphatically. "The alarm clock certainly isn't, believe me. You should hear what Mother Walter has to say when she thinks someone's tampered with it!"

"Oh, well, I suppose you know best."

"Honestly, Sister, I used to think all these things were ridiculous too, but now I see it differently. You've just got to be ready to lay aside your own judgment, as the rule says."

"But there's no sense in some of these things," Sister David insisted. "Sister, I hear you being sick every time we have cheese for supper."

"Not every time," I said thankfully. "I'm getting used to it now."

"But, Sister, you obviously can't eat cooked cheese; it's bad for you. You look all white and wobbly the next day. And there's this ridiculous rule that says we not only have to eat everything set

before us, but we actually have to eat two helpings! Of course I can
see that we mustn't be fussy and obviously it's important for us to
eat enough, but you're going to do dreadful things to your stomach
if you go on like this! Have you told Mother Walter that cheese
makes you sick?"

"Yes, of course," I said. We had to tell our superiors when we
were ill; that was in the rule too.

"Well, what does she say about it?"

"She said that I'd just have to conquer myself and that I'd get
used to it. And I am, too!"

"But what about all these other rules! We're never allowed to
talk in twos at talking times; we have to wait till a third person is
present. What on earth are they afraid of—that we'll all turn into
lesbians?" I did a double-take. I'd never have dared express the
thought, but I'd found myself wondering the same thing. "We're
not allowed to sew on Sundays; we're not allowed to drink water
between meals without asking permission; we're not allowed to cut
our hair without permission. When we mend our knickers we have
to show Mother Walter the darn before we wear them again. It's
treating us like kids! And we have to obey people even when they're
clearly making a mistake. Like yesterday. Sister Griselda told me to
sew up that skirt in a way that was obviously wrong and when I told
her so I got an earful from Mother Albert about Sister Griselda
being in charge of sewing that morning so that she was a minor
authority and had to be obeyed. But Sister was wrong; the way I've
had to do it means it's going to fray in a couple of weeks. It's all so
stupid."

"It isn't, Sister; it's just that we've got to train ourselves not to
hang on to our own ideas."

"But why has God given us brains if we're not allowed to use
them?"

It was then that I noticed through the smoked glass doors the
unmistakable bulk of Mother Walter, who had clearly overheard the
conversation.

Only much later could I begin to understand something of what
must have been going on in Mother Walter's mind at that moment.
A few months before she'd have come straight into the boot room
and given Sister David a piece of her mind. Firstly we were having

a conversation "in a two" and thus falling into the danger of particular friendship, which she regarded as a major evil. If a nun's affections were involved at all with another sister's, how could she give all her love to God? But even worse than that, Sister David's view was antagonistic to her concept of religious obedience. Of course novices were treated like children. Christ had said that it was only the person who abased himself and became like a little child who could enter the Kingdom of Heaven. Unless a novice became child-like, how else was she to stop using her critical faculty with all its unworthy rationalizations? She had always seen it as her job to check that tendency to criticize. Of course some things were senseless if they were looked at from a natural point of view, but whoever said that the service of God had anything to do with common sense? The religious life was a kind of inspired madness. St. Ignatius had compared a good religious to an old man's stick, which serves the user in every place and for every use alike. A nun had to become indifferent to herself and her own notions, her mind as lifeless as that stick so that she could be used for a higher purpose.

But things were changing. In Rome the Vatican Council was discussing the role of religious in the modern world, and from all accounts nuns would be given a lot more freedom in the future. Cardinal Suenens had inveighed against the traditional training of novices in his book *The Nun in the Modern World.* It was a book that Mother Walter had always spoken of with deep distrust. She considered it so dangerous that when she was carrying it through the Noviceship she used to try to hide it. I had once seen it poking out from under her cape, and her expression had been as wary as if she were carrying a high explosive, as if we could be contaminated by the mere sight of the book.

But of course in a way the book was an explosive, and it would shatter the teachings that Mother Walter held so dear. The church seemed to be endorsing the cardinal's views, and it may well have been suggested to Mother Walter that she should modify her training just a little—nothing drastic of course, nothing that touched the basic principles of the Order—but especially in the matter of obedience perhaps there could be a *little* more leeway given to a novice's common sense, to prepare her for the freedom that might come later.

This must have been a hard test of Mother Walter's own obedience. Of course she would obey her superiors, whatever she was directed to do, even if their orders went against her strongest beliefs. She mustn't cling to her own views any more than a novice. But she must have been perplexed to see how novices using their critical faculties could possibly remain within Ignatius' concept of obedience. He was so clear that obedience of the will *and* of the judgment was crucial. He had quoted in his famous letter on obedience, which was read aloud to the community once a month, the example of the novice who for years had watered a dry stake at the command of his superior, knowing that it would never flower but never once questioning the inherent worth of the action performed under obedience. It was an essential principle. How could she obey her superiors by allowing novices to think and criticize and still be true to the spirit of the rule?

Poor Mother Walter. The Council was taking away so much that she treasured: the plain chant of the liturgy, all the customs of the religious life of which she was the perfect, if fanatical, exemplar. Even the religious habit would go eventually. As she wrestled with the will of the church, her behavior and modes of training oscillated violently. At the time I could see nothing of all this, and her methods seemed arbitrary and inexplicable, frightening me into an ever-deepening distrust of my own mind.

She entered the boot room and we two novices jumped and looked guilty. "You seem to have been having quite a theological discussion here," she said drily. "How did it start?"

Sister David pointed to the notice. "With that, Mother. I'm afraid that last sentence seems so silly to me, and I was arguing that a lot of the rules in the noviceship are not based on common sense."

"Like what, for instance?"

"Well . . . " she sought round in her mind. "Like obeying somebody, another novice if she's a minor authority, even when she tells you to do something you know is stupid. Surely we're meant to use our heads?"

"Of course you are!" Mother Walter snapped and turned to me. "Have you no common sense at all, Sister? Haven't you got any sort of brain? I think it's probably atrophied while you've been here." I stared at her blankly for a moment before remembering to lower my eyes. What was going on? I felt bewildered but now it

didn't occur to me to answer back or say, "But Mother, you *said*
. . . " By now I was conditioned to accept anything. All I had to do
was to obey, not seek for consistency. Mother raised her voice and
shouted at me:

"You use your common sense at all times, Sister! Do you hear
me? At all times!"

So I started all over again. Insofar as I thought at all now, I
suppose I must have thought that this was just another of Mother
Walter's methods of making me distrust my mind, and how much
I needed to foster that distrust! My mind was dangerous; it had to
go. I had thought that I understood the principles of Ignatian obedience. Yet as Mother's admonitions to use our common sense continued, usually in the form of a severe reprimand when one of us
practiced obedience as preached last year, I felt more and more
confused. What was obedience? And what was I supposed to do?
Was I supposed to think and use my common sense after all? Had
I got hold of the wrong end of the stick? If so, it just proved how
unreliable my mind was. Anyway, I told myself, thinking now seems
to be the order of the day, so I tried to free my mind from the literal
way I had trained it to interpret everything. It was hard; my mind
was extremely rusty—I no longer thought easily for myself, nor did
I easily take the initiative. A few weeks before I would have thought
that a sign of victory, but now apparently it was a failure. But that
was one thing I was learning about this quest for perfection! You'd
never finish. You could never tick off a virtue and say, "Done!" and
go on to the next one on the agenda. Something always remained
to be learned, a further renunciation was always to be made, like
peeling the layers of an onion. My present bewilderment was just
another sign of that spiritual immaturity Mother Albert had warned
us about in the postulantship. In time I would see it properly and
would understand. What seemed inconsistent and paradoxical now
must blend harmoniously in God's greater vision.

Perhaps if it had not been for Mother Walter's new advocacy
of common sense I would not have made that mistake about the
bedroom slippers. A notice went up on the board one day:

"A number of professed have complained that they can hear
the novices clattering up and down stairs at night during the Great
Silence. Therefore each novice will put on her bedroom slippers as

soon as she enters the Noviceship after the examination of conscience at nine-fifteen and she will not take them off until just before
going into meditation the next morning."

The following day at spiritual reading Mother Walter asked,
"How many novices went to bed in their bedroom slippers last
night?"

Nobody stood up. There was a nonplussed silence.

"Why not? The notice was perfectly clear." Suddenly Mother
Walter shouted angrily, as though something that had long been
pent up had erupted at last, "You all exercise your critical faculty
far too much. You all think it is important to use your common
sense. Obedience, Sisters, is literal and total! Of the mind *and* of the
judgment. It has nothing to do with earthly prudence or 'sensible'
behavior."

Involuntarily Sister David and I exchanged bewildered glances.
Where did the truth lie? The pendulum swung madly.

Then I saw it all. Mother Walter gave the sign for spiritual
reading to begin and I turned to my sewing. The thing to do was
to abandon thinking altogether. To search for a rationale for behavior was worldly. St. Ignatius said that obedience had to be "blind."
Right. I'd got it now. I was blind in that I couldn't understand the
underlying principle. And that was what I was supposed to be.

One day that I particularly remember, I was sewing in the small
sewing room. I was surrounded by bales of pillow ticking. Feathers
filled the room in soft white drifts. Periodically I sneezed, for they
were irritating my nose. I was standing over a table, carefully cutting
out yet another round of pillows—fifty pillows had to be completed
by the end of the week.

The door opened and I was dying to look round to see who had
come in, but that was not allowed—it was undisciplined. Mother
Walter stood at the door and watched me for a while, consideringly;
then, nodding to herself as though she had decided on a course of
action, she strode into the room. She was carrying a length of white
material and a pair of scissors.

"Oh!" she sounded impatient and put out. "You're here!"

I jumped guiltily, though it was difficult to say why. "I'm so
sorry, Mother," I said apologetically.

"I wanted to use the table," she said with evident irritation. "But of course"—sarcastically—"I can't possibly disturb *you*, can I? Not when you're doing such valuable work!" "I can easily go somewhere else."

"Oh, no," Mother replied heavily. "I wouldn't dream of disturbing you, Sister. No," with a martyred sigh, "I'll just have to make do with the floor."

In spite of my obvious distress, she lowered her vast frame to the floor, spread out her material, and with much sighing and groaning, proceeded to cut it out.

"Mother! Please!" I pleaded. "Please have the table!"

"No." She crouched over the material, wincing at the discomfort. Airily she said, "Please don't dream of disturbing yourself on my account."

We continued with our work in an uneasy silence. At first, I jumped at every sigh from the floor, but as the minutes wore on the guilt gave way to suppressed anger. As I bent once again to the ticking my lips were compressed in a hard line. Mother looked up at me and watched for a while, sizing up the situation. Then she picked herself up, advanced to the table, and started to examine the small pile of completed pillows.

"This is disgraceful work, Sister!" she bellowed, rending the room with her anger. A feather must have gone up her nose for she started to sneeze mightily, her diatribe and dignity temporarily ruined. Recovered, she continued. "Look at this seam! And this! I gave you this job to do because it was so simple. I thought that even you with your limited intelligence couldn't make a mess of it. But look what happens. What use do you think you're going to be in the Order, Sister, if you can't even tackle this kind of work with any reasonable success? You are useless! A hopeless, useless person, Sister!"

Something seemed to snap in me. I threw down my scissors, narrowly missing the Novice Mistress, tore from the room, slamming the door, and proceeded to pelt up the stairs with Mother in hot pursuit, veils streaming, rosaries clanking, crucifixes swaying wildly from side to side. Eventually she caught up with me, shook me by the shoulders violently and yelled into my face: "How dare you! How dare you! Go up to the attic now, get down your trunk, and sit on it for the rest of the day. Why do I ask you to do this? Because we can send you home, Sister, at any time. Do you hear me, Sister? At any time!"

The anger had long since faded. The reminder about being sent home had sobered me considerably. It was, I knew, a real possibility. Only a few weeks before Joan had disappeared from our ranks because she was not considered by the Provincial Council to have a strong enough vocation. And Joan had never done anything like this. Slamming a door in the middle of a reprimand from my superior, throwing the scissors at her! I sighed miserably, looking round at the cheerless attic with its dusty piles of trunks. I was overcome with disgust at myself.

What right had I to be angry? I, whose noviceship was drawing to a close. Who was supposed by now to be like that dead body, allowing myself "to be treated in any manner whatever." Just when I thought I was winning the battle, something like this happened to show me that I had made no progress at all.

A half-forgotten line from Shakespeare echoed in my mind. "Is there yet more toil?" And I knew the answer. I would be fighting this battle with myself until the day I died. Did I want to go on? I didn't have to think very long. Yes, of course I did, if today's escapade was not going to send me packing. The self-pity I had been feeling was just another sign of self-love. If I left, all I would have would be this self of mine. If I stayed and won my battle I would have God. Was there really any question? He had challenged me and I must continue until there was no self left—only God.

8 · BURIAL
1963-1965

I was kneeling in church, making my morning meditation. It was then past six. Morning prayers had been completed; we had stood silently to make an act of the presence of God, bowing low in reverence. Then we settled ourselves to begin and the silence in the church intensified except for the beating of the November wind, which made the leaded windows rattle. The church was dimly lit and, flanked by the other novices at the back, I squinted to look at the notes I had made the night before, opening my New Testament at St. John's Gospel:

"Unless the grain of wheat dies it will remain nothing more than a grain of wheat. But if it dies it brings forth much fruit."

The text had seemed so inspiring last night, but now, as happened so frequently, I couldn't concentrate on it at all. I was so tired. Every night, when the bell tolled three times at ten o'clock to tell us to put the lights out—one toll for each member of the Blessed Trinity—I fell asleep heavily, and the call was a shattering experience. I never seemed to get enough sleep. And last night I had been sick again after two helpings of cauliflower and cheese. I felt ghastly, slightly giddy and hollow inside.

Suddenly I became aware that the light in the church had changed. It seemed harsher, and . . . something seemed to be flashing, slowly at first but gradually increasing in tempo. I looked around. No one else seemed to have noticed it. Sister Jocasta next to me placidly turned a page in her book. I hid my face in my hands to try and blot it out. Then I became aware of a terrible smell— sulphuric and choking—that made me gasp. What was happening?

I was shaking all over, I noticed vaguely, and to keep my balance I clung with whitening knuckles to the bench in front of me.

Then it hit me. Waves crashed around me, and I lost all sense of what or where I was. I looked ahead at the altar, the crucifix, the glimmering red sanctuary lamp—they became more intensely, sharply red and then suddenly flickered and lost their identity. I had never seen them before. Lights flashed. Sweat trickled down my back. I was trembling with fear, my brain licked to a frenzy, fighting to breathe against the ever more powerful stench. And then darkness, blessed darkness, and a long silent fall down a bottomless pit.

Dimly, a long way away, I could hear voices. They were faint but clear, as though they were ringing down a long silvery tunnel. I couldn't move, couldn't speak. I just heard the words striking against my mind without making much sense of them. I knew the voices. Whose were they? Numbly I lay there, wrapped in the shiny darkness.

"Has she come round yet?"

"No, but she's not so stiff now. What do you suppose it was? It seems too long for an ordinary faint."

"Surely, my dear Mother Albert, that's quite obvious. Hysteria. That's what it is. Try slapping her on the face." I could feel something hitting me sharply and tried to respond. But I couldn't. Without fear, feeling nothing in fact, I lay there and listened. Mother Albert spoke next.

"She's very highly colored, isn't she? And her breathing's funny. Do you think we ought to get a doctor?"

"If she doesn't come round soon, perhaps, but not otherwise. This is pure nerves and attention seeking. You've said yourself how nervous and emotional she is. She's just got to learn to control it. There's no real strength of will here, just messy undisciplined emotion."

I knew that voice now. It was Mother Walter's. Suddenly I seemed to fall back into my body. I opened my eyes gingerly. A hard band of pain pressed down across my eyes, making me wince. I was staring at something shiny and red. Where was I? I was on the ground. It was cold. So cold. My tongue felt bruised and swollen as though I had bitten it hard, and as the world became clearer, I found that I was filled with a desolation too strong for tears. I shifted uneasily, trying to find a position where my head wouldn't hurt anymore.

"She's coming round." Which one was that? It sounded like Mother Albert. Hands seized me and pulled me roughly into a sitting position. My eyes focused gradually on Mother Walter's face. It was red with fury, tremulous with contempt.

"How dare you, Sister! How could you make an exhibition of yourself like that?" I blinked at her, bewildered. What was she talking about? What had happened? "If you feel faint," Mother almost spat the words into my face, "it is quite simple. You sit down and put your head between your knees. Then, if you find that you are no better, you leave the church as unobtrusively as possible and get some fresh air. You do not disturb your sisters' prayer by falling about on the ground in that disgusting display of hysteria."

I could understand very little of what she was saying to me. "Faint? Did I faint, Mother?" The words seemed to come from a long way off.

"Indeed you did," Mother snapped. "And religious do not faint, Sister. It is pure self-indulgence."

I looked from Mother Walter to Mother Albert, stunned by the force of their disapproval. Slowly things were beginning to come back to me—the terror, the stench, the loss of identity. Self-control? What had happened to my body? I knew that it had been beyond my power to control what had happened to me. I shifted my swollen tongue uneasily in my mouth and felt the throbbing in my head. What if there was something terribly wrong with me?

"I—I—couldn't help it, Mother," I said. I knew that I was justifying myself but I felt that I had to try and share with her what had happened. "I got all bewildered and frightened and—something seemed to take me over."

"Precisely," Mother Walter said angrily, "and I'll tell you what did take you over. Your feelings, raw and undisciplined emotion."

I could feel the tears rising. The sense of desolation was now compounded with a terrible feeling of failure. I felt quite helpless.

"You see," said Mother Walter, indicating the tears. "Look at you! Weeping when your superior corrects you. You are here to learn your faults, Sister, and how can you possibly learn them unless I tell you? And here you are, giving way to self-pity on top of everything else. I am deeply disappointed in you. I think," she added after a pause which let her words sink in, "that you had better go and lie down, Sister, until you are in a better frame of mind."

I stumbled up to the dormitory. I felt so ill. Suppose I was physically ill and nothing was being done about it? But no, I told myself. Of course Mother was right. I was an emotional wreck. I was oversensitive; look at the way I was crying now, tears that would not stop. But how terrifying to feel that my emotions were so powerful that they could cause this. I passed a hand over my throbbing head. Was Mother right—was there something wrong with me? I shook my head. Even if Mother was mistaken, my job as an obedient religious was to accept her decision blindly, because that would be what God wanted. But how could I control these feelings, with their sudden, violent effects?

Mother Albert pushed aside the curtains of the cell and looked toward the bed.

I was perched on the end of my hard iron bedstead staring straight ahead. My eyes were puffy and red and I know their expression was a frightening mixture of fear and despair. My face had lost its hectic purple color and was now muddy grey. I had taken off my cape and veil and wimple, and my cropped hair stuck up like a toothbrush all over my scalp.

As Mother Albert entered the cell I jumped and turned to her with an expression that cried out for help. "Mother, I'm so sorry, I know I shouldn't have done it. I don't know—"

Without a word she walked across to the bed. Then silently but firmly she put her arms round my trembling figure and pulled my cropped head against her breast. She could feel a slight stiffening of surprise, and then with a despairing cry I relaxed against her.

"You feel too much, Sister," Mother Albert said gently. "You mustn't. Feelings don't count, you know, feelings don't count."

"But Mother," I said despairingly, "I know that, but how can I stop feeling things? I try and I pray about it all the time." That was what I had been going to meditate on that morning, I remembered suddenly.

"You can do it, you know, Sister," Mother Albert continued. "I know you can. You're much stronger than you think. It is an attitude of mind. Tell yourself that these feelings don't matter. It doesn't matter whether you feel you love God or not. Feelings of love are worthless. What does matter is the will—hanging on to God's will nakedly in faith."

I nodded. I felt so safe, so calm suddenly. I could smell the musty, damp serge of Mother Albert's habit. Closeness to another human being after these years of silence and distance.

"But how can I stop feeling lonely?" It was warm here in this cell, but once I had put on my habit again . . . I thought back over the months since I had arrived here as a new postulant. I saw vividly the bland faces of the professed as I opened doors for them, bowing to me expressionlessly, their eyes staring right through me so that I felt invisible. When I poured out tea in the refectory they held up their cups and coldly stared back at me, no smile of thanks ever. I thought of the steely atmosphere of the chapter of faults. Of the noviceship recreations where none of us was in touch with anybody else because we were not sharing our thoughts and feelings on any real level. The perpetual silence driving me back into myself. The ban on friendship. No talking in twos, ever, because friendship was dangerous. The odd sentences from the rule: the sisters shall not touch one another even playfully. How strange that sounded now as I sat hearing Mother Albert's heart beating steadily, her silver profession cross pressed against my cheek. I knew that this was only a concession to my weakness, that it would never be repeated. That she was doing it because I had failed.

"How can I stop wanting people to love me?" I asked in a small, muffled voice.

"Try to be more peaceful about it," Mother Albert said quietly. "You can't stop feeling lonely all at once, but you can accept it positively instead of battling against it all the time. We have to accept loneliness on a human level. All our love is for God. You remember the rule? How we have to 'strip ourselves of all affection for the Creature so as to place all our whole affection in the Creator.'"

"Yes," I said. "I do want that, Mother. I pray all the time for God to take my feelings away. Not to love anybody anymore. How can you help loving some people more than others? The rule says we must love everybody equally—but *how*?"

"You can't help liking some people in the community more," Mother Albert said. I breathed a sigh of relief. There were novices that I liked and would love to have had as friends: Sister Rebecca, Sister Jocasta, Sister Griselda. And now, shaky with gratitude, I loved Mother Albert. I had always liked her better than Mother Walter. She seemed more solid, somehow. I felt safe with her.

"Then how can I strip myself of that love?"

"By not indulging it at all. Ever. You have that rule, haven't you"—I heard Mother Albert sigh with—was it, could it be—impatience?—"that says on Saturday afternoons or feast days you can't talk to one other novice alone? Use that as positively as you can, as a safeguard against letting one friendship grow so that it excludes other people and takes away your love for God. You know," she said, "there are one or two people in the Order that I like very much indeed. Do you know Mother Cyprian?"

I nodded, amazed. I had never thought that Mother Albert was a prey of her feelings. She seemed so detached. I had seen Mother Cyprian once or twice from afar when she had visited Tripton. "Well, when she comes here we never go for a walk together or make any attempt to have a 'special' conversation in talking time. We've never said anything to one another about it. It's just that we know we could become close friends and we both know that that is something we have to sacrifice. Do you see?"

"Yes," I said. Life stretched ahead as a long, solitary path. These moments with Mother Albert were all the more poignant because I saw them as an unrepeatable oasis in a lonely desert.

"After all," Mother said, "no human person can ever satisfy us wholly, you know. Only God can do that. And the emptier your heart is of all other loves, the more He can fill it with this love. And it's worth it in the end. But you have to be prepared to suffer first. Are you ready for that?"

I thought hard. Again it was the old story. I felt that I couldn't bear what lay ahead but that was just one of my limitations. Once I'd forced myself beyond that, then I'd find the perfect and infinite love of God. Of course it was worth it.

"Yes, Mother," I said, "but do you really think I can do it?"

"I'm sure you can. Quite sure. You just have to stand firm. Don't let all these turbulent feelings destroy your peace of soul, Sister. They're not worth it. Look what happened this morning."

I thought again of what had happened, the terrifying loss of control, the throbbing pain in my head, the convulsive shaking, and the merciful fall into oblivion.

"I couldn't help it, Mother. I felt so ill." She held me a little away from her and searched my face worriedly. I tried to describe my symptoms, but suddenly, as if remembering a prior decision, her own obedience, probably, to Mother Walter, she cut me off.

"It was all hysteria, Sister. You can help it, you know. I have faith that you can." But it was kindly said.

There was silence. The last few seconds of human warmth.

"Now," she said firmly. And I knew what she meant. Now I had to resume the battle with my feelings. And the battle with my body, with its violent rejection of the discipline of the convent: its vomiting, its fatigue, its convulsive fainting.

"God bless you, Sister." She made the sign of the cross on my forehead and then she was gone.

With heart beating, a few months later, I went into the little disused dormitory in the Noviceship tower and locked the door. It was a strange thing that I was going to do. "Corporal mortification," Mother Walter had said, "is valuable. You have been learning how to subdue your body by disciplining it to do the will of God when you eat what you don't like, get up the second you are called in the morning, and endure the normal physical hardships of our life. But now you are ready for the next stage."

I pulled the little bag from my pocket and stared at it. I had been shocked when Mother Walter gave it to me. I had always thought the nuns so restrained in their piety. Never had I expected here the excesses that I associated with the more frenzied Christianity of the medieval period. I had read in church history of the old Irish monks of the seventh century who used to stand naked all night in the freezing sea and of the fathers in the desert who whipped themselves until the blood ran. But . . .

I drew out the discipline: a small whip made of knotted cords. Those fathers in the desert had seemed tasteless in their fanaticism. But now, in the heart of civilized Tripton in the middle of the twentieth century, I was being asked to emulate them.

I knelt down to pray, as Mother Walter had recommended. I remembered St. Paul's words: "I buffet my body and make it my slave." Perhaps this really would help to subdue this unruly body of mine. I had had two more of those frightening fainting episodes and grown to dread them, not just because of the horror of the experience itself but more because of what they showed me about myself. To make my body the slave of my will, that was what I had to do. How else could I possibly love God? Help me, I prayed meekly. Of course for a rebellious body like mine, the mere tool of my emotions, violent measures were essential. Nothing else seemed to work. Try as I would I could not stop those attacks.

Quickly I took off my veil and wimple and laid them carefully on one of the beds. Then I picked up the whip and began to beat myself over the back of the neck. *Harder and harder,* I muttered to myself through clenched teeth. The cords bit into my flesh, smarted, and stung. I felt sweat standing out on my brow and felt myself trembling all over. *It has to really hurt. Really hurt,* I thought, *or else how can it work; what's the use of it?* Tears now filled my eyes, tears of pain. *It's got to work,* I thought, *please, please, let it work!* It was not just my body I wanted to hurt; it was myself. As I went on I no longer felt the pain. Just this dark and reckless excitement that grew steadily, blotting out everything but itself. And then there was a huge sense of release.

I knelt, leaning against the bed, my face hidden in my hands, my body quivering in every limb, my breath coming in sharp pants. Shakily I tried to make the sign of the cross but the action seemed too strenuous and positive for the dreamy lethargy into which I had fallen. Exhausted and, in some strange sense, satisfied, I waited for my heart to steady itself and for the throbbing sensation deep within to cease.

I looked up at the crucifix on the wall as my numbed neck began to prickle painfully into life, bewildered by the excitement that had possessed me. Where had it come from? Instead of beating my body into subjection the discipline seemed to have roused it to a new life, touching something in me that left me frightened, tingling, and alert. It was my mind that had been stilled, while my body knew an intensity that I had never dreamt of before.

Slowly I got up and pulled on my veil and wimple, wincing as the stiff linen rasped against the tender flesh. Then I sat down on the bed to think. Some burden or pressure that I had been unaware of in myself had been lifted. I felt entirely transformed. Clean and hollowed out. Profoundly relieved, too. And what kind of satisfaction had the penance given me? Penance wasn't supposed to be satisfying and exciting. It was meant to kill, not to arouse. Perhaps some destructive force had been beaten out of me. For a time. And then perhaps the devil in me would grow again and I would have to come back here to this room to thrash it out again.

I looked again at the crucifix on the wall. The silver figure glinted in the sunlight. "Where do you come into this?" I asked God. Usually penance was very austere and Christ-centered. In the refectory when we kissed the ground in penance for faults against charity or humility, we prayed: "O God have mercy on me, a sinner." When I kissed the feet of the community in the refectory, crawling under the tables and pressing my mouth to the bunioned black shoes of the professed, the dreary prosaic lowliness of my position impressed on me a sense of my own insignificance in the Divine scheme of things. But this penance had blotted out God entirely, blotted out everything but that strange drowning sense. That peculiar pleasure.

I couldn't be doing it right. Something must have gone wrong. Now I felt barren and empty. The satisfaction had given way to a gnawing restlessness and some odd craving. Craving for what?

This, I thought, *is something I don't understand.* I didn't want to understand it; it hinted at too many fundamental difficulties. But I knew I had to try and face them. I'd have to take my perplexities to my superior.

"Come in!"

Mother Walter was sitting at her desk, smiling her restrained, ascetic smile. I went and knelt at her feet. "Yes, Sister."

"Mother," I said, and I could hear the words coming out in an urgent rush, "please, I want to talk to you . . . to ask you about the discipline."

Mother smiled again and gestured to the chair. It was a small, hard chair, the kind that is used in infant schools. It had always made me feel like a small child to sit there, so close to the ground. And today for some reason that seemed reassuring.

"You sound worried, Sister."

"Yes, Mother, what's it supposed to do to you?" She looked perplexed.

"I thought I'd explained all that, Sister."

"Yes, I knew what it's supposed to do. It's meant to beat the body into subjection. But . . . " Suddenly I broke off, feeling confused and embarrassed. Mother Walter's calm, pale eyes regarded me curiously. Could she ever have felt anything like what I had just experienced?

"Go on, Sister."

"I found that it roused my body to life in some way," I said slowly, not wanting to meet her eye. "I seemed to forget all about God, all about everything . . . I found it . . . exciting." I stopped short and looked down at my hands.

There was a silence. "Sister!" I looked up. A dark flush had spread across Mother Walter's face, and around her mouth there was an expression of distaste that I could see she was trying to get the better of. "I'm glad you've come to talk to me about this. This is a difficulty that some nuns have—some more than others," she said evasively. "But don't discount the discipline; it can help you. You see . . . " she continued awkwardly. *Why can't she just get it out once and for all,* I thought impatiently, *instead of going round in circles like this?* Then I checked myself quickly. "You've got strong passions, Sister. We've already seen that. You get very emotional—there's all that disgusting fainting. You tend to react to things too strongly. It's all part of your undisciplined body and mind that's got to be quelled."

I took this in. "But how can I control all this?" I pleaded. The fainting, the surges of feeling, and that heady excitement just now came up unbidden. I never sought them out.

"Bodily mortification will help," Mother replied firmly. "This passion—*excitement* I think was the word you used. It's something that you are going to have to give up and get out of your system. It's something you'll have to fight hard all your life. Because you're going to make a vow of chastity."

"Does it mean that I'm not suited to the vow," I asked anxiously, "because of my passions?" I wanted to talk about these more fully. But Mother Walter didn't want to go into it, I could tell.

"No, not at all. It just means that you've got to work hard to subdue these bodily . . . instincts. The rule says that we have to live like angels. Angels, as you know, have no passions; they are pure spirit, pure intellect and will directed wholly toward God. You have to make yourself into an angel, Sister. Not a cherub on a Christmas card. But a spiritual, not a bodily person."

"But if the discipline rouses these passions, Mother, isn't it just going to make me less spiritual?"

"No, not if you persevere. Beat yourself harder. Make it unpleasant and painful. You know, I gather psychiatrists these days tend to use something called 'aversion therapy.' If somebody is an alcoholic, for example, they feed him a drug with alcohol that will make him ill."

"So that he associates the pain with the addiction?" I asked thoughtfully. "If I beat myself harder, then, it'll make the discipline more effective."

Mother nodded. "That's the idea. And not just the discipline. Fasting helps too. You'll be fasting once a month from now on, keeping the bodily appetite low. And all our rules of religious modesty, custody of the eyes especially, and making yourself eat things you don't like. All these things will keep the bodily urges down, weaken them, bring them right under your control."

I breathed deeply. It seemed like a massive undertaking.

"It's a full-time job, Mother."

"Yes, but it's all for one end. To let God take you over wholly. Let Him possess you."

I thought of the crucifix in the dormitory and how coldly separate it had seemed. "It's so hard to feel God, though. So often it feels in prayer as though He's abandoned me. I *know* He hasn't, but it's hard to keep on sometimes, feeling so empty."

Mother picked up the small crucifix lying on her desk. "He experienced that too. Do you remember? He cried out, 'My God! My God! Why hast Thou forsaken me?' "

"And then He died."

"Yes. Then He died." She looked at me appraisingly for a moment and then nodded, as if satisfied. "You are beginning to die. It's a slow process, you'll be at it all your life. But you're beginning."

One evening I was sitting in the Noviceship garden, looking out over the peaceful countryside. I was sewing my profession habit. I could hardly believe that I had come to the end of my noviceship. In only six weeks' time I would kneel at the altar and make vows of poverty, chastity and obedience. Sometimes when I thought of it I quailed inwardly: it wasn't that I was afraid of the commitment or was worried that I was doing the wrong thing. Far from it: I was overwhelmed with gratitude to have been admitted to profession. What worried me was whether I was really ready. So often we had been told that our response to the intensive training of the novice-ship would condition the whole of our religious lives. I knew how far I fell short of the ideal.

I was sitting on a bench near the Postulantship. Inside I could hear energetic housework going on: the clatter of chairs and the rhythmic swish of the heavy floor polisher. Mother Albert and the first years were preparing the Postulantship for the new postulants who would be arriving in September. I thought back to my own postulantship. It had seemed so simple then. I smiled wryly to myself. If I kept the rules, I'd thought, I couldn't fail—it would be steady progress toward God. I knew better now. Keeping the rules was not just a matter of external observance: it meant endlessly struggling with myself to hold nothing back from God. Novices spent the last eight weeks of their noviceship in special seclusion. It was like going back to the first year again: once more we were confined to the Noviceship; we didn't study but spent the time preparing ourselves for the great step. After profession we would go immediately to London to continue our training in the Scholasti-cate. It would be so odd to leave Tripton after these last three years.

Suddenly I heard a footfall on the grass behind me. I looked round quickly and saw Mother Walter coming toward me. She sig-naled to me not to get up and came down to sit beside me. What could she want? Her face was preoccupied and serious.

"Sister, your parents came this afternoon. They'd been to visit friends in Bedfordshire and had to pass through Tripton. So they dropped in." She smiled as though I'd be delighted to hear the news. My heart sank. I knew just what was coming. "They asked permission to see you, but of course I couldn't let them do that. Not during your last eight weeks, when you are all in strict seclusion."

"Of course not, Mother," I said, with as much serenity as I could muster. I understood about the last eight weeks. But how could they? I could imagine only too well how the conversation would have gone. They would have stood nervously in the parlor.

"Do you think they'll let us see her?"

"Don't see why not." My father would have been dubious at first but would rapidly have gained confidence in his rights. "Dammit, we practically had to pass the front gate. It'd be bloody inhuman if they didn't!"

And my mother would pick up the tone, defiance creeping into her speech: "It seems fair enough. We are her parents, for God's sake! We've given her up very nicely, not made any fuss. They've got her now, permanently. The least they can do is let us see her for half an hour!"

But then Mother Walter would have come in, grasping their hands with a radiant smile: "How lovely to see you! What a lovely surprise!" She would have asked questions about their journey, about Lindsey, as though they had dropped in for a chat with her, knowing full well what they really wanted. Finally they would have asked to see me for half an hour, for fifteen minutes. There would have been a pause and then: "I'm sorry." A polite but firm refusal.

I looked back at Mother Walter, searching her face for some indication of how they had felt. She smiled back at me cheerfully.

"They quite understood, bless them! I explained that you mustn't be distracted at this time or distrubed in any way. After all, they saw you five months ago," she laughed roguishly in an attempt to lighten the moment. "No. They realized that it wasn't a good idea."

Did they? I knew them too well to believe that. "Rules are rules," Mother Walter would have smiled. And my mother would have bitterly reflected that Mother Walter was a walking rule book, dead to all human feeling. And why would it "disturb" me to see my own family? she would have asked angrily. Was my vocation such a fragile thing that it was endangered by a few minutes' conversation with my parents? And my father, unable to hide his disappointment, would have stared solemnly at the carpet, not wishing to witness the pain in my mother's eyes.

I nodded. "Yes, Mother. I'm sure they understand," I said calmly.

Mother Walter sighed happily. "You have wonderful parents, Sister. God will bless your little family for their sacrifice."

I hoped so. Yes, of course He would. But somehow that didn't make the prospect of their present pain any easier to bear.

Mother got up to go. "They sent you their love, Sister."

"Thank you, Mother." I turned back to my sewing, heavy with the thought of my parents driving sadly home. Without me.

It was 25 June 1965. The morning of the profession. There were four novices being professed that morning. Only four left of the ten apprehensive postulants who had had tea in the big parlor on that September day three years ago. Gradually the other six had dropped away, silently disappearing back into a world that now seemed unreal. I felt exhilarated to be one of the survivors, to have seen the whole thing through. But it was also humbling to think that God had chosen me, with all my faults, and not the others.

Each of us novices had been through an entirely separate experience in the noviceship. I could see the change in Sister Griselda. Her honest, plain Irish face was more serene now than it had been when she was Sister Edna in the postulantship. She moved more quietly, and her endless concentration gave her a puzzled, questing look. Occasionally there would be a flash of the old humor, but she was more thoughtful now, silencing her eccentricities in the nunlike demeanor that now seemed an essential part of her. Sister Carmel's head leaned slightly to one side. She had grown fatter during her three years in England but still walked with her old Nigerian roll; even the rules of modesty had not been able to change that. She too was quieter, absorbed in a spirituality that sometimes made her look drugged, as though the ordinary world hardly existed. She walked forward in the procession like a sleepwalker, on her lips that peculiar secret smile that made her look as though she were hugging a hidden joy, a silent joke that she would never share with anyone else. Sister Jeremy, the youngest novice, seemed unchanged. Her pink and white prettiness, her placid, dreamy eyes looked calmly out onto the world as they had when she was Margaret, the postulant. Perhaps she would always go through life without agonizing, without drama, troubles and reprimands rolling off her, leaving her unscathed. But that was probably presumptuous. Nobody but God and our superiors knew about the trials and testing each one of us had undergone in the noviceship in preparation for this day.

Much of the ceremony was the same as for the clothing: the long procession of nuns headed by the crucifix, the joyful "Magnificat," the solemn interrogations at the foot of the altar. But there were also important differences. No parents filled the chapel. They had already made the renunciation and given their daughters to God. They were not invited today. The profession was a private ceremony for the Order only. And this time there were no brides, just four novices, walking one by one up the aisle to lay their lives on the altar. That is why the ceremony took place in the morning, during solemn sung Mass. As Christ's sacrifice was reenacted sacramentally during the Mass, the novices made their vows, joining their sacrifice to His.

The vows came during the Communion. The priest stood before each novice, holding up the small white Communion wafer as she read the vow formula.

"I vow to Thy Divine Majesty poverty, chastity, and obedience," the threefold sacrifice of the body and the mind. "I humbly beseech therefore," each completed the oath, "that as Thou hast been pleased to accept this sacrifice in the odor of sweetness, and as Thou hast been pleased to give me the grace and desire to offer it, so Thou wilt enable me to fulfill the sacrifice." And, as a token of Divine assistance, at the end the priest laid the host on her tongue, giving God to her just as she had given herself, body and soul, to Him.

Then came the solemn betrothal. Each novice knelt in the sanctuary at the priest's feet and her white novice's veil was exchanged for the long black veil of the professed nun. Then she said, "He has placed a seal upon my forehead that I may admit no other lover but Himself." It was a renunciation of all earthly love, all ordinary satisfaction and fulfillment. And then the small gold crucifix ring, which had been laid beside the tabernacle for the last month, close to God as the young nun will be all her life, was placed on the third finger of her right hand, and each novice spoke this time not of what she was giving up but joyfully of what she was receiving.

"I am the bride of Him whom the angels serve, at whose beauty the sun and moon stand amazed. My Lord Jesus Christ has led me into the bridal chamber. As a bride He has adorned me with a crown." For that no sacrifice was too great.

Finally the choir began to sing the Litany of the Saints, the great devotional prayer of the Jesuits, calling upon all the saints in Heaven for aid in the immense undertaking. Two novices walked slowly up the aisle from the back of the church, carrying between them a heavy funeral pall, the same one that was laid over a nun's coffin when she died. They reached the top of the church, bowed low to the altar, and then began slowly to unfold the heavy black material, holding it up so that gradually an immense black screen appeared, shutting the four newly professed nuns off from the rest of the congregation.

Then, behind the shadow of the pall, with a swift movement, the new professed prostrated themselves, lying face downward on the ground, their arms flung out in the form of a cross. Nailing themselves with Christ to the sacrifice of their lives.

Slowly the pall was laid down over the prostrate bodies, covering them entirely, shutting them into the death they had voluntarily embraced. They were entirely buried, dead to the world, just as they would be when their coffins were laid to rest in the cemetery and were covered with the thick black earth. "You are dead," wrote St. Paul, "and your lives are hidden with Christ in God." The young nuns had disappeared completely, their own individuality blotted out by the heavy black material, indistinguishable one from another.

And now Mother Walter walked up the aisle and knelt beside the pall, offering her novices to God. Her work was over. She had trained each one in the personal way of death God had appointed for her. Each of them now was responsible for completing the symbolism of today's ceremony and making her life a daily dying, which the final death of her body would complete.

The Litany flowed on for a further twenty minutes or more, while the young nuns lay buried.

Lying under the pall, my hands clenched tightly, my eyes shut against the hot, musty darkness, I was doing the hardest praying of my life. It did indeed feel like burial. I could hear the choir, but only far off, as though the sounds came from another world. I knew that death was not accomplished in one quick ceremony. *Help me to die,* I prayed. From today I would be dead to the world. There could be no looking back now. I had to die, so God could raise me up.

As if in answer to my prayer, the pall was suddenly lifted and the daylight hit me, dazzling in its brilliance. I blinked hard, dazed, as I rose to my feet, reborn. Joy filled me as I looked at the world anew, and with deep thankfulness I joined with the choir in the "Te Deum."

9 · THE SCHOLASTICATE
1965-1967

Only a day later I found myself in a different world. Deafened by the din, I stumbled through the maze of the London Underground. Everywhere people seemed to be pushing. They elbowed their way aggressively to the ticket machines, swarming in untidy, thrusting crowds. No one stood back to let others go first with the self-effacement that I had grown so used to. People swore impatiently as they struggled through the turnstiles. On the escalators I couldn't believe the advertisements—bodies, nearly naked, displaying breasts and legs; pictures of long cool drinks whose brand names I had quite forgotten, speaking of pleasure and frank sensuality. And all around people's faces were set in hard, strained masks. They glanced uneasily at me as my veil billowed into their faces, and I picked my long skirts up round my ankles to stop them from getting sucked into the machinery. No, I thought, this is not my world. I don't belong here anymore. And then eerily in the long echoing passage I heard music pounding. I glanced at the faces of the passersby, who didn't seem at all concerned or surprised. Then I saw him, the ragged guitarist with a beard, long hair—down to his shoulders!—and tattered jeans. With his head thrown back, lost in his music, he ignored the coins that were being flung carelessly into his empty guitar case. He was the first man I had really looked at for three years. What an extraordinary creature! As I hurried past I heard the words of the strange song he was singing: "We shall overcome."

After this the Scholasticate seemed a haven of peace and so familiar. The house, with its four floors and thirty rooms, was like a doll's house after the vast bulk of Tripton: the little dormitories, with only three or four beds to a room, the tiny refectory that just squeezed in the fifteen scholastics and that overlooked a little Kensington garden with a mulberry tree at the bottom. And how odd to have next-door neighbors! In identical houses. A princess lived on one side, I was told, and on the other side was an embassy. I wondered what they thought of us.

I tapped on Mother Bianca's door. We were going in one by one to meet the Mistress of the scholastics. I tried to remember what I had been told about her. She was, I knew, very ill indeed and had only just left the hospital. She was also deaf. Thirty years ago when she'd been in her late twenties she'd lost her hearing and had had to retire from teaching. Three years ago she had been appointed Mistress of Scholastics, but most of the intervening time she'd spent as Clothing Mistress at Tripton, repairing sheets and darning lavatory cloths. What a terrible life, I thought. Would God ask such a sacrifice of me? When Sister Carmel left the room, I knocked at the door for my interview.

"Come in!" the voice was old and crackly; it sounded as though it were disconnected and hadn't been part of the speaker for a long time. I entered the room and looked nervously at the desk.

Mother Bianca looked up and smiled, and I found myself smiling back with genuine pleasure. I was looking at one of the most serene faces I had ever seen in my life. It was a thin face; the cheeks were shrunken, or rather sucked in as though poised in a continual gasp of pain. There was pain too in the lines around the eyes and the mouth. But the eyes themselves were entirely free of strain— they radiated kindness and warmth, which was odd because they were such a pale, cold blue. And the smile was kind too. The kindness came as a shock after the years of austerity at Tripton.

I knelt at her feet, unable to take my eyes off her. "Sister Martha," she said. It was not a question. It was an acceptance of me. All that I was.

"Yes, Reverend Mother," I replied, mouthing the words clearly, so that she could read my lips.

"Sit down, Sister." As I did so I noticed a spasm of pain pass through her body. She shifted slightly in her chair, breathing hard, trying to settle herself. I looked at her anxiously, but her smile never faltered. It was not a strained smile. I didn't feel crushed by the suffering that filled the room, because it was totally accepted by her. There was no struggle, no outrage. I sat back in my chair and relaxed.

"Well, Sister," she began, "you know what the Scholasticate is for, don't you?"

"Yes, Reverend Mother. I'm here for two years to continue my spiritual training and begin to train professionally for the work of the Order."

"Good," the eyes approved me. "A clear answer and I can follow your lips, too. Don't shout at me, that just muddles the sound of my machine." She pulled out her deaf-aid, which crackled and spluttered alarmingly. "Just use your lips as well as possible. I hope you've got good eyes, Sister?"

"Yes," I said, bewildered.

"Good, because if you ever go deaf you'll need them to lip-read." I blushed at the matter-of-fact tone in which she spoke of this possible disaster. "And I hope you rub your hair bone dry after you've washed it."

"Well, no, Reverend Mother. There isn't time usually. You know, we start our bath at nine-fifteen each week and lights go out at ten."

"Of course, but you must *not* go to bed with wet hair. Sit up in bed and keep on drying it. I went deaf because of that."

I blinked at her. The quirky tone of the conversation with its free and easy moves delighted me but surprised me too. She was talking to me about herself. She was personally involved in the conversation, which didn't follow the usual lines of well-planned admonition and impersonal rebuke I had grown accustomed to hearing from my superiors. But how terrible to think that she had gone deaf so needlessly! I made a firm resolution on the spot to rub my hair bone dry in the darkness of the dormitory before lying down to sleep, however tired I was.

She smiled again, that rare, transfiguring smile that made me feel happy and secure. "Well, Sister," she said, "I expect you want to know what the Order plans to do with you?"

I nodded, hardly daring to breathe. I was now about to receive a life sentence. The day before, when I'd made my vows, I had promised absolute obedience. The Order could throw me into any job at all, however uncongenial, and that would be God's will for me, to be endured to my dying day. I looked at Mother Bianca. Thirty years of sorting out the laundry despite her university degree clearly had not left her bitter and twisted. She seemed joyfully accepting. Would I respond so faithfully?

"Yes, Reverend Mother," I said at last.

"You're going to go to Carter's, Sister. That's the crammer that Sister Jocasta is going to at the moment. You're going to study English there." I breathed a sigh of relief and joy. Literature again! How good God was to me! "And we're hoping to get you into Oxford."

I gasped. Oxford! I hadn't read a single book or poem for three whole years. However would I measure up to the intellectual demands of Oxford? It seemed like an impossible dream. I'd never do it, but I knew that I'd have to try. And this time it wouldn't affect just me, my success or failure. The Order had a huge stake in it. The responsibility to do well sank heavily into me. I forced myself to listen to what Mother was saying.

"Then, after you've got your degree, you'll be qualified to teach in one of our schools. Besides English, of course, you'll be carrying on with the diploma in theology, scripture, and church history. Your examination results were very nice last summer, Sister. Only another two years before you've finished that. And then you'll be learning to cook."

I gaped at her. "Cook, Reverend Mother?"

"Yes. The Order has decided that all the choir nuns have to learn to cook. We're not getting as many lay sisters as we used to and it may prove necessary in the future. So every Wednesday you'll be the housekeeper, spending the whole day in the kitchen and cooking all the meals for the community."

I flinched. I hardly knew how to boil an egg, let alone cook full meals for twenty-five people.

"Then, I think I'll teach you logic. After the chapter of faults on Friday evenings, by yourself. I think you'll find that helpful in your studies. I tried teaching Sister Jocasta last year but she couldn't follow it. I think, yes," her eyes appraised me shrewdly, "I think you'd take to it quite well."

I watched as the color suddenly drained from her face. Her lips turned slightly blue and she arched her neck backward, her mouth opening slightly, and a strange clicking noise came from her throat.

"Are you all right, Reverend Mother?" I asked, terrified.

She swallowed, and I watched the Adam's apple move convulsively in her throat; then she smiled again at me.

"It's my back, Sister," she said simply. "Could you get that cushion and put it behind me?" I did so, watching her lean cautiously against it, with every movement defending herself against pain.

"Is there anything else I can do?"

"No, Sister," she shook her head. "I've got pills but they make me too sleepy. I just feel diabolical today."

"I'm so sorry." I felt helpless, but not dwarfed by her bravery. There was no martyred act, just serene resignation. What courage, I thought. And something else, too, that took me a moment to lay my finger on. Yes, my superior was admitting to pain and weakness. She was not complaining, just letting me in on it. We were talking to one another directly, not taking refuge in impersonality.

"Sister." She fumbled among her papers and handed me a list. "Here's the reading list Carter's have sent you." I glanced at it and went dizzy with joy: Jane Austen, Keats, Wordsworth, George Eliot. I felt like a starving person about to sample a banquet. Struggling hard, I tried to still my joy. I shouldn't take pleasure in this. I recalled Mother Walter's strictures about intellectual pride. I fought my way hopelessly toward indifference.

"Thank you, Reverend Mother," I said, trying to sound calm as I knelt down to receive her blessing.

"Enjoy it," she said. What? I looked up at her, astounded.

Her eyes twinkled. "You'd better get started right away. God bless you, Sister," and a great peace filled me as I felt her making the sign of the cross on my forehead. Who could have stripped herself of herself so thoroughly as Mother Bianca? But she seemed to be telling me that despite this, humanity and warmth were possible in the religious life.

"I hope you'll feel better, Reverend Mother."

She laughed in a tone of genuinely delighted amusement as she gestured that I should leave the room. "Go in peace, Sister."

I did. The room had seemed holy somehow. But there was more than peace. There was hope, too, in my heart.

Besides our studies and our cookery, it was also deemed advisable that, very occasionally, we watch news shows on television. It would give us some indication of what was happening in the world that we would soon be working in. New names hit me. Vietnam, for example. I gazed horrified at the carnage that had been going on during these last years that I had known nothing about. There were other things. Youth seemed suddenly to have grown very important. When I left the world in 1962 we had been miniature adults, disregarded under the parental thumb. Watching massed rallies on the television screen, I recognized the song the boy had been singing in the Underground: "We shall overcome." Were young people planning to take over the world? Technically I myself was young. I wasn't yet twenty-one, but as a young professed I was absolutely insignificant in the Order. I stared at the long-haired youths and shockingly miniskirted girls. They were of my generation, but I felt as though I were watching creatures from another planet.

One night there was a program on cancer. As I heard the inexorable statistics and saw the graphs, listened to the interviews with the wasted sufferers, I felt a lump rise in my throat. The room was very still. None of us dared to look at one another. The word had never been spoken in connection with Mother Bianca, but we knew, somehow. *She shouldn't be here, watching this with us,* I felt myself crying inwardly. *How can she bear it?* Hardly daring to breathe, I stared hypnotized at the screen. I could feel that all our eyes were glued there, drawn as by a magnet. *Take refuge in impersonal fact. Don't exchange glances. Otherwise it will be worse for Mother.*

At length I could bear it no longer. I stole a sidelong glance at her. The convent cat, Tess, had jumped onto her knee and was purring loudly. Mother smiled down at her, stroked her lovingly, and then turned her gaze back to the screen. The strained, hot-eyed intensity that I could see in everybody else's stare was entirely absent from her face. Calmly, her eyes shrewdly intelligent, she watched, the receiver of the deaf-aid in her hand turned to the television to catch every word. The other hand stroked Tess. A smile of interest and calm detachment played over her face.

Mother Bianca's courage only underlined my own sense of inadequacy over my own trifling ills. Food was becoming abhorrent to me and now I found that I was vomiting nearly every night, cheese or no cheese. Working in the kitchen didn't help. I grew to dread Wednesdays. The day started at six-thirty in the morning when I left my sisters meditating peacefully in the little chapel and began to peel the potatoes. Mountains of them. The morning was entirely taken up with preparing dinner—sausages, very often, with waterlogged cabbage, followed by rice pudding made with powdered milk and stewed in the double boiler. The afternoon was spent on my hands and knees laboring over the kitchen floor, which was composed of white vinyl tiles that had to be scrubbed—all fifty square feet of them—with scouring pads to erase the muck of the morning and the scars of my rubber soles, which left black gashes everywhere. Then, having reheated the tea left over from breakfast —now a bright purple hue—I began supper. One afternoon I spent two hours trying to mince warm, red liver to serve on toast. The slimy stuff remained bleeding but intact despite my sorties with a blunt knife, leaving me nauseated, my hands dyed red and reeking with the smell.

My usually disastrous efforts were supervised by Mother Constantia, a freckled Irish nun with an enormous, rather vacant face. She wrote out the menus and instructions and periodically appeared in the kitchen to gaze lugubriously over the lumpy custard or the watery stew. "Reverend Mother just won't be able to eat that marmalade pudding, Sister. Just won't be able to touch it!" The community too learned to dread Wednesdays. It was even more humiliating when Mother Constantia tried to mask my errors with encouragement. "Sister," she drawled to me one day, "your brawns were beautiful: I loved the way you set those hard-boiled eggs across the top. There was only one thing"—I looked at her sardonically— "a mere detail of course, quite unimportant. They had a very peculiar taste."

I found myself thinking critically of her intelligence sometimes. Reading was again sharpening my wits. But usually nausea coupled with physical exhaustion reduced me to a mindless and obedient robot. That's the point of it, I told myself. My studies were going well, but Wednesdays always brought home to me my basic uselessness. There was no chance for intellectual pride to go unchecked. What was the mind when I saw my sisters charitably chewing my burnt offerings with patient smiles of forebearance?

One evening after a particularly disastrous dinner, Mother

Constantia appeared as a freckled reproachful ghost in the kitchen. "Sister! After today's terrible dinner we'll cancel the supper menu." She smiled, her thick lips screaming forgiveness and despair at my efforts. "We'll just have soup and cheese. And Sister, I want to ask one thing of you. Just one thing. It isn't much to ask—God knows —after what you put the community through at dinnertime." Smitten with remorse, my head bursting after two hours of bending over the floor with my scouring pad, I waited in suspense. "I want those soup plates hot, Sister. Scalding hot. Please," she pleaded, "surely you can do that for the community, Sister."

Right, I thought, as I melted the bulk-bought powdered soup in a saucepan. I turned the oven up to its highest pitch and threw the soup bowls in. This was what God was going to ask of me tonight. Fidelity in little things. I cut up the plastic cheese into neat squares and, as directed, for dessert I hacked at the rock-hard dates, peeling oblongs of sticky, solid dried fruit, wondering how long it had been since they had seen a palm tree.

Flushed with a sense of success, I heard the gong ring for supper at seven-thirty. For once I was ready. There had been days when the community had sat in silence in the refectory while I frantically dished up the vegetables. Sister Jocasta bustled in in her white serving apron. Trying to erase my smug smile I waved at the soup tureens as I climbed out of the stifling white nylon overall. "Where are the soup bowls?" she hissed.

"In the oven," I said as I scrubbed at my hands, trying to eliminate the dirt of this morning's potatoes. I breathed a sigh of relief. They really should be hot by now. At least I'd done that for God today.

Sister Jocasta stood at the oven open-mouthed. "Sister!" she breathed. "Whatever is it?"

I peered into the oven. There was a pile of ten china soup bowls. But on top of that flowed a strange meringuelike concoction, monstrous and deformed. Sister scrabbled in the oven and carried it out. Aghast, we stared at each other. Then Sister Jocasta collapsed. Weeping with laughter she clung to the kitchen table. "God help you, Sister," she gasped. "You'll be slaughtered!"

Half the soup bowls were plastic.

A few nights later I went up to Mother Bianca's room for my logic lesson. I enjoyed these, delighting in the cut and thrust of her mind, which seemed unclouded by pain and sickness. However had she endured all those years sorting out the laundry? Surely she must have felt frustrated sometimes. How was it that her mind had never gotten swamped by those soft mounds of underclothes? But then one look at her face gave me the answers. She had joyfully accepted God's will. And in being prepared to lose herself completely, she had found herself. She was the most individual of the nuns I had yet come across in the Order. It was an inspiring example.

Tonight, however, as I pulled the chair round so that I could sit beside her at the desk, Mother Bianca stopped me. "Sister," she said, her odd crackly voice sounding concerned, "you're getting very thin."

I stood before her, blushing awkwardly. "Lift up your cape," she said, "and let me see. Your habit's far too loose. Can't you pull the waiststrings any tighter?"

I pulled up the long, prim cape to reveal the habit hanging slackly round my waist. She plucked at it and looked up at me, her kind eyes sharp with anxiety.

"No, Reverend Mother," I said flatly. "The strings are as tightly drawn as they'll go."

"But that habit was made only four months ago! Have you lost all that weight so quickly?"

I nodded numbly. I had noticed my dramatic loss of weight and couldn't understand it. After all, I was eating everything I had to: two helpings of every meal, tea, and elevenses. The trouble was I couldn't keep it down. The mere sight of food sometimes sickened me. Today was Friday—two days since my cooking day—but I could still smell the onions on my hands and in my clothes, and the smell nauseated me.

"Sit down," Mother Bianca patted the chair next to her. "You look very pale, too, Sister. Have you been sick at all?"

"Yes, Reverend Mother."

"How often?" She sounded cross but I knew somehow that she wasn't angry like Mother Walter. Just worried.

"About four times this week."

"Why ever didn't you tell me?" She brought her fist down on

the table sharply. Her voice was anguished. I looked at the lines of pain on her face, at the tense back. I looked down at the desk and at the floor, which were both covered with soft, white drifts of her skin, which she shed daily so that her room had to be swept twice a day. She was dying inch by inch. How could I have bothered her with my silly little gastric troubles? Anyway, I knew what was the matter with me.

"I think it's just weakness of will, Reverend Mother," I said. "That's what Mother Walter always said it was."

She looked thoughtful. "You are overanxious, Sister," she replied slowly. "There's all that fainting. You must try to get the better of all your nerves and worries."

Who better to tell me? But there was no condemnation in her voice. Just a gentle, firm admonition.

"Yes, I know, Reverend Mother. I will try."

She smiled up at me suddenly, that rare smile that made you forget what she was suffering, just for a second. *Don't worry about me,* I said to her silently. *Keep yourself well.*

"But this sickness is quite a different matter," she went on. "You might have a stomach ulcer, Sister, and that's an awful thing." I looked at her, astonished. Nobody had ever suggested before that I might actually be ill. Besides, I wasn't, not ill like she was, anyway. "But you're much too young for that. You're only just twenty-one. I want you to go and see a consultant. If it is nerves, then we'll know where we are. Is there anything that you know always makes you sick?"

"Cheese," I said promptly, "and too many milky things."

"Then you mustn't eat them!" she said, bewildered. "Why have you been?"

"Mother Walter—" I began.

"Yes," she spoke shortly, sighed, and shook her head. "Well, the noviceship's over now, Sister. I'll speak to Mother Constantia and when we have cheese, you're to have a boiled egg. Mind you, another superior may make you go back to eating everything. But you don't eat any more cheese as long as I'm your superior."

I was stunned. No more of those terrible struggles to force the food down my throat. I could scarcely believe it. Mother Bianca matter-of-factly opened the logic book. "Now, where have we got to?" she said.

As I bent over the exercise with her she glanced at me again. "Your collar's chipped," she said critically.

"I know." Those stiff plastic collars were endlessly breaking and cracking on me. "I must have a funny-shaped throat."

"Have you asked Mother Constantia for another one?"

"Yes, but she said I broke too many collars and that I'd have to make do with this one." I hadn't queried that decision. It was a matter of Holy Poverty. If I was careless, I had to suffer. A poor nun had no right to automatic restoration of property.

Mother Bianca sighed again, this time with exasperation. "Mother Constantia gets far too upset about these things," she said. "Wait a minute." She got up and rummaged in her cupboard. "There," she said. "Take these."

She held toward me about five or six collars. I stared at this unprecedented wealth. "Reverend Mother, I can't take all your collars," I protested. "You won't have any left for yourself!"

She tapped my hand lightly with her pencil and smiled at me again. A smile of pure amusement. "Sister," she said quietly, still smiling. "I'm not going to need any more collars. Am I?"

She held my gaze in those calm, kind eyes. *Don't die,* I wanted to say. *I need you too much.* But that was unworthy.

There was a long silence and I found myself smiling at her. "No, Reverend Mother."

It was odd lying under the thin sheet on the consulting bed of the hospital. When the doctor lifted the sheet I blushed uncomfortably, turning my face to the wall with shame.

"Does it hurt here? Or here?" he was saying. "Try to relax. I can't examine you, Sister, while you're so tense." I took a deep breath and tried to loosen my muscles against the prodding intrusive fingers, but I felt my breath stick in my throat. It was the shock —tender, probing hands against my vulnerable flesh. Flesh that hadn't been touched for years.

The doctor had kind eyes. I tried to look at them hard to take my mind off my own nakedness while he questioned me about my bowels, my eating habits, my sickness. He watched me shrewdly as I answered, nodding slightly.

Suddenly he sprang. "Are you happy, Sister, in this—er—

setup?" he asked, embarrassed in his turn, not knowing how to phrase his question.

"Oh *yes,* Doctor," I said.

"Quite sure?"

"Of course." He sighed and covered me up again with the sheet.

"Because I don't think there's anything physically the matter with you. There's no trace of an ulcer. I've taken tests but I don't think we'll find anything wrong."

My heart sank. I should have been pleased, but a physical illness would have been so simple. Instead it was my wretched emotions again. And try as I would, I couldn't control those. How could I stop myself being sick?

"It's nerves then, is it?" I asked, my voice dead and tired.

"Yes, probably. You say you eat regularly, that in fact you have to eat a certain amount every day." He paused. "Do you find that difficult?"

I explained about the cheese and the vomiting during the last three years and saw him press his lips together impatiently. *Poor man, he can't really understand why I had to do that,* I thought.

"But now you don't have to eat dairy products anymore. Is that right?"

"Not under my present superior. But another might change that again."

"Do you find food rather disgusting at the moment, whatever it is?"

"A bit," I said brightly, trying to be brave and positive.

He shook his head. "That's why I'm asking you if you're happy. It may be that this kind of life isn't for you." He looked uncomfortable. A bit out of his depth.

"No, Doctor, it's not the life. It's me."

As I got dressed I couldn't help overhearing Dr. Saunders' conversation with Mother Constantia through the thin hardboard partition. I heard him sitting down at his desk and sighing. He sounded tired and discouraged. Then he cleared his throat self-consciously.

"Are you Sister Armstrong's—er—superior?" he asked.

"Oh, no, Doctor. No. Reverend Mother wasn't well enough to come. Is there anything wrong with Sister Martha?"

"Nothing physical, as far as I can see."

"Thank God," Mother Constantia exhaled devoutly. I could just imagine her rolling her eyes piously heavenward. There was a pause and then she continued, tartly. "So why is she being sick?"

"Probably for nervous reasons." Again I felt the depression sink right through me like a heavy weight, and now it was mingled with contempt. How I despised myself! Nerves! I sounded like a Victorian miss with the vapours. But what could I do about it? I reached out for my veil and became aware that Dr. Saunders was still speaking.

"But I think," he was saying firmly, "that you ought to watch her carefully. She's underweight. Not gravely so at present, but I believe the weight loss has been rapid and marked." He paused interrogatively. There was a noncommittal noise of assent from Mother Constantia.

"I suspect," the doctor went on, "that her eating habits of the last few years have given her a neurotic distaste for food. I think you should watch her carefully; you might have an incipient case of anorexia on your hands."

Whatever was that? I looked up from my dressing sharply. Mother Constantia sounded as bewildered as I was.

"Anorexia?"

"*Anorexia nervosa.*" Dr. Saunders sounded impatient. "An inability to eat resulting in drastic loss of weight."

"Oh, no, Doctor." Mother Constantia sounded amused in a superior kind of way. "That's not possible. Sister eats very well. She has to under Holy Obedience. And," she added defensively, "we give her a good healthy diet."

"I'm sure you do, Sister," Dr. Saunders said politely, but the irritation he felt was barely concealed. "But anorexia isn't only caused by starvation. She's already finding trouble keeping her food down. I understand that some of the regulations have been waived in her case? Good. Well, that should help. Because if she goes on with this vomiting I think you should get her looked at again."

"You mean," Mother Constantia said after a puzzled pause, "it's just her nerves."

I sighed as I pulled on my stockings. That's what it came back to, really. Nerves. And all this talk about anor . . . anor—what was it?—couldn't disguise the fact. There was one cure only, as far as I could see. I'd have to strengthen my will. It was because my will was flabby, I thought with disgust, that all this fuss was happening. The doctor couldn't be expected to understand the self-discipline that was essential for every religious. I thrust my feet into my shoes, furious with myself.

"Is she nervous?" Dr. Saunders was asking. "Are there any other neurotic symptoms?" I blushed, shamed at hearing my feebleness discussed like that.

"She faints quite often, Doctor."

"Really? Tell me about that."

Oh no! I thought. *Couldn't we all just go home and forget about it?* This doctor was here to look after people who were really ill, not waste his time with a hypochondriac like me.

"There isn't much to tell. It's just hysterics. She falls flat on the floor. She's very sorry afterward."

"Has she seen a neurologist?"

This was ridiculous. I pulled the laces of my shoes into a tight double knot and stood up, my face burning with embarrassment. The doctor was being very kind but he didn't understand. I could hear in his voice that he thought the religious life was unnatural and unhealthy. But that was a worldly view. The fault was me.

"I'm sure there's no need," Mother Constantia was saying blandly as I went back into the consulting room. "It's just her nerves."

Dr. Saunders looked at me. His eyes were troubled and he rubbed his hand over his forehead as though he wanted to scrub something away. He took a breath as if to speak and then looked at Mother Constantia again. He sighed, glancing up at the clock, and shook himself.

"Well. Yes. Yes. I see." He sounded depressed. "That will be all. I'll be writing to your own doctor." He pulled a sheaf of papers from the file in front of him and didn't look at us again as we left the room.

Under the merciful dispensation from cheese, the vomiting became less frequent and I began to gain weight again. But still I was left with that nagging disgust with my rebellious body. Other aspects of the Scholasticate I enjoyed. Work was going well at the crammers and I was getting good reports. They thought I had a good chance of getting into Oxford. Reading again was sheer joy and I was beginning to worry about the pleasure I took in it. Fortunately, though, I had little time to indulge my love for literature with all my theological studies for the diploma. My mind, I noticed, was beginning to work in two quite different ways. With literature I'd start on a train of thought and follow it wherever it led me. This was exciting even though I was sadly aware of how rusty my mind was. Still, that was just part of the sacrifice I had made. What did it matter if my brain was not as good as it might have been? It belonged to God, and anyway that kind of intellectual freedom was dangerous.

I was becoming increasingly aware of this in my theological studies. Here you didn't have the same kind of freedom. When I started to write an essay I knew what conclusion I had to come to in order to remain orthodox. My job here was to juggle facts and material to produce that correct conclusion. This, I recalled, was what Mother Greta had found difficult. But, I told myself firmly, this was the way it had to be. If I let my mind go it would fly away with me and take me away from God, away from true obedience.

This attitude was put to the test in my first experience of teaching. Every Sunday morning Sister Jocasta and I set off with Mother Bianca to teach in a Sunday school in the East End of London. We went armed with a pathetic collection of visual aids to try to anchor the attention of the children. How to bring them to God? It was an unequal struggle. As Easter drew near we decided to have a Paschal meal with the children to bring home to them the reality of the Last Supper. For weeks beforehand we explained the ceremony and they drew pictures of the plagues of Egypt and Paschal lambs. When finally we sat them round with meager scraps of cold roast lamb, our bunches of watercress and salt water, grape juice for wine, and our homemade teethbreaking unleavened bread, the failure was only too apparent. For the children it was just a laugh, a chance for a picnic.

They were a nice bunch of children, and increasingly I grew to respect them in their struggle to survive in terrible conditions. Tough, hard-eyed Cockneys mingled with Indians and West Indians, whole families crowded into a tenement room, but the children were immaculately turned out.

"Hello, Miss," they'd scream as we entered the room.

"You've got to call me Sister," I'd have to protest each week, "not Miss."

"Sorry, Miss!—I mean Sister!" They'd shrill delightedly, darting away to rampage around the room. They quieted instantly, however, as soon as Mother Bianca started reading the prayers. She stood on the little platform in the dusty hall, emaciated, swaying with pain, her voice hoarse and deep. And the prayers she said were the old-fashioned ones she'd learned herself as a child, to "Little Jesus meek and mild" and to guardian angels. I knew from my studies that angels had been exploded theologically. But trendy theology and trendy prayers didn't seem to count here. Nothing could have seemed less relevant to the children's lives, yet they were won by Mother Bianca herself.

I was trying to prepare a class of seven-year-olds for Confession and was getting worried about it. My worries came to a head one Sunday when Veronica, a flaxen-haired, angelic child, struggled through a "practice" Confession with me as the "pretend" priest.

"I've been naughty, Miss—I mean Sister—I mean Father," she paused, bewildered. I couldn't blame her.

"In what way, Veronica?"

"Well, I tickled my little sister, Miss, and I stuck me tongue out at me dad when he came home late from the boozer."

I bet you did, I thought wearily. I could see it all. The drunk father, the harassed mother, the children frightened out of sleep in the close, hot little room.

"But Veronica," I tried to explain, "those aren't really *sins.*" *Not sins at all,* I added to myself firmly. "When you go to Confession you've *got* to have at least one *proper* sin to confess. Have you told any lies, for instance, or stolen money, or anything . . . " I petered off lamely in the face of her obvious bewilderment. Even if she had done any of those things, I wondered, would God really be sitting up there counting them as sins when she was living like that? It was a disquieting thought.

"What's a lie, Miss?"

What was the church asking me to do? Here I was, pumping these children with the Catholic mechanisms of guilt that would probably haunt them all their lives! Was that what the love of God was all about? I was startled by the violence of my anger. Where had

198

that criticism welled up from? A year ago I couldn't have had an idea like that. Did it mean that I was intellectually proud? Or—and this was a staggering thought—*was I right?*

There was one way of finding out. At the end of the lesson I went in search of the parish priest. "Father," I asked, "do we have to put them through Confession yet? They're not ready. They've no idea what it's all about!"

Father Flannigan looked back at me, a mulish expression filling his bleary, red-rimmed eyes. His cassock was shiny and stained all down the front. And there was an unmistakable smell of whisky. The hall of the presbytery where we were standing was covered in dark green paint and smelled sour and uncared for.

"Sister," he said heavily, "I don't care what trendy nonsense you're learning these days in your theology. I want those kids *done*. Done, Sister! The sacraments work automatically. We know that by faith! I want them done now, so that we've got it out of the way!"

I stared at him, horrified. The voice of the church. Then I took myself in hand. No, it wasn't the church. It was a bad priest talking. My theology, the documents that issued from the Vatican Council backed me up. I had to obey this priest; I knew that, but as I went upstairs to Mass I was feeling rather shaken. I had thought something out; I had argued and maintained my position. I was right. But I'd have to watch myself carefully. I could one day argue and be wrong. *Don't let me be proud,* I prayed, kneeling beside the children in the gallery.

Looking down at the scene in the church I could see why Father Flannigan clung to his belief in the automatic operation of the sacraments. If they didn't work automatically there was no hope for this loft. The church was a converted music hall. We sat round the front row of the circular balcony that hung directly over the altar. On the far side of the circle I could see Kim and Simon hitting each other over the head with hymn books while Sister Jocasta struggled over ten children to try and part them. Julie and Peter had improvised paper darts, which they were shooting down on the heads of the congregation below. Veronica and Nigel were engaged in a wrestling match. By the time I got round the huge circle to them, Danny and Steve, who were kneeling quietly beside me, dazed with boredom, would perpetrate some new atrocity.

Beneath us the Mass droned on. Mechanical, soullessly gabbled

Latin. So different from the prayerful calm of the convent church.

"*Pax vobiscum,*" said Father Flannigan crossly, turning with arms outstretched to the congregation. Then without pausing for breath he shot one hand up, pointing menacingly at the gallery, and yelled: "If you kids don't shut up once and for all, I'm coming up there in person to belt you!"

And then he swung wearily round to exchange the kiss of peace with the pimply acolyte.

On the way home Mother Bianca closed her eyes and leaned back against the seat of the bus, absolutely exhausted. *She shouldn't be coming with us,* I thought; *it's far too much for her.* I watched her emaciated frame shaken and jolted as we ground our way across London. As we neared home Sister Jocasta and I exchanged glances. We were getting near the danger spot. If we traveled another two stops the bus would deposit us at the end of our road. But it would cost another four pence each and Mother Bianca was always adamant. "We can walk!" she said emphatically. "It'll be good for us. Holy Poverty! We can't throw away an extra shilling like that." It might be good for us, but it was too much for her. I looked outside. Time for action.

"Reverend Mother," I began. She opened her eyes and smiled at me, denying her pain, eager to hear what I wanted to say. I started to tell her about my dilemma with the first Confession group. Sister Jocasta joined in and Mother became wholly involved in the conversation.

"Yes, you were right to represent it, Sister. Those children probably aren't ready. But you were also right to obey Father Flannigan instantly." Sister Jocasta and I dared not look at one another. It was working today; sometimes it didn't. "He is our superior, and an act done under obedience to a priest is never wrong, never wasted—oh, dear! We've gone past our stop!"

"Oh, I'm so sorry, Reverend Mother." We struggled to our feet and made our way toward the conductor. Sister Jocasta winked at me and I smiled back.

"Here!" Mother Bianca was waving a shilling at the conductor. "We've gone past our stop. We're so sorry—it was a mistake. You must let us pay you!"

"That's all right, Sister," said the Irish conductor. "I'm a Catholic myself. It's been a pleasure to have you on the bus."

We got out at the top of the road and I tried not to watch Mother's expression of agony as she struggled down to the pavement.

A month or so later our doctor brought a specialist to see Mother Bianca. They were up in her room for an hour. I was housekeeper that day, and when I heard the bell tinkling I ran upstairs, knocked, and entered the room. Mother was sitting calmly at her desk and the doctors were hovering and bidding her goodbye. She smiled at them peacefully.

"Sister," she said, her eyes bright now with pain but so kind. "Would you be good enough to take these letters to the post? And show these gentlemen out."

They followed me downstairs silently. I crossed the hall and opened the door for them, politely and discreetly.

"My God," said the doctor as he crossed the threshold. His voice was awed and shaken. "What is that woman enduring?"

The specialist joined him on the top step. He looked out onto the sunny Kensington street, now full of summer leaves and cheerfulness, and then turned back, listening to the silence of the house.

"If it were you or me," he said at last, "with that pain you'd hear us screaming all the way down the road."

"It's terrible. I can't bear to think of it," I said a few days later to Sister Jocasta. We were walking down Kensington High Street on our way to Confession at Our Lady of Victories. It was Saturday afternoon and recreation time. For the last three days that snatch of conversation had remained in my head. I watched Mother gulping down our unpalatable meals in the refectory, getting up every morning at five-thirty, giving us instructions, giving lessons, taking recreation. Of course I had been aware of her pain. But that two doctors who must have seen hundreds of cancer patients had been shaken by her endurance had terrified me.

Sister Jocasta frowned. "I know," she said quietly after I told her what the doctors had said. "It was the same last year. You know she was in the hospital last summer, nearly a year ago?" I nodded.

At Tripton we'd been praying for her recovery. "Well, I wasn't supposed to know this, but when she came out, the hospital had given her three weeks to live. At the outside."

"So when we arrived at the Scholasticate she should have been dead."

Sister nodded. "And she's kept going for another whole year. Apparently—I heard all this in Blackpool during my rest and change there in the summer—they've given her drugs to try to ease the pain a little. But she won't take them."

"Why not?"

"Because she says that she is responsible for training young nuns, that the drugs make her sleepy, and therefore she can't take them."

We walked on silently. I turned over the heroism in my mind. It was superhuman. And yet that wasn't the word to apply to her. Mother Bianca was very human.

"It's monstrous," Sister said suddenly and her face was suffused with anger, "the way they've treated her! Kept her in that clothing room for thirty years, wasting herself, making her feel a failure. And then, when she first started complaining of the pain, they told her she was imagining it and not to make a fuss! And now! Why on earth have they kept her in office?"

"It's for us," I said at once. "I'll never forget this year. Never."

"All right, it's wonderful for us. An inspiring example for the rest of our lives. But what about *her*?"

We walked on. It was the first condemnation of the convent's ways that I had ever heard in the religious life. And the awful thing was that part of me, that dangerous part that had tackled Father Flannigan, was drawn to her point of view. But I struggled hard against that: it was a worldly view.

"But Sister, she doesn't mind; she never thinks of herself. That's what has made her such a marvelous person. She *is* stripped, emptied—all those things they've been preaching to us as ideals for years."

"Yes, but she's a saint," Sister replied curtly. "I mean that quite literally. And there aren't many saints around, are there? Look, let's face it—how would you or I get on if we'd been treated like that? We're not saints and we'd be wrecks!"

"But, Sister, that's a fault in us: we're not here to seek our own self-fulfillment."

But despite my ardent denials, my thoughts were still churning as we knelt in the queue at Our Lady of Victories. Did Mother Bianca's sanctity really excuse her superiors for the inhumane way they treated her? And could treat me? Did the end really justify the means? But I had to resist this. Now that I was using my brain again I must be careful to keep it in check or it would run away with me, away from my vocation.

But beneath all that there was another worry. Mother Bianca would die soon and I found the thought intolerable. I loved her. I knelt in the large echoing church and faced the fact. I wasn't loving her "in Christ," or with a vague, general diffused affection. I loved her particularly. And where did that leave my detachment? If I loved Mother Bianca in the way that I should, I should be delighted that she was going to God. Death in the Order was a subject for rejoicing. That had startled me at first. On the day that somebody died in the infirmary at Tripton we always had cake for tea and talking at meals. Not to cheer us up but as a celebration. It was logical, really. A nun had spent her whole life preparing for union with God. Of course we should be glad.

One evening we had been eating supper in the refectory at Tripton in silence. Sister Jocasta had been reading aloud a series of somebody's devotional letters. We had known that Mother Maria had been dying all day. The silence meant that she hadn't died yet. One or two terrible stories had filtered through to us via Mother Albert. Apparently Mother Maria was not slipping away peacefully: she was fighting and kicking, trying to get out of bed to escape from her death and from the "Abbess" she could see standing beside her. This had shocked me. That a nun who had spent her life preparing for death should at the last fight so desperately against it seemed horrific. Had she sensed some awful failure or some more frightful void beyond the grave? Mother Albert had shrugged nonchalantly: "It sometimes happens like that. It's just a last trial that God sends." And now as I ate my sardines on toast and listened to Sister Jocasta's clear voice above the clattering cutlery, I wondered whether Mother Maria were still fighting against the inevitable.

Crash! We all jumped and involuntarily turned to the door.

The superior had walked into supper, throwing the door back so that the heavy brass knob banged against the wall. She was smiling from ear to ear. *"Deo gratias!"* she shouted. Thanks be to God—the signal that we could talk. "Mother Maria has gone to God!" The community burst out laughing and supper commenced anew, light-heartedly. But underneath the joyful chattering I had worried whether, after such a death, rejoicing was appropriate.

There had always been death at Tripton. One summer some-one had died every week and we started calling Monday "Funeral Day," growing used to the long procession through the Cloister to the cemetery, to the open grave. We knelt beside the dead body to say good-bye, looking at the waxy skin, at the face, often unrecog-nizable once the spirit had left the body. It was difficult to imagine that the nun was in heaven and to take in Job's words from the dirge that we sang round the coffin every evening: "In this flesh I shall see my God!" remembering that discarded husk.

And now, kneeling in Our Lady of Victories, death hit me in a new way. How could I eat cake at teatime, laugh happily in the refectory when Mother Bianca died? Her death would leave a huge absence in my life. I shouldn't mind. But I did, and an overwhelming desolation filled me.

A few weeks later in the autumn of my second year in the Scholasticate, Mother took to her bed. It was the end. We knew it and crept about the house, listening to the silence coming from her room. They were going to take her to Tripton to die. *Why can't they leave her here?* I thought unhappily. *We can look after her.* I hated the thought of that journey for her—an ambulance, a train, another ambulance. All that shaking and jolting. How would she survive the journey?

On her last evening with us she called us all into her room to say good-bye. We sat round the bed on the floor while Mother was propped up with pillows, even thinner and more gaunt than before. Her face was grey. But her rasping voice was still firm, though sometimes she had to wait to catch her breath.

"As you know, I'm going to Tripton tomorrow. I don't expect I'll live very much longer." How could she be so matter-of-fact? "But Mother Frances is coming to take over here. She's just what you need—younger than me. It'll do you good to have someone young and healthy. She's supposed to take over on the fifteenth of next month and I'm meant to carry on till then." Suddenly she laughed—that cracked laugh of pure amusement—and she spread out her hands, eloquently inviting us to share the joke. "I'll be dead by then!" We tried to smile but I felt the tears welling up instead. *I mustn't cry,* I thought, *not in the face of such courage. I mustn't be weak and self-indulgent. Because it's myself I'm sorry for.* "However," Mother was continuing, smiling wryly to herself now, "superiors never take account of things like that," and she grinned at us again.

I wonder how often they've asked you to do impossible things in the past? I thought, still struggling with my tears. *And if you don't obey them this time and give in to the ultimate human weakness, it'll be the first time.* She was a superb nun, I knew, and I knew too I could never be as good as she.

"Well," she finished, "I shall be watching you all from Heaven and following your careers with love and prayers, you know." Then she put her head to one side. "Of course," she said thoughtfully, "theologically we don't know whether souls in Heaven can see the world in the Beatific Vision. But *if* I can see you, then I'll be interested. Anyway, we'll all be together in God—you by faith and me in reality. So it's all the same."

She made a signal for us to leave. Struggling with my feelings, I got up.

"Sister Martha," she said suddenly. "Will you stay behind?"

I heard the others leave the room as I went and knelt by the bed. I stared down at the grey blanket that swam before me. Then I blinked my tears back, striving to be worthy of this gift she had given me of a few last words.

I looked up at her worn face for the last time. She started wishing me luck in the Oxford entrance examinations that were only a few weeks away. Even on her deathbed she was so at home with God that she was making jokes, puzzling out theological problems, thinking about my exams. Never a single stab of self-pity. She could face death so calmly, I knew, because she had been dying all her life, just as a nun should.

"Thank you, Reverend Mother, for all you've done for me." There was so much I wanted to say and the empty little formula sounded so trite. "You've given me more than you can ever realize."

She reached out and put her hand on my head. We looked hard at one another and she smiled.

"When you came here, Sister, I was told that you would be difficult. And I want you to know," her voice became emphatic, "that you have never been any trouble to me. You've been a good scholastic . . . you're a good girl, Sister. Remember I said so."

Mother Frances' arrival made me realize even more clearly all that I had lost. She was a large middle-aged woman, with a pleasant face and a calm smile. Her eyes were small, though, and had a slight cast in them so that she never seemed to be looking at you.

That was the trouble, I decided. Mother Bianca had always engaged directly with me, but Mother Frances returned me sharply to the usual impersonal treatment of the Order, though she was never unkind and we got on perfectly well. I got into Oxford that autumn, and she was pleased because I was going to her old college to read English, as she had done before she'd entered. It was just that there was a dimension missing. I mustn't be unfair, I said to myself. I can't expect everyone to be like Mother Bianca.

She had announced Mother Bianca's death to us one hot September evening before instruction. For weeks we had been expecting the inevitable news from Tripton, but somehow it still came as a shock. Mother Frances gave us the facts, even now sounding cool and ironic, her bright eyes glancing away from us and from the sadness that filled the room. There had been a silence as each one of us stared at the table top, lost in reactions that we would never share. I struggled with the lump that rose immediately to my throat and blinked away the rebellious tears that showed me how far I was still lacking in religious detachment. I knew that I should be glad that Mother Bianca had gone to God, but all I could feel was a heavy loss. That evening nobody mentioned the subject that filled our minds. We chatted brightly and cheerfully about trivia, but for all that there was a sense of strain at that recreation. We all smiled happily at Mother Frances, knowing that God had sent her to be our superior. But how strange and sad it was to see her sitting in the chair that had so recently been Mother Bianca's.

One morning, shortly after the exams, I came down to breakfast feeling terrible. I had been sick again during the night and had had to sit down during Mass that morning. I still felt unwell and found it physically impossible to eat. I knew I should eat, but the food would not go down and I felt the well-known waves of nausea engulfing me. I sipped half-heartedly at a cup of tea and left the refectory as soon as I could.

I was sweeping the front hall when Mother Frances passed me, tapping me on the shoulder. "Come upstairs, Sister," she said coldly. I followed her, heart sinking. I knew what was coming.

"Sister," she said as we reached her room—the room that had been Mother Bianca's—"why did you not eat any breakfast this morning?"

"I felt sick, Reverend Mother. I was sick last night and I didn't think I could keep anything down."

"I see." She looked out the window and I, kneeling beside her desk, looked at the floor. "There's absolutely no need for you to be sick, Sister. I gather from Mother Constantia that you saw a doctor last year and that this vomiting is simply a matter of nerves."

"Yes, Reverend Mother."

"So, no more sickness, please. If you are weak enough to allow yourself to be sick, you are to eat more than usual at mealtimes the following day. I will not have you seeking attention and sympathy as you did at breakfast this morning."

"I'm sorry, Reverend Mother."

"And I gather that Mother Bianca gave you leave not to eat cheese. I'm afraid I think you used this privilege to pander to your nerves. So you will resume eating cheese today."

"Thank you, Reverend Mother."

I wasn't surprised. The tone, the message was all very familiar. But something was different. What? I knew suddenly that the difference was in myself. Mother Bianca had inspired me as much by her humanity as by her sacrifice. And now I was back in the old isolation. Was it really so necessary? Was it really so wrong for me to have felt love for such a magnificent human being? As the year wore on that dimension that was missing in the Order and in my life began to trouble me more and more. I began to be sick again frequently and once again I noticed that my habit was hanging loosely round my waist.

The strain grew considerably by the end of my scholasticate. It was a hot summer. As I toiled through the London streets, sweat poured off me. I thought I'd gotten used to being endlessly sticky and smelly, but disgust with my body became steadily more acute. The real problem was my underwear. The large skirts of my habit swirled around and sucked up filth and grime from the Underground into a kind of vacuum. Each night I stood in my cell gazing in amazement at my legs. They were black! That was no exaggeration: they were caked with black soot that would only come off if I scrubbed my legs with a nailbrush. But at least I could get that off. My underwear remained black, and it would be days before I was allowed to change it. It was in a bad state; the long legs were patched and darned and even the laundry could not get out all the soot, which clung in grimy little crevices to the darning cotton.

One Saturday afternoon after tea we sat down for afternoon reading. This was a weekly recreational period when the superior read us a secular book as a treat while we did our mending. Since a good many books were unsuitable, for obvious reasons, travelogs were usually chosen. For the past five years I'd listened to accounts of Tibet and of Antarctica and ventured into the interior and ascended Everest. I came to associate the smell of darning cotton with haversacks and tents. That afternoon we were trekking across the Gobi Desert. The book had lost me completely. It merged drearily with all the other travelers' tales we'd ploughed through. I picked up my darning gloomily. The brethren seemed to share my opinion. The boredom in the room was almost palpable.

"Are you enjoying the book?" Mother Frances asked. "I find it most interesting."

Automatically we all looked up and smiled slightly and obediently. Sister Griselda nodded solemnly:

"Oh, yes, Mother," she spoke for all of us as the eldest scholastic. "It's absolutely fascinating. All those yaks!"

Yaks? What on earth were they? I'd not been listening when these creatures had been described but the Gobi seemed full of them. Did Sister Griselda really know herself? I glanced at her caustically as Mother started to read, and she grinned back suddenly and gave a faint shrug.

I returned to my darning. I felt bored, dirty, and suddenly hopeless. The arid wastes that were being described in Mother Frances' passionless voice seemed to sum up my life at the moment.

Scarcely knowing what I was doing, I reached for a pair of scissors. I wanted to show somebody, somehow, what I was feeling.

I heard Sister Griselda gasp slightly as, with a huge feeling of relief, I slashed the legs off my long underwear.

Of course my act was noticed, as I had intended that it should be, but by the time my shorn underwear came back from the laundry I was feeling calmer and rather shaken by my own behavior. What had got into me?

I waited apprehensively for the bombshell. It came at spiritual reading the following Wednesday.

"I gather," Mother Frances sounded bewildered, "that somebody has cut the legs off her underwear."

That was the way a public rebuke always began. In impersonal terms. The guilty person was supposed to rise instantly to acknowledge her fault. I stood up feeling fairly calm. *The only thing to do is to be honest,* I thought. *If she asks, explain why you did it and she might be able to help you overcome this rebellious tendency.*

"But Sister," Mother wasn't angry, exactly. Just astonished. "What do you want? *Briefs*?" It sounded on her lips like an obscenity.

"Yes, Reverend Mother!" I heard myself saying. "Briefs would be marvelous!" They would, too. No more dreary mending, clean clothes every day. A picture of bliss. But what was happening to make me say what *I* wanted and criticize the practices of the Order? Astounded at this emergence of my critical faculty, I listened to myself saying: "My long underwear gets so filthy, Reverend Mother, and, in the world, I was accustomed to change it every day."

"Good gracious!" She sounded amazed. "In my day that would have been considered the height of fastidiousness. Do the rest of you feel like that?" I looked at the others threateningly, and miraculously they didn't let me down. The subject was too near to their hearts. They nodded at Mother Frances over the generation gap.

Mother was really trying to be reasonable, I thought with sudden liking and respect. For some reason she wanted to help with what she could see was a difficulty. In the end I had to keep my "briefs" as they were and do a penance in the refectory for a fault against poverty in destroying what didn't belong to me. But though we still weren't allowed to have more than two pairs of underwear a week we could, while the weather was warm, wash them out and hang them out the windows to dry overnight.

That night the princess who lived next door had a party. Champagne corks popped; light, civilized laughter floated into the air.

"All quiet in your nunnery tonight, I see," one of the guests said, perhaps, glancing up at the tall silent house. "Good God! Do you see what I see?"

The laughter must have grown more delighted and less civilized, as one by one the distinguished guests saw the airtex bloomers festooning the windows of the convent.

Before going up to join the Oxford community I was sent to Tripton for a rest and change. Nuns weren't supposed to have holidays; that was too worldly an idea. So we had a rest and change instead, R and C for short. There was a joke in the Order that young nuns never had a rest; they only had a change. I could see the truth in this as I was set to moving furniture all round the vast school. Sister Jocasta and I seemed to be endlessly wedged in awkward corners of a winding staircase with a table or a cupboard pinned between us.

It was strange going back to Tripton, seeing the long line of novices in church and in the refectory, and not being a part of that world anymore. Mother Walter and Mother Albert smiled politely to me across the refectory, as though to a mere acquaintance, with a detachment that was, in my present state of mind, chilly and disturbing. The community too carried on its business. No one spoke to me. In between furniture removals I sat in the school library working through the reading list that I had been sent from Oxford. But no one spoke to me at recreation after lunch. It wasn't that they meant to be unkind; kindness just didn't come into it. Young nuns were to be seen and not heard. How different they all were from Mother Bianca! And which example was I supposed to follow? I felt lonely and shut out and then guilty for my weakness. I had no business with this maudlin self-pity. That was something I had vowed to leave behind when I left the Noviceship.

How little I had achieved in these last two years. But then I knew that I mustn't expect to see any progress in my spiritual development. That could only lead to pride and complacency.

One afternoon as the community dispersed for informal recreation after lunch, Mother Katherine touched my elbow.

"Let's have a talk, Sister."

I was delighted. It seemed ages since I'd spoken to anyone at all. I followed her into the garden where we sat in the shade of a large cedar tree.

"Well, how are you?" she asked. Her eyes searched my face anxiously. I could see that it was not just an empty greeting. What could I tell her? I felt tongue-tied and shy. It seemed another world, those conversations that we'd had at school; we'd chatted and laughed together and I'd felt so certain of what I wanted. I'd known just what I wanted to say. But now I felt an empty vacuum inside me. All the time I was thinking what I ought to say, what was expected of me. I didn't know who I was anymore.

"I—I'm—" I stuttered and colored, looking down at my hands. Mother Katherine would think I'd become a gibbering idiot. I could see her looking troubled, as though she were trying to match this nervous young nun with the happy, eager schoolgirl she had known.

Suddenly I found my tongue. I knew that she wouldn't be shocked by what I had to say. "I don't like it here," I said bluntly. "I know I shouldn't say that, but coming back to Tripton has been awful."

"I know," she nodded. "I always feel the same when I come here. It's a very cold community, isn't it?"

"Mother"—things that I'd been damming up for so long came rushing out—"is it really necessary for us to behave so coldly to one another? I know I've got to be prepared for sacrifice, and I am, really I am! And I know I can't expect human warmth and companionship, but often I feel so starved."

She sighed and looked away from me for a moment, studying the grey stone of the buildings. Her face looked sad and tired. I felt contrite. I'd put her in a difficult position. She'd just been appointed superior at Skipton in the north of England. She could hardly discuss and criticize the policy of the Order with a young nun. I tried to help her.

"Not all of you seem to be so chilly and distant. You're not. Mother Albert isn't always. And Mother Bianca wasn't. And nobody could have been holier or had a stronger will than she did."

"I know; she was a marvelous person."

"That's the trouble. She's the kind of nun I'd really like to be, but I feel it's hopeless."

Mother Katherine looked at me quickly, her eyes apprehensive. "Hopeless? You're not thinking . . . ?"

I stopped short, horrified at myself. Good heavens, I thought, if I encourage this kind of thinking I will lose my vocation.

"No, Mother," I said slowly, shaken out of myself. "Oh, no, I couldn't give up." Of course I couldn't. Abandon the whole thing just because things were difficult? I remembered our conversation at school all those years ago, when I'd been so ardent and ready for sacrifice. "I don't know where all these thoughts have come from," I said slowly. I traced the steps in my mind. There was the danger of my studies beginning to lead me into intellectual pride; there'd been the conflict with Father Flannigan and that talk with Sister Jocasta. Had I really been severe enough with myself then, implying disobedient comparisons between Mother Bianca and Mother Frances? And the long underwear. One little thing leading to another. How careful I'd have to be. "I hope Oxford won't make me too critical. I hope it will let me stay humble and obedient."

Mother's eyes were troubled. "So do I," she said quietly, but somehow I felt that we weren't talking about the same thing. "Sister, sometimes God asks us to hang on," she said urgently. "Keep going in the darkness no matter how hard things are. Promise me that you'll keep going next year."

Again she looked away from me, preoccupied, as though she were trying to find a way of saying something rather difficult. "Oxford," she said, and I saw her sigh impatiently. Suddenly she turned back and the doubt had gone from her face. Her eyes were blazing urgently. "Look Sister. Use your brain." I was startled by the vehemence in her voice. "God has given it to you. It's a great gift. Use it."

I stared at her. "But, Mother . . . " What could she mean?

"Yes, I know all about obedience!" She waved her hand impatiently. "Of course you must be obedient. Always! But that doesn't mean that you have to stifle all your own gifts. And now the Order is sending you to Oxford, precisely to develop your mind. So use the opportunity."

I sat back, stunned by the impact of what she was saying. Just now I'd been chiding myself for letting my own thoughts get out of hand. I glanced at Mother Katherine, who was once more looking pensive. What was she so worried about? There was a short silence. What she must mean, I thought slowly, is that I have to let Oxford develop me academically. I'll have to master my subject if I'm going to teach it well. After all, she'd stressed the importance of obedience. Thinking about literature would be one thing, but I must never pit my thoughts against my superiors'.

"You see, Sister," Mother Katherine said carefully. "You may find it difficult." She stopped. "At Oxford."

We looked at one another and I knew that I mustn't ask her anything else. What was she trying to warn me of?

"Pray," she went on quietly, holding me with her eyes. "Keep near to God and you won't have any need to worry. You will promise me to hang on, won't you?"

I didn't have to think. "Yes, Mother. Of course I promise!"

10 · OXFORD

Oxford. City of dreaming spires. Broad leafy streets, soft-stoned cottages. Bells summoning the students to intellectual endeavor, to develop and grow.

Our day was a frenzied rush. There were two of us student nuns. My companion was Sister Rebecca, who was now in her final year at the university reading French and Italian. It was good to see her again, still serene and calm. But, like me, thinner. Much thinner.

Our day started at half-past five, of course. Then prayers, Mass, breakfast, a little bit of manual work, and at nine we started work. We studied or went to lectures and tutorials all morning. After lunch we said all our prayers—one spiritual duty after another—for an hour and a half. Then at three o'clock the two of us were sent out for a walk. Sharp, medicinal recreation. After tea, work again until suppertime. A solitary life, secluded from the other members of the community in the interests of our studies.

I had been at Oxford for a month and was halfway through my first term, sitting in a seminar. Literary forms was the topic, an introductory class for freshmen. Outside I could see undergraduates in their short skirts and long hair scurrying between the halls of residence, noisy and happy. In front of me the tutor sat, a lean, glamourous woman with a caustic tongue and a mind like a laser. We were discussing the novel, or rather the rest of them were. I sat at the side of the room listening in awe to these girls, all of them years younger than I was, playing with ideas, tossing the ball of discussion one to another. Many authors were mentioned whom I had never read. However could I catch up? I watched Elizabeth, the

215

scholar, with her long black gown slipping off her shoulders as she leaned forward lost in her own argument. In the competitive entrance examination, Elizabeth had achieved high enough grades to be awarded a college scholarship, which gave her 50 pounds a year and the prestige of wearing a more elaborate gown than the rest of us, whose more lowly status gave us the title "commoners." If only I'd been able to prepare for Oxford properly during the Scholasticate. The crammer had put me through a few authors to enable me to get through the entrance papers, but now I saw with frightening clarity that this was just not enough. These girls had a wealth of culture at their fingertips. It seemed hopeless.

And the other students seemed so confident, too. It wasn't that I couldn't understand the arguments. The broad general lines of the discussion I could follow clearly and I knew that later on in the convent library I'd be able to think it all out more peacefully. It was the quick critical cut and thrust that paralyzed me in this class, making me aware of a yawning emptiness where ideas of my own should have been. I felt the lethargy of my mind, which had been numbed by misuse. And how I found myself longing for that mental agility that I knew I'd had once. But of course I'd had to give it up. I wasn't questioning that.

One o'clock. The bell rang for college lunch and the girls gathered their notes together and left the room, chattering together cheerfully. I tried smiling at one or two of them; I had to behave in a friendly way, I knew. Not start a friendship or anything like that, but by my black-robed presence offer them some witness of the love of God. They didn't seem to be aware of that at all. One or two gave me a quick embarrassed smile and hurried past while the rest stared at me blankly or averted their eyes and passed by. I couldn't blame them. What had I got in common with them or their newfound freedom, friendships, loves, and intellectual confidence?

I made my own way to the door. "Sister!" I spun round. The tutor was beckoning to me. I went over apprehensively. Her elegance and sophistication daunted me as much as her brain did. What a ninny she must think me. Perhaps she had already regretted admitting me to the college.

"Sister," she said, leaning back in her chair, legs crossed, her pale wheat-colored suit shrieking of worldliness, her eyes sharp and appraising, "you don't say very much at these classes."

It was quite an understatement. "No. I'm so sorry."

She waited, smiling slightly. It was not an unfriendly smile.

"I find it difficult. To speak. My mind is working slowly at the moment. I'm sure it'll improve," I added hastily, "but I'm just not used to discussing things."

"No. I do understand that. But try, won't you? You know your written work is good. It's very promising." I gasped incredulously, feeling a warm gush of delight.

"It's easier on paper," I explained, trying to appear cool about this unexpected praise. "When I've got time to think. It's just here. The others are *so* clever, and they know so much, I . . . I feel paralyzed by them."

"I wouldn't let them do that to you." She smiled as if amused. "Look, don't force it, but try to make yourself say at least one thing at a seminar. Take it gently. It'll come. I don't suppose," and there was an ironic edge to her voice, "you have much of a chance to meet the others socially."

I shook my head. I knew that she was a Catholic, used to the ways of nuns, and would understand this.

"Well, as I say, don't rush at it but just try to get used to discussing things again." She picked up her books and made off, her gown billowing behind her. Then, looking over her shoulder, "You see, you've got a lot to contribute."

I flew to my bicycle almost giddy with happiness. I wasn't a total dolt then! Tucking up my skirts, I mounted the bike and perilously pushed myself into Banbury Road. We'd just been given permission, Sister Rebecca and I, to ride bicycles, and very odd it felt, too, perched on my bustle with my veil flapping wildly in the breeze. I pedaled faster. And faster. I'd got to hurry. I'd missed first-table dinner, of course. Sister Rebecca and I usually did, and, even though the twelve o'clock lecture might let us get back at three or four minutes past the hour, we still weren't allowed to go in late. Which meant that getting through all my prayers—a quarter-hour's examination of conscience, half an hour's spiritual reading, half an hour's silent prayer, and the Rosary—all by three o'clock was a terrible rush. Sometimes, if I got in by five past one, I could make my examination of conscience before second table at one-twenty, but that rarely happened and was quite out of the question today.

Locking up my bicycle, I hurried into the convent and made my way into the community room in the basement. Sister Rebecca was sitting there, eyes cast down, hands folded. How pale and strained she looked. I was worried. I knew she worked slowly, and with finals coming up she was very worried about her work. I was bursting to tell her about my conversation with Miss Jameson, but of course it was silence time. I knew she would understand. She too felt dumb and vacant in discussion, even after all this time. Looking at her, my heart sank. Would I be able to unlock my mind, to succeed where she had failed? The little rush of confidence I'd felt started to evaporate.

I looked up at the clock. One twenty-two. I was starving. Hadn't they finished yet? *Hurry up!* I thought frenziedly, looking down the dark passage to the refectory. We had to be in church, kneeling down and starting our prayers, on the dot of one-thirty. That left us eight minutes—no, seven and a half now, to eat lunch and wash up. I sighed impatiently. If only we could be allowed to leave for our walk a quarter of an hour later. We could still be back at work by 4:00 and have had a walk. But no, the edict stood firm. I *must not* criticize, I said to myself through gritted teeth.

Thank God! I could hear them saying grace. Soon they'd begin the "De Profundis" and start the procession up to the chapel. Sister and I moved down the corridor ready to race into the refectory the second the last nun left. Meals were always rushed these days, I reflected, as I stood with my eyes fixed not on the ground where they should have been, but on the clock. It was no better at supper. At that meal Sister Rebecca had to serve the community—putting round the dishes, clearing them away, putting out the pudding and the washing-up tins—while eating her own meal. And I had to read to them for twenty minutes, then get down and have my supper in ten minutes flat so that I wouldn't miss Compline.

"*Requiem aeternam dona eis, Domine,*" Mother Praeterita said, halfway up the stairs at the head of the line.

"*Et lux perpetua luceat eis,*" the community replied.

The last nun left the refectory. We dove in.

"*Requiescant in pace!*" the echo came down the stairs dimly. May they rest in peace.

Six minutes.

I threw the food onto my plate, picked up my fork, and then stared at it. The gravy had gotten cold in the kitchen and had a thick, glutinous skin. The potatoes had been put into the warmer for us and had hard, yellowy crusts. The meat looked like animal sinew and fat. I laid my fork down and breathed deeply, trying to fend off the nausea that was rising. My hunger had vanished. At the moment I could imagine nothing worse than eating—pushing that stuff down my throat at top speed, feeling it churning around while I knelt in the chapel, wincing with indigestion, and finally throwing it all up again. What was the point? I was sick nearly every night at Oxford.

I glanced at Sister Rebecca, noticing that she had only put a tiny portion on her plate. She swallowed with difficulty and took a gulp of water after each mouthful. Seeing me looking at her, she smiled at me pallidly.

"Only take a little bit," she whispered. I looked at her in astonishment. It was strictly forbidden to talk in the refectory and so unlike Sister to break a rule. "It's better in the long run to eat just a tiny portion of both courses. Otherwise you just can't keep it down. Not in the time." It was good advice. I'd follow it in the future.

Saturday night. Six o'clock in the evening. Instruction with Mother Praeterita. A night in "drear-nighted December." Keats knew what he was talking about: "The feel of not to feel it." Numbness and emptiness.

Sister Rebecca and I were sitting in front of Mother Praeterita's desk. Every week young professed had to go to their superior for an instruction on the religious life, just to make sure they were not losing sight of their original ideals. I sat tensely upright, gripping my hands tightly together. These occasions were becoming more and more of an ordeal. At first I had sat back drinking it all in, as I had during the past six years. Passively. Waiting for my final spiritual maturity to make all the difficulties clear. But now . . .

Mother Praeterita's long elderly face loomed a dead ivory color in the lamplight. The large bags under her eyes fell into deep shadows and the flesh hung in wrinkled folds as she gazed intently over our heads at a point on the ceiling, slightly to her left. She never looked at us. And she mumbled. Sometimes if her thought was complex she lowered her head and whispered stammeringly into her left shoulder. Poor Reverend Mother, I told myself firmly. She can't help stammering. Somebody had told me that she had been born left-handed and had been forced by her parents to use her right hand. That was why. But if only she'd talk to us instead of the ceiling!

I pursed my lips together. Tonight was going to be different. I was not going to allow it to upset me. I had no business letting it upset me. This was my religious superior. She represented God to me. But it was so hard. Miss Jameson's advice about the seminars was working. Now when I attended a class in college I could think while the others talked. Often I found myself saying something, carried out of myself by the force of my reactions to what was being said. But that is college, I said to myself grimly. That is Oxford. This is my home. I pressed my feet firmly together. Taking a deep breath I looked back at Mother Praeterita, willing my eyes to be calm.

"Well, it's the end of another term." As usual the mumbling voice sounded disembodied. It floated round the room like a ghost, refined out of feeling or involvement. "For you, Sister Martha, the end of your first term here."

I felt a sinking gloom. No more college. *Just as well,* my nun-self replied tartly. *Now you can become fully integrated here, as you ought to be.*

"So let us review the blessings of being a student nun." She paused, burrowed in her notes and then turned her face to the ceiling again. "First, there is the great blessing of loneliness. It is lonely being a student nun. You see very little of the community because of your studies. And of course you see very little of the students. And that is a great blessing. Because, Sisters," she turned a page, "it gives you a chance to realize your dependence on God, to rely on Him alone."

I had heard it so many times before, but something in me now was exploding in protest. It was my Oxford self—that part of me that was trying to drag me away from the hard road of the religious life.

"And so, Sisters," Mother was reaching the end of her first point. "Let us thank God that you are so lonely."

Aghast, I heard myself say, not angrily but calmly and logically, "Reverend Mother, I think it's bad for us to be as lonely as we are. I don't think God wants it at all."

Silence deepened in the room. Mother Praeterita flinched as though she had been shot—young nuns did *not* talk at instruction.

But that part of me that was learning to argue had gotten switched on and I couldn't find the knob to switch it off:

"It's bad for us," I was saying. "We have nobody to discuss our work with and that is holding us back in our studies—it must! Sister Rebecca and I see no one but each other. You say that particular friendships are wrong. But you're forcing us to be friends. We go for a walk together every day; no one else has a clue what we do with ourselves all day; nobody's interested. So we're friends now. And I think that's a good thing!"

Part of me was appalled. Such worldly, unspiritual views! But the person who was talking believed them. I realized that somewhere, in some buried part of me, I had believed in them for years but I'd kept them hidden even from myself.

Mother's face pressed against her left shoulder. Her hands were shaking. "Sister! Sister! What can you be thinking of? We *know* the value of solitude, the danger of friendships."

Leave her alone, I thought. *Think your own thoughts; don't shatter her with them. It's not fair. My mind is quick; I mustn't press her. She even has to read these instructions.* But I couldn't. Something was forcing me to go on:

"We say that God is a God of Love. St. John says that if we don't love our brothers whom we can see around us, then how can we love God Whom we don't see? Why have we got to turn in on ourselves and let our thoughts and feelings dry up and turn bad inside?"

There was an inarticulate moan from behind the desk: "God won't let us dry up if we really turn to Him."

I looked despairingly at Sister Rebecca, who sat, her eyes big and unhappy, torn between the two of us. She shot me a quick smile of support. And I felt better, less alone. *And that's what it's all* about, *all that I'm trying to say!* I thought. *Just that our life is hard, and why can't we make things easier for one another sometimes—in love?*

"Sister, you mustn't harbor these thoughts. They are dangerous." Mother leaned across the table, a fragile old lady no longer, her eyes hard and angry. "You know, this attitude comes of thinking too much about literature."

"But, Reverend Mother, how can literature turn me away from God?" It was a question I would not have dreamed of asking six months ago, but now it burst from me eagerly.

"Because it appeals to the senses too much. There isn't enough grit in it."

I looked at her speechlessly: "What can I do then? How can I stop myself liking it so much?"

She brightened, feeling on safer ground now. "Oh, it's a matter of constant self-discipline, Sister. Not letting yourself delight in the words all the time. I used to enjoy reading very much myself, you know," she smiled as if at a past folly. "But I don't anymore. Now when I read a book it's a chore. And I've got into the way of just tearing the heart out of a book, leaving the inessentials. Try doing that. The next book you have to read, don't linger over it. Just tear the heart out of it. Otherwise your indulgence in literature might destroy your vocation, and then how can you stay with us?"

No! I thought, horrified. No, I didn't want that. To give up all hope of close union with God. And to go back to the world! Those confident, pretty girls at college. I could never really cope in that world full time. I wanted to continue. I pursed my lips tightly shut. But my mind raced on: Jesus had the Beloved Disciple, He had friends, He wept when Lazarus died. He was passionate and involved. He wouldn't want this; He couldn't.

How could I stop my mind now? Oxford and literature had woken it up and it was growing stronger every day. It had a life of its own that was getting bigger than the rest of me.

Would it take me away from God?

It was Christmas Eve. The church was darkened. And we were kneeling, making our meditation. In half an hour midnight Mass would begin.

It seemed so much easier here in the darkness. The silhouettes of the nuns, the silence all speaking of prayer and dedication. I was turning over the Christmas mystery: God, laying aside His power and strength and becoming a helpless Baby. Couldn't I lay aside my own strength and do the same for Him?

Suddenly that old sensation: the lights, the stench, the flashing images. *Oh no!* I thought. It had been four months since the last time. I'd hoped it was all over. Shaking convulsively, I tried to get to my feet but then felt that falling, down, down, down . . .

A finger jabbing my shoulder. Raising my bursting head from

the chapel floor. The infirmarian whispering. I was to go to bed. To miss Mass. Reverend Mother displeased. Weakness.

I staggered to my feet and swayed drunkenly up to the dormitory. Outcast and disgraced.

It was a cold, wet Christmas. The community were not allowed to speak to me. Sister Rebecca did, briefly, on the stairs, her eyes worried but sympathetic.

"I couldn't help it," I whispered.

"I know." A glance of mutual understanding. And she had to go.

"Peace on Earth to men of good will." But my will was not good. It was weak. It allowed me to fall hysterically to the floor; it let my emotions knock me over. My head was splitting with pain. I deserved it. My tongue was bitten and swollen—a punishment for my words of criticism.

I deserved to be exiled from the life of the community. It would help me to accept being alone not just as a punishment but as a means of coming close to God.

It was February. Soon I would be taking my preliminary exams. I wasn't worried about those, but how was I faring as a nun?

We were having revision seminars. And I was giving a paper. I'd been nervous, but as I went on I forgot my diffidence and started to enjoy unfolding my argument. I made a joke: the students laughed. I felt the thrill of contact, of mind teaching mind. They asked questions, and I was answering them, I realized, with a flush of excitement. The hour sped by: I felt transformed, exhilarated.

"Thank you, Sister. That was an excellent paper."

I felt my cheeks, already glowing from the thrill of the last hour, flush with pleasure at Miss Jameson's words. An accolade, welcoming my mind back into the world. Then the students started leaving the room to go to dinner. I gathered up my books. It was over. Suddenly the emptying room looked sad. I fastened my shawl with a pin, ready for the ride home. Home. I felt that leaden weight descend on me as it had done once or twice recently. How could I share this sudden excitement? I heard Mother Praeterita's chilling words again: "Tear the heart out of it!"

A few weeks later I was standing in the hall. It was ten to seven in the morning. As the youngest member of the community I had to leave the chapel at six forty-five and go down to wait for the priest who came sometimes to say Mass, finishing my meditation on one of the hall chairs. "Brrr." A short, discreet ring of the doorbell. I got up and opened the door in silence.

Father strode in. He was a large, plump man in his late sixties. He had a bald shiny head with a few black strands draped carefully over it, and blotches of brown freckles on his scalp. Normally he nodded affably to me and went up the front stairs to the sacristy, knowing, of course, the rules about the Great Silence.

This morning, though, he stopped short halfway across the hall. "Sister?" A whisper.

"Yes, Father."

"Are you coming up to the sacristy now?"

"Yes." That was part of my job, to ring the bell to summon any of the few students who lived in the hostel and the *au pairs* to Mass and then to go through the sacristy and light the candles on the altar. "When I've rung the bell."

"Good," he said. Why did he say that? I wondered.

I entered the sacristy quietly. Inside the chapel the nuns were settling themselves for Mass, kneeling down, opening their missals. I went across to light the taper. Father was resting in the corner.

"Sister." I turned to him. He did seem in a talkative mood this morning. What had got into him? "I don't think I've got this vestment on straight. Can't get it to hang. Could you just fix it on my shoulders?"

"Certainly, Father." I stepped up to him. The vestment was slightly askew. It had been made for a slight man. I pulled at it, appraisingly.

Suddenly he trapped both my hands in his and pressed them against his shoulders. Startled, I looked at him sharply. His eyes were closed and he seemed to be having trouble breathing. He must be ill!

"Are you all right, Father? Can I get anyone?"

He sighed. A shuddering sigh. Then he opened his eyes and gave a nervous, tremulous laugh. "Yes, yes, fine, just turned a little giddy."

"Would you like to sit down, Father? Shall I get Reverend Mother?"

"No, no! God bless you. No, I'm all right."

He still had my hands pressed against his shoulders. I made to release them. With an abrupt, snatching motion he squeezed them hard for a second, then kissed them quickly before he gave them back to me.

I stared at him, astonished. "Thank you for looking after me. I'm quite all right now. Off you go."

Vaguely disturbed, I stepped through the sacristy door into the sanctuary and lit the candles.

The cats had gotten into a fight.

There were two cats, a Siamese called Ming and a tabby called Sebastian. For the last nine months I had watched in surprise while the community fawned and drooled over these two sleek, well-fed beasts. There was a Ming faction and a Sebastian faction. The merits of each were hotly disputed every evening at recreation, the rival parties picking the animals up, holding them close, speaking to them softly and lovingly in a way that they never spoke to their sisters in Christ. Once Sebastian got locked in the air-raid shelter. No one knew where he was and for three days the house was plunged into mourning. When Sister John discovered him one evening and carried him in triumph into recreation, Sister Rebecca and I exchanged ironic looks amidst the general tumult.

It was not surprising, therefore, that the cats themselves should start to feel some kind of rivalry. One evening after Compline I had gone into the pantry to do the washing up to find fur flying and claws flailing. Agonized shrieks issued from both the protagonists. The community clustered behind me and the air was rent with wailing and lamentation. I rushed to the sink, filled a pitcher of water, and threw it over the cats who, with discontented yowls, fled in opposite directions. Their distressed partisans followed. Ming was discovered under the sink with a bleeding ear.

SuddenlyI was aware that in the midst of the soothing clucking going on around me there was a terrible sobbing. Mother Imelda, onetime superior and member of the Provincial Council, now infirmarian at Oxford and leader of the Ming party, was leaning against the wall, her face ashen, tears rolling down her plump cheeks. Her body was shaking with sobs.

"Mother! What is it?" I rushed over and tried to take her arm. She pushed me away roughly. "Are you not well?"

"Poor little lad!" she hiccupped between sobs. Then, her face red with anger, "I'd like to kill Sebastian. Kill him! Ming, my Ming! Let me get to him."

Then she staggered slightly. Hands caught her and she was led away, still sobbing. "Never mind me!" she was crying. "Get my darling lad's ear seen to."

I stolidly began the washing up. What a fuss! They celebrate when one of their sisters dies, but look at the emotion produced when something happens to a cat! There was something wrong here. Something I did not want to understand.

Now the pantry was empty, and Sister Rebecca appeared at the door.

"Did you see Mother Imelda?" I asked.

She nodded. We stared at one another dumbly.

"Am I going mad or is everybody else?" I cried. "Look, doesn't this prove what I said to Reverend Mother!" I swished the water round angrily with my mop. "If there were enough scope for friendship in the Order there wouldn't be any need for this kind of thing."

Sister Rebecca looked at me, her eyes deeply troubled.

"Yes, Sister. You're right."

Mother Imelda had to stay in bed for three days. The doctor was called in. *Why did they call a doctor for that and not for me?* I thought angrily. *Isn't this just as much of a weakness as my fainting?*

Ming was carried into her cell. He lay on the bed with her all during her illness, purring and complacent.

What was going on that Mother Imelda was in love with the cat?

I was studying in the library one day after tea when a long shadow fell over my books. A peremptory cough. I looked up to see Mother Praeterita, her usually pale face flushed with agitation.

"Yes, Reverend Mother?"

"Sister, there's a—a person to see you in the parlor."

"Somebody to see me?" I said, astonished. "Who is it, Reverend Mother?"

"One of the students." Mother Praeterita's lips quivered with distaste. "She arrived a few minutes ago, pushed her way past the portress, and insisted on seeing you, even after it was explained to her that you were working."

A student? To see me? "I'm so sorry, Reverend Mother. I can't think who it can be."

"Please don't let it happen again. A religious has no business to fritter her time away in the parlor in useless conversations. Remember how St. Teresa said that to frequent the parlor and involve herself with seculars was one of the gravest temptations for a nun. You must not involve yourself with the students, Sister. Try to get rid of her quickly."

I hurried to the parlor and pushed open the door. There, pacing up and down the dark little room, was Julie, a cheerful, extroverted girl who had been my tutorial partner last term. We had had one or two dead-end conversations and I could not imagine why she should come to see me. When she saw me she wheeled round angrily.

"Sister!" she exploded. "I've never seen anything like it!"

"Like what?" I asked, bewildered by her indignation. What had I done to make her so furious? Anxiously I searched my mind for any occasions when I might have offended her by mistake, but I couldn't think of a single occasion when I had even seen Julie recently. She had resumed her angry progress up and down the room.

"Well," she said defiantly, "I just dropped in to see you. There's nothing so terrible in that, is there? I mean, people in Oxford do it all the time, don't they?"

Did they? I didn't know what people did in Oxford. I smiled uncertainly. But Julie didn't wait for an answer. "I wanted to talk to you. About Christianity. That's what convents are for, surely? I'm not a Christian, you know, but lately I've started to get interested. I *mean*," she shrugged impatiently, "I don't know whether I believe it yet, but it's a good system. You know, love thy neighbor and all that. I wanted to find out more about it and you seemed the obvious person to ask. So I dropped in. Well!" her indignation started to gather force. "I rang the bell. Some wizened old nun answered—well, she can't help what she looks like, I suppose, but Christ! She might try to be a bit more welcoming. You know—knock and it shall be opened to you? Is that right? Something like that, anyway. Well, this old *bag*!" I closed my eyes, dreading what I knew was coming, "looked at me very dubiously and said, 'Who are you?' I ask you! Bloody rude! Anyway, I walked in and explained that I'd like to see you and she still looked at me as though I was something the cat had brought in, mumbled something about having to ask Reverend Mother, and shoved me in here. Honestly! It's a ghastly place, dark, smelling of breakfast for some reason, obviously intended for third-class visitors. Then there was a lot of whispering about me outside, about how regrettable it all was and how it mustn't happen again. And then you came in, looking absolutely terrified!" Suddenly Julie stopped pacing and faced me. We stared at one another helplessly. Whatever she saw in my face made Julie lose her anger.

"Sister," she asked, in a shocked but gentle voice, "is this a Christian place?"

Manual work. A day in early May. Sunlight slanting through the lavatory window making the red tiles gleam as I rubbed the polish off. A tap on my shoulder. I sprang up to face Mother Praeterita.

"Sister, Father would like to see you in the parlor."

"Me, Reverend Mother?"

A hooded glance that meant: a religious superior must never meddle with the private conscience of one of her subjects if she wishes to confess to a priest. I could see what she was thinking, but I had nothing to say to Father. I had worries, yes, troubles. I seemed constantly to be kicking and then forcing myself to stay in harness —I must! But I had nothing to say to *him*!

Warily, I entered the parlor, the small one with the little frosted window. He was having breakfast and the air was warm with coffee and bacon. There was a mess of crumbs and china on the white tablecloth. I remembered that odd scene in the sacristy when he had been ill and acted so strangely. Perhaps he wanted to apologize. I sat on a hard seat by the door.

Jovial remarks: wonderful examination results, you clever girl! —enjoying the summer term—remembered himself as an under-grad—was wondering, would I like to join the choir at his parish church?—couldnt' sing?—nonsense, of course, he was sure I could —must speak to Reverend Mother—nuns ought to be more in-volved with the life of the parish—come and see me—talk it over— Vatican Two and all that . . .

I got up to go, bewildered by the frantic rush of his speech that never once paused for a reply and ignored my stumbling, evasive interjections. I looked at him. His forehead was wet and shiny. He giggled nervously. I noticed he hadn't got his teeth in. How could he eat without his teeth?

"I must go, Father." He got up and made as if to open the door for me. "I have to be at work in the library at nine." He must be under a strain. Perhaps his heart, poor man. His breathing was awry, rough and ragged.

"Nice to see you, Sister . . ." a pause; his hand was on the door knob. "We must talk about the choir . . . involvement . . . Oh, God!"

With a shock I found myself crushed by the weight of his arms around me, pressing me against the door. Rigid with disgust I turned away, trembling, trying not to see his clammy forehead, not to feel the fumbling hands, not to smell the stale egg on his breath. Sickening waves of disgust . . . my body . . . his old body. Hands freckled like toads . . . how to get away—?

This episode ran as a worrying commentary on my reading of the modern novel, which I had begun during the Easter vacation. This reading wasn't compulsory, but I'd heard these novelists mentioned so often that I felt I had to discover them for myself to try and fill some of the huge gaps in my education. I didn't ask Mother Praeterita's permission.

Sitting guiltily in the library reading William Golding and Angus Wilson, I began to discover a new world, the world outside the convent gates. And I discovered sex.

The sexual incidents described in *The Pyramid* and *Pincher Martin* confirmed my view of sex as something horrible and frightening. I thought back to the revulsion I'd felt when I'd seen Anthony and Suzie kissing all those years ago: the fumbling, the clashing of teeth, and the disgusting exchange of saliva. Anthony's wet hands kneading Suzie's neck. Far more recently, there was that encounter with Father in the parlor. How right I'd been to reject all such unpleasantness.

But these novels did more than confirm that. They imprinted on my mind a set of vivid images that seemed indelible. As I knelt in church, these pictures of limbs tangled in improbable positions, of gasping, shuddering bodies filled my mind and made my cheeks burn and my guts turn to liquid. I could not, try as I would, rid myself of these images that sickened me yet at the same time attracted me in horrified fascination. Sex, which had been entirely absent from my life for years, suddenly invaded it. Of course I had a ready-made category for this experience. When we'd been instructed about the vow of chastity in the noviceship, we'd been warned about such temptations against purity. I recalled Mother Walter's calm, ascetic voice telling us that temptation itself was not a sin: no one could help thoughts entering her mind. Sin only began when these thoughts were deliberately encouraged and enjoyed. As long as we fought against such temptations we were not breaking our vow. What she had not told us was that this fight for purity only involved one in those images more and more deeply. I found myself wrestling with them as though I were myself in the grip of an obscene embrace, being raped by these feelings that I couldn't control. In combatting pictures of these couplings, I was somehow enacting them over again, and in the midst of the guilt I was enjoying it.

In cooler moments I found that the really disturbing thing about these temptations was that they revealed my basic ignorance. Yes, body fitted body, men and women groaned and panted, but what exactly were they doing? My knowledge of the male body was confined solely to dimly remembered and modestly fig-leaved pictures in art appreciation lessons at school. I hadn't a clue how this alien body worked sexually, and without this all-important information I realized that my understanding of sex was centrally incomplete. In fact, now that I came to think about it, my knowledge of my own body was rudimentary. For years I'd simply attended to its needs mechanically and fought it tooth and nail. But I'd never thought of myself as a sexual being. How had I come to make a vow of chastity with such a vague idea of what I was renouncing? That was academic now, of course; I'd made my vow and I fully intended to keep it. Besides, men for me had become unreal beings. My ignorance of their bodies was equalled by my ignorance of them as people. Women I understood and could relate to, but apart from my father and Anthony I'd never really known any men. They had never been a part of my world. Since I'd been a nun, the only men I'd seen were priests, their mysterious bodies shrouded in vestments and habits, performing the holy ritual of the Mass. Or they were an ear turned toward me on the other side of the confessional grille, a disembodied voice giving me a penance and repeating the words of absolution. The idea of having sex with a man was impossible. I felt closer to the rabbit of the biology textbook.

But if this were so, what was the powerful excitement that had been released by these tantalizing novels? Still more worrying was the fact that these sensations were not altogether new. They seemed allied to my experience of physical penance, with the yearning for affection and warmth that I'd been fighting against for so long, even with moments of prayer when my mind had seemed to rest in God for a while. What did it all mean?

The writer who affected me most profoundly was Iris Murdoch. Beneath the bizarre antics of her characters I found a philosophy of human love that was intelligent and satisfying, even though it seemed to oppose all I'd been taught. In *The Bell* the sympathetic treatment of homosexuality both shocked and fascinated me and caused new pictures to join the obscene pantomime in my head. But even more frightening was her suggestion that religious experience could be a sublimated form of sexuality and that sex could not be completely suppressed. It could erupt and overwhelm you when you least expected it, and its force could destroy religious aspiration at a single blow. Religion indeed seemed to be a fragile veneer, completely at the mercy of these imperative demands of the body. I thought again of Father's freckled hands creeping over my shoulders. And what of the sudden onslaught of sexual feelings in myself? Where had they been hiding all these years? Did sexuality lurk like a caged beast inside me, ready to spring and destroy my vocation one day? The trouble was that I was too ignorant to know how to prepare for such an attack.

I tried to dismiss Iris Murdoch's views as worldly and beneath my notice. But kneeling in the ornate little convent chapel I found myself plagued with doubts and fears. Had my desire to become a nun been some sort of adolescent sexual escape? Or had my knowledge of the ugliness of my unformed body made me believe I was unfit for love, so that I had removed myself from the sexual arena simply to forestall a lifetime of rejection? It doesn't matter, I told myself. Even if it were true, a religious vocation can begin with all sorts of unworthy motives. The only criterion of a true vocation is that it is ratified by the church through the Order. As mine was. God wants me to be a nun. I want to be a nun.

But still at night as I lay wrestling with these dark and obscure feelings I felt a curiosity that involved my body in frightening conflict. I felt it aching with emptiness, crying out for satisfaction in a new and powerful language of its own. It longed for warmth and contact in a much more explicit way. *No,* I told myself. *This is a temptation.* But this reasoning felt flimsy. How wise religious orders were to warn nuns against erotic literature. The struggle was so lonely. It filled me with desires and shame that I could never admit to others. How could I confess to this intimate muck that had lived in my mind, waiting for a few novels to stir it up like this?

"Well, that was an excellent term's work." I was sitting in a tutorial with Elizabeth. The tutorial is the heart of the Oxford teaching system. While lectures and even some seminars are optional, the weekly tutorial, when the students go singly or in pairs to discuss their essays with their tutor for an hour, receiving intensely individual teaching, is sacred. Miss Jameson's room was filled with sunlight. The pale brocade curtains, the sofa with its look of faded elegance, the antique desk and the books, hundreds of them, set the final touch to the room. It was a room in which to think, to be quiet, and to feel your mind expanding and growing.

Elizabeth sat beside me on the sofa. Her long hair was flicked casually back from her shoulders. She was wearing the merest scrap of a dress and her long slim legs draped themselves on the rug before her. I sat beside her feeling bulky, black, and hot.

"I've very much enjoyed teaching the two of you," Miss Jameson went on. "I hope I teach you again some time."

And now it would be over again. The long vacation back at the convent. None of these talks. But instead a task that I dimly knew awaited me. Something I did not, could not, must not let myself think about.

"Sister," Miss Jameson raised a cynical eyebrow at me. I wasn't frightened of her anymore. She was formidable, yes, but the tutorials this term had given me a confidence, a knowledge that my mind was enjoyed. "Reverend Mother Praeterita has invited me to tea." She made a face and, sympathetically, I found myself grinning back at her. "Is there anything behind this invitation?" she asked with a mock sinister tone.

"Oh, I don't think so," I replied. "She hasn't mentioned anything about it to me. But I should imagine she's asked you just to be polite, because it's the thing to do."

Miss Jameson sighed. "Oh dear! I do wish she wouldn't." She picked herself off her chair, stretched, and looked at her watch. "I think it's time for a drink. Sherry, Elizabeth?"

"Yes, please."

"I suppose it's no use offering you any, Sister . . . no, I know. It's a pity." She looked at me, her head slightly on one side. "It'd probably do you good!"

She settled herself back in her chair, her legs curled under her. "No, I do wish Reverend Mother didn't keep asking me to tea. You haven't been at one of these 'do's' yet, have you? Before your time, there used to be a lot more student nuns. And I'd go to tea with Mother Praeterita. We'd sit opposite one another—she not eating a thing, of course. Well, the tea tray would be between us, and I'd want some more tea. We'd both be eyeing the teapot. Should I help myself," she paused dramatically, "or should I wait for her to pour it? We'd look at one another, weighing up the situation, and then we'd both make a dive for the pot and our hands would collide. Silvery tinkle of embarrassed laughter!" She gave a yelp of amusement. "Dear me, Elizabeth," she looked at my partner, who was gazing at us open-mouthed. "Haven't you ever been to tea in a convent? Well, if you ever get the chance, don't."

In spite of myself I found myself rocking with laughter. A catharsis of merriment instead of tears. The absurdities I had been feeling acutely were being exorcised by this sophisticated outsider. A part of me felt disloyal. But I could see the thing so clearly. Mother Praeterita looking at the ceiling, Miss Jameson watching her like a hawk ready to pounce in ridicule. What an ill-matched pair! But it was only a small part of me that didn't want to laugh.

"Isn't she the daughter of———?" and she mentioned a minor literary figure of the turn of the century.

"What!" I said, appalled.

"Oh, yes. Didn't you know? Astonishing really, he was so intelligent—some of his prose work anyway."

"Oh, no! How awful."

"You're not supposed to talk about your past lives for some

reason, are you? Pity, you might pick up some interesting tidbits. He knew them all—the Rossettis, Swinburne, Conrad . . . Sister, what's the matter?" she said suddenly, noting my stricken expression.

"It's dreadful," I said. Then suddenly I started to laugh, getting the story out in gulps. "When I first arrived she asked me—casually—whether I'd ever read any of his poems and what I thought of them. And I said only one, a poem called 'To Angelina,' and that I thought it was ghastly sentimental trash!"

Miss Jameson roared with laughter and kicked her heels in the air with delight. "Oh, poor Sister! But it's even worse than you think it is!"

"Why?"

"My dear, she *was* Angelina!"

Helpless, the two of us rocked around, tears of laughter pouring down our cheeks while Elizabeth looked at us in amazement. Every time we started to sober up, Miss Jameson, who had rummaged in her bookshelves, started to read out lines from the fateful poem in her caustic tones—"Angel dimplings," "Thy wistful smile—ah sweetness!"—that started us off again. My pent-up feelings poured out of me in healing laughter. How long was it since I'd laughed, really laughed a good belly-laugh like that?

"Never mind." Miss Jameson eyed me glintingly. For the first time I felt she was looking at me as some kind of equal. "She got what she deserved. If you're going to ask that kind of loaded question it's up to you to make your position quite clear. Are you sure you won't have a sherry?" Suddenly the question seemed to be asking much more than that. Are you sure all this business is really for you, my girl?

Silence.

"I don't think I should, thanks."

"No. I do understand. But do try and laugh at it sometimes, Sister. You look a hell of a lot better already. You getting enough to eat there?"

"Oh, yes, thank you."

"Because you're absurdly thin and you've got great purple rings around your eyes." Elizabeth shifted uneasily on the sofa, reminding us of her presence. The kindness, as any kind of gentleness always did, kicked me hard in the stomach, winding me for a moment.

"You know, you're a very intelligent woman, Sister, and convents can be mad places. You *must* see it and laugh at it with me again. Really, Elizabeth, you've no idea—has she, Sister? I remember once going to stay in a convent, not one of yours. As you know I am a Catholic, and I was giving some kind of talk there to the League of Catholic Mothers, or something equally unlikely. In the evening I asked for a bath. My dear, terrible consternation! The bathroom was miles away. I was led there by a dear little nun trying to memorize the route by means of statues—you know, left at St. Joseph, right at the Sacred Heart, straight on past the Little Flower." I was laughing helplessly again, feeling once more that incredible easing of tension. I could see it all so clearly. "Well, *finally,* I got into the bath, and *wham* at ten o'clock there I was sitting in the water and the lights were switched off at the mains! Plunged into darkness, stumbling round trying to find everything—my flannel, my talcum powder, my underwear for God's sake! It took me *hours* to get back to my room in the dark. Simply *hours.* I had to stop and keep feeling these statues. Is this Our Lady?—no, it's got a beard!"

When our laughter had subsided again she regarded me shrewdly. "That's the trouble with convents, you know. They don't take little individual difficulties seriously enough. Rules are rules; lights go out at ten o'clock, regardless of the fact that some poor unsuspecting visitor might be up to her neck in bath water. No, I know all about convents, you know. I tried my vocation once."

Of course, I reminded myself on my way home, I mustn't take what she was saying seriously. It really was a worldly view. I had to shun it or risk losing my vocation. And I had to hang on. I'd made my vows for better or for worse. It would be worse than failing at a marriage. I couldn't let myself be seduced by Oxford.

But I did feel better for our talk all the same.

Dustpan and brush in hand I came down the stairs into the front hall and was confronted by Mother Praeterita. She beckoned to me.

"Sister, Father would like a word with you. He's in the little parlor having his breakfast."

"Oh, no, Reverend Mother!" I paled suddenly, feeling that sick churning in my stomach.

"I beg your pardon," she answered coldly. Shocked. Was I actually defying her?

"I mean . . . please, Reverend Mother, I'd rather not go."

"Why not?"

"Because . . . because . . . " I looked up at her; she was remote from passion, understanding nothing, thin and unworldly. The flesh and blood seemed already to have fallen away. She was now studying the chandelier in the front hall. Most of the time she just wasn't there. "I—I—think he's too fond of me."

She looked at me, bewildered. Her mouth dropped open as it seemed to do when she was surprised. For once she met my eyes. I stared back hard. Besides my own embarrassment holding me back from a full communication, I also knew that she couldn't take what I'd have to tell her. There were no concepts for it in her mind.

"What do you mean, too fond of you?" I felt myself blushing. "How dare you be so presumptuous! Here's Father giving up his time to help you and you dare to make an insinuation like that. He's a holy man, Sister; he doesn't allow his feelings to get the better of him. He knows the importance of self-control—a lot better than you do."

"It's not just feeling. It's not—not healthy what's happening between us."

She looked at me and flushed. Her long aristocratic Roman nose curled, the nostrils distending as though she were smelling something unspeakable. Then, click. I heard her mind switch off and she gazed back at me calmly. For a moment she had understood, completely. She'd seen the ugliness. The complications, having to tell Father's superiors, having to talk, to think about *it.* And she'd turned her mind away. Stopped it working. As she'd been trained to do so often in her religious life.

"Sister," her words were like chips of ice, her eyes hard. "I order you to go in to Father. Now."

I stood there with my back to the door. My hand on the handle. "Sit down, Sister? No . . . " The embarrassed laugh, the toothless mouth, the little pulse beating, beating in his temple. Eyes soggy now with—what? Hands trembling as he jabbered on. He was thinking that I looked pale; perhaps I'd like someday to take a drive with him in the country? No, I wasn't too busy, he was sure. Reverend

Mother would agree, he knew. She was worried about me and he could help me. Poor child—looked so strained. You know I'm always here, Sister, always here if you ever need me. O Sister.

He was beside me now. I stared mesmerized at his eager, frightened face. "You will let me help you, Sister, my dear." A toad hand reaching out for my shoulder, nicotined fingers stroking my cheek. "Sister, Sister."

And then my voice trembling with disgust: "Get away from me, don't touch me!" and the door slammed, crashing through the peace of the convent, and I was running away from the sickness and the crucifying need in him and the fear in myself.

In the dormitory I sat on my bed, panting, shaking still in reaction. What could I do? Where could I turn for help? Poor Father. What had happened to him? Years and years of being a priest and now this: grabbing young nuns in the vestry, in the convent parlor. A desperation. A suicidal insanity.

After manual work this morning I had planned to take the discipline. It was time. Increasingly, of recent months, I had felt a growing reluctance. But now . . . I remembered Mother Walter's advice to me to see the discipline as a means of keeping my passions under control. Surely it would help me not to become like Father.

I took the little whip out of its case and drew the curtains round my cell. Then I looked at myself. As though from a distance. Thrashing myself until the blood ran, harder and harder. The excitement. The release. The word I had used half an hour ago to Mother Praeterita—*unhealthy*—hit me with real force. Was this really the way? Had it stopped the community here from falling in love with a cat; had it really helped Father? Or had it whipped those passions in an unnatural direction?

For a long moment I looked down at the whip. Then calmly I put it away.

"Reverend Mother, I don't want to take the discipline anymore."

It was a week later and I had been summoned by Mother Praeterita for my fortnightly talk with her.

"Has what you want any bearing on the matter?" she asked coldly. "Isn't it a question of what God wants?"

"All right, then. I don't think God wants me to do it."

"Why?" Sarcasm now. "Do you think he has decreed something different for you, you alone out of the whole Order? You alone out of the centuries' tradition for all religious?"

Pride again. But was it pride? Polonius' words came forcefully home to me. "This above all, to thine own self be true." But then my self was supposed to be dead. Always this *impasse*. And yet now something in me wouldn't let go. I tried another tack.

"The Vatican Council, Reverend Mother"—she sighed despairingly—"seems to think that a lot of these practices are no longer suitable for people today. There's been talk of abandoning it altogether in the Order; I know that. The community mentioned it the other night." I omitted the disapproval that the community here had expressed at the possibility.

"But Sister, you can't just take the law into your own hands like this," helplessly, "you know that. The General Chapter of our Order will tell us what to do."

"But Reverend Mother, I can't go on doing something that I feel is bad for me."

"Bad, Sister?"

"Yes." I leaned forward again. Willing her to see what I meant. Again that frightened flickering in her eyes as they met mine. *Leave her alone, you bully,* I told myself. But I couldn't. Something was forcing its way out. I couldn't stop it. "To me it seems that flagellation is a means—a perverted means—of sexual satisfaction."

A horrified silence.

"Reverend Mother, what do *you* think about it?"

Again the click in her head. The eyes looking up at the ceiling, shying away from what she didn't want to see.

"I don't—you don't—none of us knows what we think until the General Chapter tells us."

Sister Jocasta had left the Order. The letter from the Provincial had been read aloud to us this morning after breakfast. At London University she had met a young Jesuit and fallen in love. They were both leaving their orders and were going to get married.

I listened appalled to the news. I recalled Sister's handsome face, alight with humor. I remembered her at recreation in the noviceship arguing with Mother Walter, unable to let her opinion die, clinging to intellectual integrity. As I was trying to do now. Her departure filled me with more than sadness at losing a sister in Christ. We were alike, the two of us. Would I—should I eventually go too?

The thought terrified me. Abandoning the religious life, giving in to the worldliness that could ultimately separate me from God. "Anyone who puts his hand to the plough and looks back is not worthy of Me." How uncompromising that was! I did so much want to be worthy of God. Not to fail Him. And also there was a nagging fear, pure cowardice I knew. The world. I'd lost touch with it completely. Oh, I could cope now with Miss Jameson, but the undergraduates—how could I identify with them? I couldn't. I'd be trampled over at once, disappear without trace. That vision of the world I'd had on the Underground the first morning after the profession —it was not my world anymore.

But that I pushed out of my mind. I couldn't stay in because I was a coward. Couldn't admit to myself that that unworthy fear was in me. No. I had taken vows. Hang on, Mother Katherine had said, and I had promised. It was no good just serving God when times were easy. Now, when things seemed black and impossible, was the time to renew my resolve.

On our walk that afternoon I voiced my fears to Sister Rebecca.

"I'm scared, Sister. Afraid of what's happening to me here. I don't recognize myself."

"You have changed. But Sister, that's not your fault."

I blinked at her.

"It's bad for you here," Sister Rebecca went on. "Oh, not the University. Of course not! But the community. It's an old, conservative community."

"But don't you mind it?"

"Not as much as you do," she shook her head firmly, stubbornly. Not letting me go any further, despite the strain around her eyes, her emaciated body. "You feel things more than I do. I *can* see your difficulty with Reverend Mother. The two of you just can't get on. I—I don't mind so much. My temperament's quieter than yours; I'm not so quick. My mind isn't so clear and uncompromising. Reverend Mother and I are both quiet people. We can speak to one another."

I sighed despairingly. "I feel I'm two people. Two parts of me are dragging me apart and any day I'll burst! Sister, how can they do this to us? Send us to Oxford to develop our minds and then, when we go home, expect us to stop using them?"

"Other people have done it. But the trouble with you is that you're doing what Oxford is really trying to make us do. Learning to think."

"But what can I do?"

"It isn't just thinking, is it? There's the fact that you're not well. Look at both of us. We're like scarecrows. And you faint. Whatever causes that—even if it *is* just emotional—means that something is wrong!"

"But how can I get it right? And next year"—Sister had just taken her finals—"you won't be here." Suddenly the force of that hit me. No Rebecca to share a joke or an idea with. "These walks," I groaned. "There'll be a roster on the board: 'To take Sister Martha for a walk.' Like a dog!"

Her eyes were troubled. "I know! I've been worrying about that, too. Look, you're going to Skipton to make your retreat and R and C. That's where Mother Katherine is. I know she was worried about your coming here. Talk to her. She won't be able to do anything. But she'll help you."

"I don't want to leave," I said, as we took our outdoor shoes off. "I do want to be a good nun."

I was off to Skipton. Tonight I'd go into retreat with the rest of the community there, for our usual eight days every year. Part of me was excited. The Oxford convent had become oppressive and the thought of getting right away, of seeing Mother Katherine, was marvelous. But I was frightened. The eight days' silence. The rigorous Spiritual Exercises that scoured out all the places deep within yourself that you couldn't look at. This year what would they show me?

And now I was standing in the hall, saying good-bye to Mother Praeterita. Stiffly we exchanged the usual starchy embrace. I felt suddenly a great rush of contrition. All the year I'd fought her, made her life hell. It wasn't her fault. I'd failed this year, failed to see God in my superior.

"Reverend Mother," I looked up at her, my eyes suddenly filled with tears. "I'm so sorry! It's not been good between us. I'll do better when I come back."

She shook me slightly. "Don't be hysterical, Sister." It was the tone more than the words that distressed me. "Make a good retreat."

Sister Rebecca was driving me to the station. It was good-bye to her, too. As we left the drive I saw Reverend Mother standing there, a pillar of unloving righteousness.

Purple stars flashed before my eyes. Something broke in my head. Blood poured from my nose in thick, heavy gouts and clots.

"Do you want to go back?" Sister Rebecca asked in concern.

I shook my head, clutching my crimson handkerchief to my nose. No, no.

By the time we reached the station the blood showed no sign of stopping. My head was aching and I felt a strangely growing fear.

"Look," I said nasally as Sister and I stared helplessly at one another. What a farewell! "I'd better take that box of tissues with me for the journey." I reached into the glove compartment.

"Sister, you can't." She stared at me, agonized at the absurdity of it all. "The tissues belong to the Oxford community. You know there'll be a terrible fuss. I know it's stupid, it's unkind, it's wrong!" Tears stood out in her eyes and she clutched my hand. This was good-bye. We might not meet again for years. It was all in the hands of our superiors. For a year thrown into an unlawful friendship. And we might never see one another again. I felt the tears smarting my own eyes.

"No," I said. "Of course not. Reverend Mother won't let me take them."

There was a moment of silent sharing. Then, lips pursed together, she pressed her own handkerchief into my hand. "Take that." Her voice was tight.

"I can't," I said. "You know we're not allowed to lend each other things."

She shook her head hard. "Please. Take it." She was giving me more than a handkerchief. It was an act of love.

I left her in a fog of blood and tears. The religious life, I'd thought, should be one of large, liberating perspectives. And here I was worrying about a packet of Kleenex! I suddenly recalled St. Paul's words: "God's foolishness is wiser than human wisdom, and God's weakness is stronger than human strength." That was what I had to hold on to. What did St. Ignatius say I should do? "To reject all that the world loves and desires"—all the common sense, the worldly wisdom, all love—"and become a fool for Christ's sake." It was the ultimate sacrifice. To be a fool in my eyes and in the world's —to accept insanity, if need be, giving up everything for God.

All that afternoon I felt sick, gripped by a fierce, unreasoning terror. Now, in the hot silence of an August evening, I stood shivering slightly in the Skipton refectory. That very evening the retreat would begin, taking me closer to self-scrutiny than I dared to go. The only sounds in the vast room were the clash of metal dishes and the tinkle of cutlery as three white-aproned nuns scurried round, putting the supper out on the long wooden tables, their rubber soles squeaking on the polished floor. A long sunbeam slashed through the tall windows, catching the big crucifix in a dramatic, natural floodlight, tingeing the white walls with a pink glow.

Suddenly in the special hush that heralded the deep isolation of the next eight days, a long disembodied sound broke into the waiting stillness, agonized, fighting for breath, on and on with a will of its own. What was that strange, keening scream that sounded like an animal caught in a trap? Where was it coming from? Then from a long way off I saw myself, my eyes clenched tightly shut, my mouth gaping and contorted and from it coming the unearthly cry. Nuns hurried round. They slapped me, shook me, but could not quell the sound. Finally I watched myself crumble through their arms in an awkward huddle.

Then something snapping. The sound stopped. Two selves pulled apart. Blackness.

11 · THROUGH THE NARROW GATE

"Sister."

Don't wake up. Don't feel the hands lifting me, unbuttoning my clothes. Not the disgust. Can't face it. Stay asleep forever.

"Sister! Sister Martha. Can you hear me, dear?"

Dear? A shock. No anger in the voice.

"Sister. Try to wake up. It's all right." Kind voices. Gentle hands.

I opened my eyes.

Mother Rose, so worried. Large eyes magnified by her spectacles. And Mother Jean, the infirmarian, smiling but her eyes frightened and concerned.

"There you are!" I felt the tears rise and turned my face to the pillow. *But it's too late,* I thought.

"Sister, can you hear me?" Mother Jean asked. Why isn't she angry? She will be soon. When she knows I do it all the time. Weakness. Emotional. Failure. And I wanted to be good here at Skipton, turn over a new leaf. "Look at me. Don't cry. Sister, it's *all right.*"

I looked up, speechless. I tried to smile but the smile collapsed. Water was coming out of my eyes. Silently flowing, like the blood. Was it only this afternoon?

"Say something, Sister. Come on. Say something to us."

"Mother . . . I can't."

"Can't what, Sister?"

"I can't do it."

"Do what?"

"I can't do it." Like a Gramophone stuck in a groove. "Can't do it. Can't."

Whispers. Voices. "Oxford . . . strain . . . that community . . . Praeterita . . . studies . . . not by all accounts . . . Mother Katherine."

I spoke up. "Mother Katherine?" Someone had said she could help me. I needed help.

"She's away—do you remember, Sister? She'll be back in a couple of days. Try to trust us. Just for now."

Silence.

"What, Sister? What is it?"

Why aren't they angry?

A word. Coming up. Slowly surfacing. "Retreat."

"Yes, that's tomorrow."

"I can't."

"Don't worry about that now. Sleep tonight. We'll talk about it in the morning."

"No. I can't."

"You must make a retreat, Sister. It says so in the rule . . . Sister, don't. Don't cry again."

"Can't." The retreat especially, but not just the retreat.

"All right. All right. I'll talk to the priest. Such a nice young priest. He's down there now. Giving the first talk. He might help you."

"No."

"Sister, if you're not able to make the retreat, you're not. It'll be all right. I'll ring Mother Provincial and explain. It's all right."

Peace. A flooding relief.

"Here, take this pill. It'll help you to sleep."

Waiting for sleep. Being gently wrapped in it. But why are they all so kind? Now, when it's too late.

There were days of blackness. Fatigue. Waking to feel hands, see a face. Cups raised to my lips. Sleep.

Sometimes dreams. Running in a race and never, never getting there. Hearing all the while St. Paul's words read in the toneless voice of a nun in the refectory, over and over again: "I can assure you, my brothers, I am far from thinking I have already won . . . I

244

forget the past and I strain ahead for what is still to come." Strain. Still to come. And knowing that there is no finish.

Sometimes trying to kill something growing. A plant that keeps putting out new shoots, huge monstrous growth, stabbing and thrashing at it, feeling its pain as the green sap falls in huge drops. But it never dies.

And a face. Mother Katherine's, is it? Calling my name. But why? Doesn't she realize I'm already dead?

"Try and eat something, Sister."

No, not food.

One morning—how long afterward?—I woke up and saw clearly the sunlight streaming in through the windows. I looked round the room. Small. Only one bed. How odd! A room of my own! A washbasin! White walls and thin, white curtains floating gently in the breeze.

I tried to sit up but couldn't.

"It's all right. Don't try to sit. You're too weak."

A voice I knew. I turned my head and watched my mind taking in the features, slowly composing them until they became Mother Katherine.

"That's better." She was smiling but her eyes were clearly worried. "How do you feel, dear?"

Dear? Again.

"I'm tired, Mother." I felt the fatigue aching not just in my body, but in my mind too. My soul. Tired of life.

"Yes. I know." She leaned forward and took my hand. I watched this. Astonished. As though I were someone else. I would have been glad of that once, I thought. But not now. I can feel nothing. "The feel of not to feel it." Who said that?

"What happened to me?"

"You've been upset. Too upset. It's been so distressing that it's all had to come out violently. In a rush. I *am* sorry, my dear. It shouldn't have happened like this."

We sat, silently.

"You must try and eat something, Sister. You're far too thin. And you won't feel better till you do."

"I can't."

"Please. Please try." She's a superior. I must obey her. But she's saying *please*.

I nodded. She smiled. How easy it was to give pleasure. "You'll feel stronger, then," she was saying. "How much do you remember?"

I sat waiting for it all to come back. The collage of pain. "Was that me screaming?" She nodded. What did it all mean? I ought to say I was sorry for having screamed. But I wasn't. "That scream was me."

She nodded, eyes sad. "I know."

"I can't do it, Mother."

"What do you mean, my dear?"

"Everything. Die. My feelings count too much. My mind . . . " I shook my head. How to explain? "I can't stop it. I've tried. Over and over again. But it won't stop thinking."

"It shouldn't." Her voice was angry, but not with me. Her hand gripped mine. "You have a fine mind. You must use it."

"But Mother Walter . . . "

"Yes, I know. Her thinking was wrong. Not for everybody. But for you it was wrong. And it shouldn't have been like that. She's a fanatic. It'll be different now, Sister. We're changing the way we form our young nuns. All that's over."

But not for me. I'm formed. It's too late.

"But I can't anymore." A flat statement of fact. What did I mean?

"Do you want to leave? Look, Sister, I'll help you. We all will here. There'll be no pressures. Just get better. But if you want to leave—"

"No! No!" Instinctive. Not fully thought out. "I don't want to go." Panic.

Her face relaxed. "All right." She smiled. "I'm so glad. We need you in the Order." Me? "But you're not well. Would you like us to ask the college to give you a year off? To get better?"

"No!"—another instinctive reply. Oxford was important. The thought of leaving the Order terrified me, but there was something at Oxford that I knew I had to face. I couldn't think what it was—I couldn't bear to. But putting it off was hopeless. I smiled at Mother Katherine to reassure her. "Sometime I've got to face what's there for me. I love it. The study. But I've got to find what it means to me. Why this has happened. Oxford can save me."

"And the community there?" she asked.

I thought of Mother Praeterita standing stonily like a column the last time I had seen her and shook my head. "Mother Praeterita . . ."

"That woman!" No, it's not like that, I thought. You feel that because you're hurt for me. But it wasn't just her. Better that it was like that. It had shown me something. Something important that I didn't want to analyze yet.

I fought against the light-headed lethargy that threatened. There was something I had to say. It was important.

"Mother, what's happened to make people like Mother Praeterita the way they are? Uncertain with their minds, not seeing things they don't want to see. People like Mother Imelda who seem starved inside. You're not like that. You can think and feel and still be a good nun. Mother Bianca . . ." I trailed off looking anxiously for a reply.

She paused and looked straight at me. "They've failed in courage somewhere. They've let themselves get enslaved by the training, by the letter of the rule and not its spirit. Of course we must be obedient. Of course we have to love God more than anyone else. But we've given Him ourselves and He wants *us* too. As we are, as *you* are. And the hard thing is to hang on to the inner lights that God sends you. To use your mind and your heart. The training is there to ensure that God always come first, not our petty selfishness. But God."

"How do you mean, they've failed in courage?"

"By clinging to the rules as to the rail of a swimming pool. Not being willing ever to go out of their depth and trust that God will hold them up. And, Sister, there's too much of that in the Order. Far too much. The training, the way our superiors have ruled us, make it very difficult indeed for people to stop being afraid like that."

"Just the exceptional people, then."

She laughed. "Oh, you mustn't try to flatter me. You know, for years I've had a very difficult time in the Order. All that time when I was headmistress in Birmingham I was considered dangerous and subversive." She smiled, reminiscing. "Some of my superiors gave me a terrible time. They kept me in Birmingham—as you know, it's not an important school—to keep me out of the way."

I thought of Mother Bianca and her thirty years in the clothing room. It was a daunting prospect.

"How did you manage not to get bitter and angry inside?"

She shrugged. "It was difficult. To be in disgrace for fifteen years. Hanging on to what God wants of you and not giving in, just because if you do you'll be patted on the head and called a good girl —and have an easier life."

I thought hard. It was an even deeper level of renunciation. But could I do it? Something quailed inside me.

"But didn't you ever think of giving up?"

"Not really. Not seriously. Oh, I'd have a good old moan to myself from time to time. But if you love God enough then you have to be brave. You remember what Job said: 'Though He slay me, yet will I trust Him.' "

" 'Though He slay me, yet will I trust Him.' " I repeated. "But now they've made you a superior. Is it all right now?"

She smiled. "Oh, I'm out of the doghouse at the moment. But it may not last. I may find myself washing up in some back kitchen yet as an old nun."

"But wouldn't you feel that was a terrible waste? If it happened?"

"I'd feel it, yes. But I'd feel too that I'd done whatever God asked of me."

We sat quietly together. Had I really got that kind of faith? Or that degree of confidence in myself, never mind God? Oh, I could see myself carrying on, willing to be in disgrace, perhaps, after this talk with Mother Katherine. But would I have Mother's courage? Or would I become a damaged person, maiming people around me? I didn't know. How much I wanted to stay here. The ideal of perfect self-giving and close union with God seemed more than ever poignantly beautiful. And the possibility of entering the world again terrified me. But that scream had been a moment of truth. I had to find out exactly what it meant for me. And it was no use asking Mother Katherine. Only I could learn to read my own heart. I knew that now.

"Mother," I said at last, "I've got to think."

"Yes. I see that. And what I said earlier still goes. There'll be no pressure either way. You must find what God wants for you. But, Sister, take your time about the decision. You're not well. Don't fight to arrive at a resolution. You can't at the moment. Give your mind and your body time to heal. You remember what St. Ignatius says?"

I nodded. " 'Never change a resolution in time of depression.' "

"Exactly. So stay here. Try and eat a little more. Rest. Sleep. We've got to get your body back on its feet. Then your mind. Leave the decisions absolutely alone for a month or two. Go back to Oxford. Block yourself off from the community. Mother Provincial will speak to them about it. She's very concerned that you're so ill. They'll leave you alone. You enjoy your studies. Well, enjoy them next term. Just think about literature."

"Isn't that just putting it off again?"

"No, because all the time the decision, one way or the other, will be growing inside you. You'll know when it's been made. Now, you must sleep again." She made the sign of the cross on my forehead. "God bless you."

I took her advice. I passed into a drowsy twilight time. Lying in bed, seeing nobody but Mother Katherine and the infirmarian. Trying to eat a little. Trying to read. Sleeping.

One evening I heard a tap on my door. Rather a tentative tap. I glanced at the clock. Early for supper.

"Come in!" I called, expecting to see Mother Jean.

But it wasn't she. It was Mother Melinda, who was employed in the boarding school attached to Skipton convent. I looked at her, surprised. Sick nuns were not usually allowed visits at all hours by members of the community. What could she be doing here? I hardly knew her. I'd had a glimpse of her on the first troubled evening but that was all. She was a youngish woman in her mid-thirties with an intelligent, pale face and troubled eyes that sometimes flashed with bitterness. She moved across the room awkwardly in a series of little jerks, without the graceful gliding movement of the other nuns.

She smiled down at me now a little defensively as though expecting a rebuff. How odd, I thought. I'm only a student nun and she holds quite a high office in the house. But her eyes were concerned.

"Hello," she said in a roughly offhand way. "I thought I would pop in to see you. As I was passing. Don't mind, do you?"

"No. Thank you for coming."

"That's all right." She threw herself rather unreligiously into a chair and started to pick at the chipped varnish on the armrest. Then she looked up at me and grinned. I could see that she wanted to be friendly but didn't quite know how to go about it. Neither did I.

"Well!" she drawled. "You did give us all a shock, didn't you! Screaming away like that."

I flushed, embarrassed. What would they all be thinking of me?

"Poor old thing!" she said, and for a moment the roughness had gone from her voice. She smiled back at me. "I bet you've had a terrible year at Oxford. I know. Mother Praeterita was my superior when I was there but that was years ago when she was a lot younger. I expect it's all far worse now. And there were a lot of us student nuns. That helped."

"Yes. I expect it did."

"How are you feeling now, anyway? You are eating, aren't you? You look like a skeleton!"

"I'm feeling lots better now, thanks."

"Good. Keep it up." She smiled again vaguely and started to wander restlessly round the room, humming just under her breath, as she examined with apparent fascination the contents of my tooth mug.

Suddenly she turned round and faced me.

"Sister, what do you know about sex?"

I jumped. So did she. We looked at one another, aghast at the taboo word. But the word was irrevocably out now. I stared back at her curiously. The tone of her question didn't suggest that she really meant: "I expect a lot of your illness is due to sexual problems; let me try and enlighten you." No, she was the one seeking enlightenment. From me. The youngest nun in the convent here!

Then I knew why she had asked me. It was because I had screamed and collapsed. I had put myself, for a while at any rate, absolutely beyond the pale. I was one apart from the close-knit ranks of the Order. Therefore she could ask me this more frankly than anybody else.

She was still looking at me, hanging on my words. Waiting.

"Oh, well, you know. The usual things, I suppose," I hedged.

"Yes, but *what*?" Her voice was urgent.

What indeed? I looked back over the past few years. Biology lessons about the rabbit. All that evasion of the basic facts by telling us how "holy" sex was under a few stringently vital conditions. That terrible groping with Father in the parlor. What could I tell her? Only what I had recently discovered at Oxford. At the heart of all those confused impressions I had to admit to a basic ignorance.

"I suppose I don't know very much about it at all," I finally brought out. "I mean, what kind of things do you want to know?"

"Well, not just the biology of it. But the details. They're what fox me," she waved her hands around expressing bewilderment. "I mean, what position do you do it in? I was talking to Mother Gemma and she didn't know either. But she said she'd read somewhere that you could do it in any position at all."

We gaped at one another, our minds teeming with images that made no sense.

"Honestly, Mother, I don't know either."

"It's awful, really," she leaned forward frowning, talking easily now. "After all, I should be discussing sex with adolescent girls. I should be guiding them, giving them advice. But you know, I suppose some of the older ones know far more about it than I. When did you enter?"

"Nineteen sixty-two."

"Yes," she sat back, nodding to herself. "Before it all started to happen. You know, the contraceptive pill, the permissive society."

I did *not* know, I realized, anything about all that. The sixties had completely passed me by in the noviceship and the seclusion of religious training. With the decision I had to make, this sent a pang of anxiety through me.

She got up and walked round the room again, staring out the window. Turning away from me, she said with husky embarrassment, "But it's not just that, you know, if I'm honest. It's me."

"What do you mean?" I could feel her trouble strongly, like a powerful smell in the little room. I felt helpless and disturbed. She came across and sat on the bed, again a kind of freedom that was unheard of in the religious life. But now for this moment that seemed irrelevant.

"I suppose I feel frustrated sometimes. Oh, I know it's a sacrifice and all that. That's what chastity is all about. But I do feel so funny at times—I get all trembly and fidgety. Like an old maid. All right. I know the rule says we've got to make ourselves like angels. But it's hard work being an angel."

"It's impossible." I startled myself by the clarity with which I suddenly saw this obvious truth.

We sat silently together, thinking our separate thoughts. All this bleeding, fainting, vomiting—I suddenly wondered, was it because I was forcing myself to achieve the impossible?

"But what's the answer then?" I asked at last. "I mean, I don't really think it's impossible to be celibate. Some people, like Mother Katherine, aren't odd."

"Perhaps fewer people can really be celibate than is usually supposed," said Mother Melinda slowly. "It does say in the Gospel that there are only a few who can do it."

We stared at one another. Not daring to voice the personal implications for each of us. Then she brought the topic firmly away from the particular.

"I was at a course last year. A priest who is a psychologist. He goes round talking to disturbed nuns. Perhaps you should try and see him? I'm sure they won't let you go, though. He was saying that the traditional way of training nuns has been to keep them in a prepubertal state by treating them like children—you know, do as you're told, no responsibility, no mention of sex, no men, no freedom. It's an awful thought, isn't it?"

It was. "But I can see what he means."

"So can I. And then he said that often, when nuns are about my age, it can all start coming out. And this kind of restlessness and frustration gets very strong. Because the nun knows, somewhere deep down in the subconscious, that if she wants to have children it's a case of now or never. That's why a lot of people tend to leave during their late thirties."

"It makes sense, doesn't it? But does the explanation make it any easier to cope with it?"

"'No, not really. You're in a state at the moment, and I expect

252

you've got all sorts of theories about why this has happened. But it doesn't help, does it? The feelings are still there."

" 'Feelings don't count,' " but I could hear how I'd put ironic quotation marks into my voice.

"They do, you know. That's something I've learned. And don't you forget it." She got up. "You look ghastly, Sister. Have I tired you out? I'm sorry! Bothering you with my problems at the moment. You've got enough of your own."

"It's all right," I said. "You've been making one or two things clearer to me. It's not nice. But necessary. Thanks."

She looked at me. "Take care of yourself," she said. And was gone.

I went back to Oxford for the autumn term. And I did what Mother Katherine advised. The community treated me with wary politeness. Mother Praeterita and I avoided each other and when we had to converse her eyes were fixed even more firmly on the ceiling. There were no more instructions. Just prayer and work.

Prayer for those eight weeks was a dark numbness. Gazing blankly at the tabernacle, unable to feel or even to will very much at all. God was there, somewhere. I knew better than to expect revelations, visions, or voices telling me what I must do. That happened only to a very few. Always those words "a very few." Very few nuns can love enough, think humbly but remain true to themselves, trust God enough, successfully live a celibate life. Very few. It was a daunting thought. I felt exhausted spiritually. And I knew enough about prayer to realize that I'd just got to hang on, being there physically, receiving the sacraments, doing my best.

Work was easier. It absorbed all the tormented indecisions of the summer. I refused to let myself think about my decision. Instead I plunged into eighteenth-century literature. The Age of Reason. Cool, severe, and healing. Thank God we weren't doing the Romantics this term, I thought ironically. As usual the work excited me; my mind was growing stronger.

And that term, too, I watched the students. A silent observer. I didn't know them at all. I recalled Mother Melinda's words about how youth had changed in the sixties. As they trooped into the lecture theatres with their casual clothes, their long floating hair and beards, and their loud easy confidence, I thought back to my own adolescence. We had most of us looked middle-aged, youthful copies of our mothers. There had been the Suzies, but even she didn't have the sense that youth was important. The students here were seen carrying banners and slogans through the college every Saturday afternoon. Demonstrating. An extraordinary idea to me! Legalized protest. And they wandered through the streets, men and girls with their arms draped casually around one another. I remembered the Birmingham streets late at night. The doorways filled with couples frantically embracing before the appearance of the last bus. Here there was obviously no need of that. There was no last bus. Could they possibly be having premarital sex? The unspeakable bogey of my adolescence? If they were, they looked remarkably well from it. How on earth would I ever fit into their world? None of them would have any idea about the experiences I'd had during the last seven years.

One evening I went into the college to get a book out of the library and I passed the dining hall. I stood and looked through the glass doors. The hordes of people, the noise, the complete opposite of all I'd been accustomed to. I felt a cold fear clutching me. I could as easily walk through that door and sit at one of those tables as fly. I tried to take myself through the experience. Collecting my food, walking up to an empty space, watching the other people at the table eyeing me. Would they ignore me? Probably. But the loneliness and the humiliation. Or even worse, would they try to make friends? With hideous clarity I saw that I wouldn't know how to respond. I thought over the friendly moments of the last seven years: Mother Melinda and I talking in the Skipton infirmary, Mother Albert holding me to her in the Noviceship dormitory. Moments snatched out of time. Mother Bianca—but that wasn't friendship because it wasn't between equals. There was Sister Rebecca, of course. But we'd *had* to be friends; there'd been no choice. And we completely understood each other's background. But none of those students would have an inkling of my background and my preoccupations. And, given a choice, who would want to befriend me? It was impossible to imagine. I hated myself. Could anyone ever like me?

As I walked away from the dining hall I found tears pouring down my cheeks. I'd been hankering for friendship and closeness for so long, and now I knew that the capacity for it had been starved out of me. Even if I did manage to begin to approach someone else, wouldn't I be crippled by the old mechanisms of guilt that I could see were not going to disappear overnight?

I was not to spend Christmas at Oxford, I was told. I would spend the whole of my vacation at the Scholasticate with Mother Frances. That was a relief. Memories of last Christmas, that terrible attack on Christmas Eve, the ostracism and self-disgust of Christmas Day, still burnt in my mind too painfully. How considerate the Order was being. In a way it made it so much harder. Never had I felt fonder of them all than I did now; never had they shown themselves kinder to me. When . . .

I flinched at what I was thinking. It was time to make my decision. It should surely have emerged by this time. But I still felt the same dizzying confusion. The pull toward the old ideals, the sheer comforting familiarity of convent life compared with the terrors of the unknown world.

That first evening at the Scholasticate I went to see Mother Frances. Her manner was so much gentler than it had been before. How odd it was to be back in this room where I had studied logic with Mother Bianca. Where she had told me I had been a good Scholastic. To think of all that had happened since.

"Well, how are you, Sister? I'm sorry, so sorry you were so ill."

"Oh, I'm much better now, thank you, Reverend Mother."

"Hmm. You still look pale and thin. Please try and eat a little more. You can't go on like this, you know."

"Yes, I do know that. And it's not just the eating. It's—Reverend Mother, I've got to make my mind up, haven't I, about whether I'm going to stay or not? I know I'm not supposed to strain about the decision. But it's time now, isn't it? Nothing's being solved by this shilly-shallying. It's only making matters worse."

She had been watching me shrewdly while I was talking, her small brown eyes narrowed in concentration. Then she spoke. Very quietly.

"You've already made up your mind, haven't you?"

I looked at her, startled. "Yes," I said. It was true. It had happened. There it was: my decision. "I don't want to go," I cried. "So much of me wants to stay here. But for the wrong reasons. For cowardice, partly. But I must leave."

"Yes," her voice was sad. "Yes, I think you're right. You must."

"But how will I bear it?" I saw her wincing at the complexities that my question raised.

"You'll be all right." She was trying to be brisk and matter-of-fact. "You'll carry on at Oxford. You're doing very well there. There'll be no problem."

"There will," I said, forcing my fears outside myself. "And you can't help me with it, I know. But how on earth am I going to get used to people again? I'll be on my own. Up till now wherever I've gone outside I've been a representative. Not just me. Me in my own right, standing for myself. I've stood for God—just by my clothes —for all of you. Now I don't stand for anything. I've got to be myself. And I don't know who I am."

"There is a lot of what you were still there," she said. "You can't feel it at the moment, but I can see it. You couldn't do your work so well if you weren't alive somewhere. Not literature. That's you responding to those books."

"But what about other people?"

She shook her head. "I know. It will be hard. You'll have to build yourself up again bit by bit—all of you that you've taken to pieces here. It will probably take years. But you will do it in the end. You're stronger than you think you are."

"How can you say that after what happened in the summer?"

"It was an explosion. It was because it wasn't God's will for you anymore. Of course it suddenly went wrong."

"Did God change His mind about me then? Did I throw away my vocation?"

"I don't know. I can't answer that. And I don't think either of us should speculate about it. It won't help you. His will is clear enough now, though. Concentrate on the future."

The future. It stretched ahead bleak and empty. Out there, apart from books, there wasn't a single thing waiting for me. It was like being born again. But this time nobody would be there to receive me.

"You can still live a Christian life in the world, of course. God will help you."

God. Learning to live with Him in the world. Would my faith, that now seemed suddenly so thin and insubstantial, stand up to it? I felt that I'd failed Him, put my hand to the plough and looked back. I'd failed His challenge and knew I'd have to live with that always.

"Now, there are practical things to do. I'll ring Mother Provincial and tell her your decision and she'll come up and see you here. Don't worry; she'll be very understanding. And you have to write a letter to the bishop telling him you want to be released from your vows and asking him to forward your request for a dispensation to the Sacred Congregation for Religious in Rome. For goodness' sake be positive in your letter; don't tell the Bishop you've been under a strain because all he'll do then is write back and tell you to delay your decision until you're feeling better! Tell him that you've decided that your Christian vocation lies in the world, something like that."

"I see," I said faintly. How horribly official it all sounded. A few minutes ago I hadn't realized my decision was made. Now it was rapidly becoming a reality.

As I got up to go, Mother Frances looked up at me. "You're looking for something in your life. You don't know what—neither do I, but you're obviously looking. I hope you find what you're looking for, Karen, whatever it is. You haven't found it here."

The hard part. Writing to my parents. As I sealed my letter I wondered what they'd feel. They'd be pleased. But sorry for me. I shuddered. Our relationship had been carefully severed and like the rest of my life would have to be built up again, brick by brick. It would take a very long time. Inevitably I realized that they must think that basically I was still the same person that I had been at seventeen. And, like all parents, they'd find it hard to accept that I was now somebody quite different. Someone they could no longer mold. For the last seven years I'd let my superiors mold me. Now I mustn't let my parents start.

I sat talking to Mother Provincial. She'd been such a remote figure all my religious life and now she was so gentle and considerate. They all were. It was breaking my heart. If they'd apply pressure or be angry and reproachful, screaming at me that I was a wicked woman, leaving them would be so much easier. To go in anger rather than in sorrow, feeling I was heroic and conquering. Not like this.

"We're sad that you're going, Sister. We'd much rather you stay. But I do respect your decision. It's the right one, I think, and I'll pray for you. We all will."

I looked back at her dumbly. What was there to say?

"Now," she said. "The dispensation will be here in three weeks, just in time for you to go back to college."

Three weeks! I stared at her, appalled. I'd imagined that it would take months while the Roman wheels of bureaucracy ground slowly on. Comforting months. While at least I'd have time to adjust to the changes and could still cling to the familiar.

"I didn't think it would be that soon, Reverend Mother," I said quietly. I had started to tremble. I felt sick with sudden fright.

"Oh, yes. It's not good for you or for any of us to have you in this halfway state. It's a very unreal position for you. The sooner the better. You've made your decision; you mustn't be kept under any other strain."

I knelt down for her blessing, for the last time.

"We'll miss you, dear. You yourself. But you must find your own peace. God bless you."

Afterward I fled to the bathroom to hide my tears. I felt quite alone and very frightened of the ordeal ahead. I was in a state of limbo—neither in one world nor in the other. In fact, there was nowhere I felt I belonged anymore. Yes, I had made the right decision, but now I felt bereft of all the ideals and hopes that I had lived by for so long. Destitute.

I wouldn't be physically destitute, however. The Provincial had explained that I'd get a student grant and that until that came through they would give me some money. I would have a check for 100 pounds and 25 pounds in cash. I'd been appalled.

"I won't be able to take that money, Reverend Mother," I had exclaimed. It seemed wrong that they had invested so much money in me and would get no return for it. And there was something else too. Obscurely, I felt that I was being paid off in some way.

Reverend Mother had waved my protests aside. "We have to do it. It isn't charity," she had explained. "If a sister leaves us, we are bound to provide for her as long as it's necessary."

And all this would happen in three weeks. In so short a time I would be leaving here forever and living a life I could not begin to imagine.

Sadly I bathed my eyes in the washbasin, and as I did so I looked at the small mirror. There I was, my face hidden almost entirely by the habit. What would I look like without the wimple? I'd forgotten what I had looked like before. My hair! I thought suddenly. Cropped all over. Horrified, I pulled my veil off and looked.

My hair was long. Rather hideous to be sure, all different lengths, covered with starch from the cap, dull and sticky, but a passable length. Bewildered, I ran my hand through it. Then the significance of this hit me. I must, without realizing it, have been growing my hair for months to get it to this length. For years it had been automatic to crop it regularly a quarter of an inch all over. But I hadn't done that. Months ago, at one level, my decision had already been made.

It was 6 January 1969. The feast of the Epiphany. Every year on that day it was the custom in the Order for the nuns to renew their vows. Vows had, of course, been made once and for all on the profession day, and this was only a reminder, an act of devotion. Yearly we remembered that we had given our lives to God and laid them at His feet, just as the Three Wise Men had given their gifts to the Infant Christ.

I knelt in the Scholasticate chapel with my head hidden in my hands, so that nobody could see that I wasn't joining in with the vow formula that the scholastics were saying in unison.

I listened sadly to the familiar words of the vows. "I vow to Thy Divine Majesty, poverty, chastity, and obedience." I had thought that God had called me to this closeness, but I hadn't been up to it. Never had the ideal seemed more beautiful than it did now I was outside it all, waiting for my dispensation. Complete self-sacrifice. I recalled Christ's words: "Enter by the narrow gate, since the gate that leads to perdition is wide, and the road spacious, and many take it; but it is a narrow gate and a hard road that lead to life, and only a few find it." How often I'd read that, but now the last few words hit me hard. "Only a few find it." And I was not one of those few. I wasn't strong enough. Perhaps not many nuns who stayed in really were. But for all my sadness I knew I had made the right decision.

For me the narrow gate would lead only to death, not life. The kind of death I had seen in the last year at Oxford.

Now the choir were singing the prayer of St. Ignatius, the prayer that was always sung at professions. I felt close to tears as I thought of my own profession day, now soon to be canceled. The words, softened by the haunting melody, struck me with their austere strength:

> Take and receive, O Lord, all my liberty; my memory, my understanding, and my will. All that I have, all that I am, Thou hast given me, and I give it all back to Thee to be governed according to Thy will.
>
> All I ask is Thy grace and Thy love. With these I am rich enough and I do not ask for anything else.

It was the last words that stung. I did want things other than God's love. I wanted human closeness, beauty, freedom of mind. I probably wouldn't get them but I wanted them. God's love should have been enough. It was in one sense everything. But I did ask for other things, and if I stayed I'd be grabbing at little unworthy human satisfactions, as the Oxford nuns grabbed at the cat.

The prayer left an aching sadness. That perfect self-giving. That image of God as Everything that still couldn't satisfy me. How could I be happy when I'd rejected Everything? I'd undergone a training that had been planned by St. Ignatius and refined for four centuries by his successors. It was meant to last for life. Kneeling there that day, fighting with my tears, I knew it would. Always some part of me, perhaps the deepest part—who knew?—would love this ideal and mourn its loss. In one sense, vows or no vows, I should be a nun all my life.

Thursday, 27 January 1969. A visitor had arrived at the Scholasticate from Tripton and had gone straight up to Mother Frances' room. I knew who it was, though no one else did. All around me the scholastics rushed about their daily tasks. Someone was in the kitchen and Mother Constantia was bemoaning the custard.

"Just look at these lumps, Sister! I could weep. I could just weep!"

Everything was the same, and it would be the same after I had gone, the waters of the religious life closing over me without a ripple. A scholastic came into the room. She beamed at me.

"Sister Martha, Reverend Mother wants you upstairs."

I smiled back. I felt calm now that I'd come to it. Calm and yet sad. But it was right. I had to go on.

Behind her desk, Mother Frances stood with a sheaf of papers in her hand. She eyed me levelly and her voice was formal. We were going through a ritual. There was no room for personality here.

"You have to sign these papers, which release you from your vows of poverty, chastity, and obedience. You must understand that the moment you take the papers into your hand you are no longer a nun. You will then be released from your vows. If, five minutes later, one minute later, you change your mind, it will be too late. You'll have to start all over again as a postulant." She paused.

"I have to ask you formally whether you want to take these papers into your hands."

We stood in silence. Our eyes met in a salute of farewell.

"Yes, Reverend Mother." My voice was surprisingly calm. "Yes. I do want them."

We looked at one another again. A long, long silence.

Then I held out my hands for the papers.

"God bless you, Karen."

Slowly, I pulled off my profession ring, unwreathed the huge rosary and crucifix from my waistband, and laid them all on her desk. My life as a nun was over.

The coach crawled slowly up Uxbridge Road, caught in the lunchtime rush. I stared out the window, fighting back my tears.

Nostalgia was pushed aside for now and panic took over. I had written to the principal of my college explaining my decision and she had given me a room in one of the new buildings on the campus. What would it have been like to have nowhere to go? The idea of finding a room, a job all at once would have been terrifying, whereas I had a certain continuity built into my life. The next day the new term would begin with all its familiar rituals and commitments. By this time tomorrow I'd have been assigned a tutor and a tutorial partner. All much as usual, except for the radical change that was becoming more frightening minute by minute.

It was almost dark when we hurled up Cowley Road, even

though it was only three o'clock. The windows of the bus were black and shiny now that they'd put the lights on. Magdalen Tower was floodlit like a beacon, a signal that my new life was about to begin.

Curious, I pushed open the door of my room and looked around. Directly opposite was a large plate-glass window overlooking the college grounds, with a broad wooden window seat. There were a desk, a bed, a reading lamp, an armchair. A letter on the desk. But what immediately startled me was the color. The room positively glowed—the bright orangey curtains and matching bedspread, the burnished cork tiles, the brilliant white walls. After years of unbleached calico, thin white bedspreads, and old serviceable curtains the room seemed aggressively assertive in its call to comfort and enjoyment. I stood in the center of the room uneasily.

I was drained. Apart from the emotion of the day, there had been that exhausting walk from the bus station lugging my bag and books, which had proved crippling. It would have been sensible to take a taxi—it wouldn't have cost very much—but I found the idea impossible. It didn't matter how firmly I told myself that I was now a free agent and no longer vowed to poverty and the renunciation of comfort and luxury; I couldn't do it. I pushed the trunk to a corner of the room and looked for somewhere to sit down. There was a choice: the desk chair or the armchair. It never occurred to me to sit on the divan. Instinctively I went toward the desk and pulled out the leather cushioned chair. Then I stopped. *No,* I told myself firmly. *You've got to start somewhere.* Gingerly but determinedly I sat down in the armchair. It felt very odd. There had been no armchairs in the convents, of course. "In the religious life we do not loll in armchairs," I imagined Mother Albert saying. But I wasn't in the religious life anymore. I was in the world. Everywhere I looked in this little room told me that. My back was still aching and my legs and arms were weak with reaction. I tried to lean back in the chair, but it was impossible. Again there was that strong sense of something forbidden. I reclined stiffly and awkwardly for a moment and then gave up the struggle, resuming my accustomed upright posture.

I remembered my parents' telling me how they had gone over to Dublin for a weekend during the war and how they'd gone mad with delight at the unrationed food and drink. But it wasn't like that for me. I couldn't relax. I was a person who could no longer sprawl in a chair.

I gave up altogether and turned to the letter on my desk to keep the problem at bay. I was puzzled by the postmark—the University Registry—and even more so by the address: *Miss Karen Armstrong*. Why had they not used my religious name? They couldn't possibly know about the dispensation yet. No, this must be some circular or other I realised after a moment. Officialdom always used my secular name. I opened the letter and read it through.

At first the words on the page meant nothing to me. I stared at the letter and started to read it again. It must be a mistake; it can't be true, I thought incredulously. But no. "Dear Miss Armstrong." It was true. I had won a Violet Vaughan Morgan Prize for Literature.

The college had entered Elizabeth, my tutorial partner, and me for the prize examination. I'd spent the whole of the last day of last term in a gloomy room in the examination schools with men and women from other colleges. We had written essays on the novel, on ideas of tragedy, on verse satire for six hours. Toward the end my pen had felt leaden; the words I was writing had seemed turgid and stupid.

But I had won! In one area at least I could hold my own in the world. Suddenly the room seemed less alien. The letter and the check for 100 pounds that was the prize money seemed like a welcome, a certificate reassuring me that I could cope.

Suddenly I knew what I had to do. I had to make myself plunge into the world outside this room. All over the college now people would be having tea. Already I could smell toast and hear girls on the landing outside arguing about the communal kettle. I had to make myself join in while the glow of euphoria about that prize was upon me. I needed help. I couldn't do it alone. There were two girls reading English in my year who were Catholics: Rose and Bridget. They had been to convent schools. They knew about nuns—or rather, I corrected myself wryly—they knew a little bit about nuns. I would go to them.

But first there was something else I had to do. I stood at the college pay phone. Around me the students bustled, poking into the pigeon-holes, greeting one another cheerfully after the vacation. I stuck my head into the inadequate little hood trying to acquire some tiny measure of privacy.

I heard the telephone ringing at the other end. Silly to ring at this time of day, really. There probably wouldn't be anybody there. Just as I was about to give up I heard my mother's voice.

"Hello?"

"Hello," I said nervously. "It's me!"

"Oh!" She sounded quite taken aback. It must be years since we'd last spoken on the telephone. "Where are you?"

"At Oxford, at college," I said. "I didn't think you'd be at home."

"We had the afternoon off." A pause. Then, in a rush, "When are you leaving the Order?"

"I've left," I said weakly. "I'm out."

"You're out!" she screamed, astonished. "Oh. Well. Are you all right?"

"Yes, fine!" I lied breezily. Again I wanted no emotion. Not yet. I couldn't face it. "The dispensation came through this morning. And I'm back here because term starts tomorrow."

"Do you want to come home?"

"Soon," I said. My earlier instinct was still wrong. I'd got to do this thing on my own. Somehow the family were both too close and too far away to help me at the moment. "But I will be home."

"And you're all right?" she repeated anxiously. How could I answer her really? What did people say to one another on this occasion after seven years of noncommunication? Now, in the crowded college lobby, I couldn't cope with too much love.

"Yes, I'm all right. Really."

"What about your clothes?" she asked, equally at a loss.

"I'll see to that soon," I said. "Not today. There isn't time. But soon."

"Come in!"

Refusing to allow myself a second to turn back and flee from Rose's door, I plunged into the room and stood there, blinking nervously.

"Sister!" Rose sounded astonished, as well she might. For the last sixteen months we'd smiled politely at each other when we passed, but that was all. She stood up and smiled at me, her bright blue eyes questioning but friendly. "Come in!" she said waving her arms vaguely in the direction of the bed. "Sorry I'm in such a mess. You don't mind sitting on the bed, do you?" Uneasily I sat on the divan and looked up at her and at Bridget, who was sitting on the floor toasting crumpets in front of the electric fire. She turned round and smiled.

"Hello, Sister." Her pretty, Celtic-looking face was flushed and hot, her curly dark hair was falling into her eyes.

Now that I was actually here I did not know how to begin or what to say. Rose, however, now that she had gotten over the shock of seeing me there, started bustling about. She was a tall, athletically built girl with a short boyish hairstyle and a lively kind of prettiness. She seemed all arms and legs as she hurried about the small room making cups of tea. I looked round at the scene. I could see what she meant by "mess." A suitcase disgorged its contents in one corner of the room, there was a pile of underwear on the desk, and the floor was covered with books, files, records, and a guitar. I thought of the absolute tidiness of the convent—the bare surfaces, the immaculate cupboards—and smiled to myself.

"Oh, Sister!" Bridget, having finished the crumpets, smiled up at me. She was much quieter than the more tempestuous Rose and spoke with a precision that sounded slightly Scots. "We must congratulate you."

"Yes!" Rose spun round and beamed. "The prize! Fantastic! You are a dark horse, you know, Sister. You sit there like a mouse, never say a word to anyone, and then go off and win a prize. You must be ever so brainy!"

"Oh, no!" I protested awkwardly. "I'm really surprised myself."

"I expect you work harder than we do," Rose said, handing me a cup of tea. "I mean, you don't have the same distractions."

"No," Bridget sighed. "It's just impossible sometimes to fit everything in when you've got a social life. How many hours of work do you do a day—in the holidays, for instance?"

"Seven and a half hours," I said mechanically. I was still trying to work out how to break it to them. How to begin.

"What!" They both stared at me, aghast.

"Seven and a half hours! In the holidays!" Rose shouted. "Every single day!"

"Yes," I said. "It's not too bad. I mean, I do enjoy it."

"You'd have to, wouldn't you?" Bridget said. "Do you have to do that, or is it up to you?"

"Yes," Rose butted in. "How much choice do you actually have about how you spend your time?"

"Well, actually," I stared down at the carpet and groped around carefully for the right words. How did you say something like this without sounding melodramatic? "Actually I'm not a nun anymore." I stopped, unable to continue.

There was a sudden shaken silence. I could feel them trying hard to think of something to say.

Rose, her exuberance suddenly muted sympathetically, gently said, "What do you mean?"

"Well. I've felt for some time that the religious life wasn't really for me. So I've just been dispensed from my vows. This morning."

How flat and lame it sounded, put like that. But how could I possibly begin to explain everything? And too many of the things I'd have to tell them were locked up inside me. I couldn't tell them to anybody, even though I was no longer bound to keep them.

"Gosh," Bridget said. "Are you pleased about it, Sister?"

"Well, I know I've made the right decision," I said smiling, determined to project a positive image.

"Yes, but how do you feel about it? I mean, are you looking forward to doing other things? Like—you know—going out more?" She paused tactfully.

"Do you want to get married?" Rose continued for her bluntly. "I mean, that's what seems to happen to priests who leave, isn't it, according to the Catholic papers. Are you leaving to get married?"

"No!" I said, shocked out of my awkwardness for a moment. "Heavens, no! I just knew I couldn't lead the religious life anymore."

"But would you like to get married one day?" Bridget asked.

"I don't know. Perhaps. I really don't know," I said. "I haven't got any plans. Just . . ." I trailed off, gazing glumly into an empty and frightening future.

"I'm not really surprised," Rose said thoughtfully. "We've

often thought you were looking awfully strained. You've gone terribly thin."

"Yes, and you've had those great black rings round your eyes," Bridget added. "We've all been worried. But of course we never liked to ask you if there was anything wrong."

I looked at them, astounded. It had never occurred to me that the students had noticed me at all, let alone bothered to discuss me.

"It must have been terrible making the decision, then," Bridget said after a pause. "It's okay if you're leaving because you're in love. But otherwise I should think you'd feel ghastly. Do you?"

"It feels . . . strange." Again that taboo, that instinctive nunlike withdrawal. I wanted so much to answer more precisely and honestly, but I couldn't. I felt my face assuming a bland smile as I looked back at Bridget, masking my inner turmoil.

"Never mind," Rose bounded forward and sat at my feet. Impulsively she grasped both my hands. "We'll look after you!"

The warmth, the spontaneous affection took my breath away. I felt dangerously close to tears, it was so unfamiliar. I looked down at my lap where our hands were entwined. Mine and Rose's. An awkward jumble of fingers and wrists. It had been so long since anyone had held my hand. Physical contact had been a constant part of our family life, but just as I'd had to hold my mother at an emotional arm's length on the phone, so now I didn't know what to do with Rose's hands. I wanted to squeeze them back, but I couldn't. My body no longer expressed me. I'd been longing for affection, but now that I had it I felt I could only respond with the deliberate coolness we'd all practiced in the convent. That bland serenity that kept emotion and affection at bay.

"Thank you," I said at last. It sounded so stiff and inappropriate. I smiled at Rose's eager, generous face. Why should she be so kind? She didn't even know me.

"You'll have to start wearing ordinary clothes again, won't you?" Bridget said. "Have you got any?"

"No. Not yet. I'll have to buy some, of course, but I thought I'd leave it for a few days because . . ." Again, I trailed off lamely.

"Are you dreading it?" Bridget asked.

I nodded. "I'll just get things gradually," I said, still stuck in my calm pose. "Get used to the idea, you know, and then—in a few days . . ."

"I think that's a terrible idea!" Rose said firmly. "Absolutely terrible. The longer you put it off, the worse it'll be. You'll spend days and days thinking about it. No," she dusted some crumbs off her lap decisively. "We've got to do it tonight!"

"Tonight!" I bleated. "Oh, no—I really don't think that's—I mean, it's too soon. It's too late, anyway," I finished, relieved. "The shops will be shut. Perhaps tomorrow." Anything to stave off the evil hour. I stared at Rose, who was pulling on an extraordinary pair of tight boots that reached to her knees. When she stood up, I stared at her miniskirt, mesmerized. No. I couldn't change tonight. I couldn't wear clothes like that.

"It's not too late at all," Bridget was saying, reaching for her coat, which was flung across Rose's divan. "We can just get down to Cornmarket before the shops shut. We'll just do it." She bent down to pick her handbag off the floor. Quickly I averted my eyes. Her skirt was so short that nearly everything was visible.

"I—I—" I began.

"Honestly, it really will be better," Rose said, rummaging in her wardrobe and bringing out a duffle jacket. "Get it over and done with! It'll be such fun!"

They were right, of course. I took a deep breath. "All right."

"Where shall we go, Rose?"

"Marks and Sparks, I think. It's too late to look round properly and their things are pretty standard and good quality. It's no good getting anything too trendy. We'll get something fairly conventional at first," she explained, and I sighed with relief. "Then you can develop your own style later."

"Have you any idea how you'd like to dress?" Bridget asked.

I stared at them and shook my head weakly.

"You'll need shoes too," Bridget looked down at my feet. "You can't go round in those awful clodhoppers. We'll just do it. Dolcis have got a sale on."

"That's a point. Have we got enough money? I've got 3 pounds. What about you, Brig?"

Again I was dumbfounded. These strangers were ready to buy my clothes. Again I felt the shock of their kindness forcibly. "It's all right," I said. "I've got 25 pounds." I looked nervously into my purse at the money Mother Frances had given me.

"Wow!" Rose said, delighted. "That's great! We can get some

really good things. We'll just get the basics now and the rest later."

"What about my hair!" I wailed suddenly.

"Oh, Lord!" Bridget looked worried. "I'd forgotten about that. Have you—have you got any?"

"Oh, yes," I laughed suddenly at her obvious dismay. "I've got some hair. But it's an awful mess."

"Don't worry," Rose said. "I can cut hair beautifully—I cut my own and half the people's on this corridor. I'll do it ever so nicely," she said kindly, coming down and sitting beside me. "Really."

Again I nodded dumbly, letting their exuberant energy sweep me along in their wake. "Yes. Thanks."

"Great!" Rose said, leaping up. "This is going to be fun!" She paused suddenly, looking at me with her head slightly on one side. "We can't call you Sister anymore, can we? What's your real name?"

Again I conjured up that name that no longer belonged to me and tested it out, experimentally, trying to attach myself once more to this new label for my new life.

"Karen," I said uncertainly.

The crowds of shoppers milled confusedly outside Marks and Spencers. I fought my way through them, trying to keep up with Bridget and Rose, who were expertly maneuvering a path to the large plate-glass doors.

"Phew! I wish they'd widen these pavements," said Bridget, as we fought our way into the vast shop. "Just done it, I think! Ten minutes to closing time!"

I stood, feeling oddly out of place. Women with set, grim faces rummaged through piles of garments on sale. Plastic breasts, hard and shiny, modeled brassieres, and disembodied legs kicked obscenely in the air, sporting sheer stockings. I instinctively averted my eyes, feeling myself locked in some strange dream.

"What are we going to do about shoes?" Rose asked. "There won't be time to go to Dolcis as well."

"What size do you take, Karen?"

"Fives, usually."

"Hmm, same as me. Look," Bridget kicked off her own high-heeled shoe. "Try that on. It's new—I got them for Christmas—so the leather won't have stretched."

Uneasily, I untied the laces of my stout black lace-ups and

gingerly inserted my foot into the strange strappy shoe. The red leather glowed weirdly against my thick black stocking, and my foot, a complete stranger to me, peered incongruously from the folds of black serge.

"How does it feel?"

"All right, I think." I hobbled a few steps on the spindly heel. "Yes, it fits all right."

Two women queuing at the cash register gaped, nudging one another. What a spectacle I was making of myself. Never call attention to yourselves in public, we had been told again and again. Any disedification reflects not only on you but on the church as well, whose delegate you are. Blushing with shame, I took off the shoe.

"Fine!" Bridget made toward the doors. "Trust me, Karen. I'll get them—you can pay me back later," and she was gone, swallowed up in the wintry blackness outside.

"Right!" Rose said. "What a stroke of luck Brig takes the same size as you. Come on!"

I followed Rose, hoping against hope that Bridget wouldn't choose a pair with high heels. I could just imagine falling over in the college hall, in front of everybody.

"Undies first," Rose shouted. Again I colored, glancing furtively around as Rose swept down on the lingerie department. "These look about your size, I'd say, though it's hard to tell with all that stuff you've got on!"

I wished she'd lower her voice a little. A passing gentleman gave me a very strange look indeed as Rose waved two pairs of bright floral briefs jubilantly at me. "Aren't these fun!"

I swallowed hard.

"Tights next," she called as we darted toward another counter.

"Tights!" I exclaimed, picturing ballet dancers and Elizabethan plays, codpieces and all. Dear God! "What on earth do I need tights for?"

She looked at me, dumbfounded for a moment at my bewilderment. Then her face cleared. "Heavens! I don't suppose you've ever worn them. They're pantyhose! Believe me, Sister—sorry, Karen—they're the best thing that's happened since sliced bread! We wear them instead of stockings. They're so comfy and much more decent, especially now skirts are so short. You pay for these and I'll go and find you a slip."

Nervously I fumbled in my purse for the money, unable to meet the assistant's eye. What must she be thinking? It felt so peculiar to be buying my own clothes. Everything had been just doled out to us in the convent. And spending money. For years the vow of poverty had meant that I'd never handled it. Every single tube of toothpaste had been bought for me. Handing over the notes to the assistant seemed fundamentally wrong. Each month we'd all written a standard letter to our superior, asking permission to use our pens, prayer books, toilet things, paper, pencils. It was a practice that reminded us that we owned nothing of our own. And here I was throwing pounds away on myself. I felt that I ought to ask permission. But now there was nobody to ask.

"Look!" Rose yelled jubilantly. "Oh, Karen, do look!" Again heads turned as she rushed toward me, brandishing a pale pink full-length slip with a border of rosebuds. "Isn't it sweet! I know that really you don't need a slip, but I do want you to have something pretty. It'll cheer you up. I'm sure this is the right size. Do you want to hold it up against you?"

"No," I said hastily. "Thank you, Rose." It was pretty but again there was that odd sense of incongruity. What business had I with pretty, frivolous underwear? There was something deeply disturbing there that I didn't want to look into at all. This couldn't be me! Rushing round a shop at this time of day, clutching slips and brassieres. I should be in the convent chapel. It was time for Vespers. In five minutes the cantor would knock three times on the pew and the community would stand up and begin the chant.

"O God, come to my aid!"

"Lord, make haste to help me!"

They'd know by now. Would they be praying for me? Again as I blindly plunged after Rose toward Ladies' Clothing, I felt a pang of homesickness so sharp that the store swam slightly as the tears stood for a second in my eyes. There was no going back—oh, no, I knew that. It couldn't be. But how I longed to be back there for a moment, safe in the world I knew.

"We're doing terribly well!" Rose said cheerfully. "Five minutes to go! Ah, here are the skirts." She rushed round the long counter while I stumbled after her. "No, not that—too garish for you; no—too dull. Here we are! What about that?"

She held up an oatmeal-colored straight skirt with a belt.

"That's nice. A classy color—you can wear loads of things with it! That's what you want at the beginning. A few basics till you decide what you really like wearing. Here—" she held it up against me and leaned back, studying the effect intently.

"Rose!" I whispered urgently, trying to look as though I were buying clothes for the needy poor. A group of salesgirls had clustered round the counter and were whispering and giggling, staring in my direction. "Rose! I can't possibly wear this. It's too short."

Held up against my habit the skirt looked absurdly tiny. It reached halfway down my thighs, where my vest finished. "I can't, Rose. I just can't."

"Yes, yes, you can, Karen." She gripped my elbow reassuringly. "It's not too short, honestly it isn't. Look at mine." She pulled her coat aside. I sighed unhappily. It was all right for her. But what about me? My legs! They were horrible, horrible. They ought to be hidden away forever. "Karen," she said, steering me firmly toward the sweaters, "you mustn't start out looking a frump. Really, you mustn't, because then you'll never be able to break out. I want you to look smashing right from the word *go*!"

She was right.

"This one, I think." She was holding up a cardigan. "What color do you like? Please—" she turned to the assistant. "Please. I know it's after closing time. But this is so important. Really it is. It's probably the most important day in her life. Please serve us."

"That's all right, dear." The girl behind the counter grinned back, caught in Rose's drama. She stared at me curiously, dying to know what was going on. "I like the blue, myself."

"What about the grey?" I asked with little hope. It was the nearest to black.

"No," Rose shook her head. "Far too dreary with the skirt. It *must* be blue or pink. You choose."

I smiled the smile of the defeated.

"Blue, please."

Dazed, I looked around my room, which was now crammed with people. The news of my disrobing had traveled fast. Leaving me tactfully to dress, Rose and Bridget had returned to their own rooms in another part of the college to collect their hair-cutting equipment. They had returned with four other friends anxious to

272

witness the spectacle. Every so often there would be a tap on the door and someone else would join the party. There must now be about fourteen people sitting on the bed, the floor, cheerfully offering encouragement.

"Rose, don't cut it too short. You have to watch her—she gets carried away sometimes."

"My God, Sister, you look a hell of a lot better out of those hideous clothes!"

"I know! I really wouldn't have recognized you."

"Yes, those other things must have been so uncomfortable. So hot and bulky. We couldn't see any of you at all."

I was sitting with a towel around my shoulders letting Rose snip and tease my long-suffering hair into some kind of shape. Yes, the habit had been hot and inconvenient, but I was used to it. Considerably more used to it than to these new garments. It had been so sad to take it off for the last time. The veil that had been pinned on by the bishop as a sign that I had renounced the world, the cincture of obedience, the black dress that symbolized poverty. I remembered the day I had arrived at Tripton, throwing my clothes away joyfully, thinking I was discarding an old life. I knew better than that now. You couldn't exchange one life for another simply by a change of clothes. Clothes were only a symbol of something far deeper. And this time too I wasn't joyful about the change. I was doing something necessary and inescapable, not rushing forward confidently to meet the future.

I looked round at the girls who were eagerly watching the transformation, lapping up the drama. Most of them must have been thinking that I was relieved to have taken this decision. After all, after years of restraint I was now free. The world stretched ahead of me with all its delights: I could travel, fall in love, make friends, wear lovely clothes. But I still couldn't imagine myself doing any of those things.

"That's fine!" Rose decided. "Honestly, Karen, I'm amazed your hair is in such good shape. It's lovely, isn't it? I mean, it falls into shape so easily. Some people have such wiry hair. I was expecting yours to be awful. All stringy and dead with bald patches here and there."

"Have you got your curling tongs, Rose?" someone asked. "I think you need to wave it slightly at the ends."

While I sniffed the smell of scorching hair, Bridget and another girl called Mary made me up. "Not makeup," I had pleaded weakly.

"Oh, yes," came a firm chorus from the spectators. I smiled back. The friendliness in the room was unmistakable. Of course I could see they were enjoying the drama and were curious, but still it was real warmth, not the cold goodwill that I'd grown used to in the Order. Someone had produced a bottle of sherry. "We've got to mark this occasion, I think, with a little booze," and not wanting to seem churlish I took a sip. The liquid burnt my throat, making me cough and splutter. There were cheers and laughter.

"Good luck, Karen!"

There was another knock at the door. A tall, snooty-looking girl walked in. She had large horn-rimmed glasses and long straight hair that fell to her shoulders. I had occasionally seen her walking round the college. When we had passed on the stairs she stared coldly through me. I looked at her, surprised. What could she be doing here?

She crossed the room, holding a large paper parcel.

"I bought this for myself this morning," she spoke coolly but rather defensively. "It's a sweater. I think it's quite nice—it'll suit you. I'd like to make some kind of contribution to this very momentous occasion."

Amazed, I looked up at her, trying to thank her, trying to let my face show the emotion I was feeling. Again I felt the same powerlessness. My words of thanks seemed weak and inadequate. She waved them aside and sauntered calmly from the room.

"Right, now, Karen, what do you think?" Firmly Rose pushed me over to the long mirror by the wardrobe. Curiously I looked at my reflection. A strange girl stared back at me—waved hair, makeup, ordinary modern clothes. The girl was a complete stranger. Of course I could see it was me. But that girl in the outrageously short skirt wasn't who I was. It was a travesty of an ideal that I was looking at. How long would it be before we joined up—the nun that I really was and that girl in the mirror? One thing I knew, though, was that it would be a long time and hard work—just as hard as it had been to make myself into a nun.

"Now," Rose was saying. "We'll all take Karen into the dining hall so she doesn't feel embarrassed. Let's put her into the middle of the group of us so that she can't feel that people are staring."

"I don't think anybody would recognize her," someone said. "She looks so completely different."

"They'll probably think you're a guest from another college," Bridget said.

It was strange going out into the night dressed like this. The shaky feeling of the wind blowing against my hair and going right up between my legs made me feel exposed and vulnerable. I cringed from the exposure, longing for the protective covering of the habit. How many things that habit had protected me from! Now I was out in the open, fair game for anyone. Out in the cold, having to start all over again.

But the friendly circle of girls surrounding me as we entered the huge, steamy dining hall reminded me that I was not completely exposed and alone. Tomorrow and the next day and the next few years would bring me the problems I would have to face, the battles I would have to fight to learn to live again in the world. There would be pain enough tomorrow.

But don't let me think about it now, I thought, *not while I am surrounded by warmth and laughter, not while there is friendship and affection around. Later, yes. But not tonight.*

AFTERWORD
1980

Yesterday I met a friend for lunch. She used to be Sister Rebecca but she left the Order a year or two after I did. I watched her weave her way through the aggressive traffic on Regent Street, perched upright on her bicycle, looking just as she used to look cycling round Oxford in her habit, her back straight and her face a severe mask of concentration. We greeted one another enthusiastically while she parked her bike, unclipping her floating Indian skirt, which she had secured with a massive paper clip.

"I can't find anything else to use," she said when she saw me laughing. "What did we do in the convent?"

"We used to tuck our skirts up."

"Yes, and wobble on an uncomfortable bustle!"

We smiled at the shared memory. We're always glad to see each other.

"It's such a relief to talk to someone who really understands what it was like," she said. "I can't talk to anyone else about it at all."

"Do you find that people seem to think it's bad for you to dwell on it and change the subject quickly?" That had so often been my experience.

"No, not really. I find that I just can't bear to tell anybody that I was a nun once. Whenever I pass a nun in the street—even one of those dowdy modern ones—I feel they must *know* and reproach me. I hurry past without even looking at them. And you know what it's like. People ask, 'What did you do before your present job? . . . and before that? . . . and before that?' I sit there dreading the moment when I've got to tell them, or go vague."

277

I did know what it was like. Unlike Rebecca, I have made a point of telling people that I was a nun if those questions are asked. Then I sit back waiting for the reaction, the double-take—"You don't *look* like a nun!" No, I don't now. Why should I? Or else their eyes glaze as at something distasteful, and they say, "Well, I'm sure you're glad that that's all over," and change the subject. Or worse, there's the "Tell us all the gory details" approach. However hard I try, I've never been able to explain adequately what it was really like, and that means that I've never been able to explain the most important part of my life, not even to the people who've been closest to me. That's why I value Rebecca. Only she really appreciates the huge task we have both got: to come to terms with those years in the convent and somehow ensure that our lives in the world keep in touch with the nuns we were and still are. We both have found very different ways of coping with the outside world, but at least we understand the nature of the struggle.

When Rebecca and I had collected our lunch, I told her that I had written this book. I was a bit apprehensive about her reaction. After all, she's in the book.

She looked at me silently for a while and then slowly a smile spread over her face. "How amazing," she said at first. Then her face became thoughtful. "It's time," she said. "How brave of you."

Again I knew what she meant. To confront those years is painful because they never die. People seem to assume that the experience is over now and that its only relevance to my life today is a fund of funny stories to tell at dinner parties. But the insight I'd had when I left the Order—that in some sense I'd always be a nun—has proved to be right. Yet I agreed with Rebecca when she said that she'd never doubted that her decision to leave was the right one. "It's the one thing I've never regretted," she said. "Heaven knows, life hasn't been a bed of roses since, but the thought of going back has never crossed my mind."

"Sometimes," I said, "when it was very hard and so lonely, I used to look back and long for someone to advise me. We had the rule and superiors to teach us how to become nuns, but nothing and nobody to help us to stop. But I knew I couldn't go back, even though they once told me I could if I wanted to."

I also find now that I can't regret that earlier decision to become a nun. Although I was ridiculously young, there was nothing unusual then in entering the Order at seventeen. But after I left they decided that no girl should enter until she had had at least three years' experience in the world after leaving school.

I've tried to write about the dawning of my vocation as it appeared to me at the time, but now I see that mixed up with all the idealism, I was escaping from a world that I felt unable to cope with. In a sense, when I decided to be a nun I was "dropping out" in the way dictated by my Catholic background. I'd never heard of a dropout, of course, but such ideas must have been in the air at the time, even in a convent school in Birmingham.

It's all very different now. The Order was transformed by the decrees of the Second Vatican Council. The nuns have discarded the habit completely, the rule of silence has been relaxed, the old rituals and customs have gone. The novices are no longer secluded from the world, nor are those trials and disciplines manufactured for them. They live in London in a lively community and are always going out and about. There's no more chapter of faults, public penance, processions down drafty cloisters, medieval underwear, austere dormitories. Nuns live in cheerful bedrooms that they decorate themselves and can invite visitors in to see them and drink coffee.

Would it have made a difference in my final decision to leave if it had been like that when I entered? I don't think so. I would probably have joined one of the stricter contemplative Orders. It's years since I've visited a convent, but on my last visit I felt disappointed and ambivalent about what I saw. It seemed that the old rituals and austerities supported the religious life with a dignity that it no longer has. Certainly there had to be changes, and the nuns would argue that nothing essential has gone. But a support system must be found to uphold the one thing that can never be changed: a nun's life is nonsense unless she is prepared to give up every bit of herself. At least the strict observances of the old days made it very clear to me what that meant.

On the day I left I knew that things were going to be lonely and difficult, but I had no idea how truly terrible the period of adjustment was going to be. For over six years I had to force myself into the world I'd abandoned so thoroughly. In the Easter of my first year in the noviceship, I remember, someone recorded us singing the chant during the Easter vigil. Mother Walter played it to us one evening at recreation, and I listened puzzled to our voices, pure and confident as choir boys' soaring in serene praise. "Mother," I said while she turned over the tape, "we don't sound at all like women. We sound like . . . " I trailed off; I didn't have the words: sexless, prepubescent, without passion. Mother Walter looked bewildered and waved my comment away as an irrelevance, but for the rest of the evening I remember looking round the table at my fellow novices. I knew how often each one cried herself to sleep in the crowded dormitory upstairs (there was usually someone sobbing at night), and from the endless public reprimands I knew how, in our private muddles and complexities, we were miles from that pure, happy sound issuing from the tape recorder. Nevertheless we had produced it; it couldn't all be a lie. A struggling group of young women produced that joyful, eunuch-like singing. All passion spent. Somewhere we were loving, sexual beings, full of depression and struggle, but we looked as peaceful as angels. "My peace is not the peace that the world gives," Christ had said, and I'd found that that was true. I rarely felt at peace, often felt very miserable indeed, but at another (deeper?) level I was happy because I knew I was where I wanted to be.

"But what a waste," people so often exclaim. "Seven years! Such crucial years. Your youth squandered unnaturally!" A few years ago I'd have agreed with them. But now I can honestly say that I wouldn't have missed the experience. At least for once in my life I tried to live absolutely and single-mindedly.

The ideal of the religious life is still, I think, a beautiful one. But only a few of those who undertake it are capable of it. My most crucial mistake was the overvaluing of the will. Rebecca and I were both ill in the Order, but such was its strength of belief in the sovereignty of will power that it never occurred to the nuns until too late that we ought to see a doctor. How lovely it would be if the will really were supreme; if the mass of emotion, bodily impulses, and disorders and the murky subconscious could all be controlled by a strong act of will. In the Order I discovered that we are complex beings, mind, heart, soul, and body engaged in a continuous bloody battle. Indeed, one of the most important things I learned from religious life was the relative impotence of the will. It's a good, though humbling, thing to realize. It brings a kind of peace with it.

I'm a better nun now than I ever was in the Cloister. You can be so fearful of loving other people more than God that you can be downright uncharitable. Surely it's better to love others, however messy and imperfect the involvement, than to allow one's capacity for love to harden. Ironically I now sometimes see in myself qualities of detachment and self-sufficiency that are so like those I was struggling to acquire when I was a nun. The sad thing is that I no longer value these qualities as I did: they can so easily become hardness and complacency.

The nuns I lived with were women of charity and integrity. They were striving for a superhuman ideal and not surprisingly they made mistakes. They did their best for me but between us we failed. Religious life is about love and love is about risk. Perhaps none of us risked enough.